DAWSON'S

to

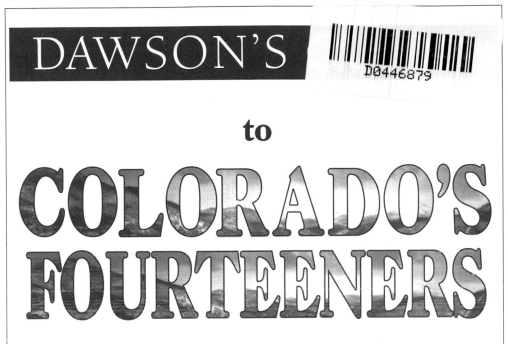

COLORADO'S FOURTEENERS

by Louis W. Dawson II

Volume 2
The Southern Peaks

The complete mountaineering guide to
Colorado's high peaks
Technical Routes
Snow Climbs
Ski Descents
Classic Hikes

Blue Clover Press

Attention Readers:
The information presented in this book is based upon the experience of the author
and his sources and might not necessarily be perceived as accurate by other persons; there-
fore, extreme care should be taken when following any of the routes described in this book.
This book is not intended to be instructional in nature but rather a guide for mountaineers
who already have the requisite training, experience and knowledge. An advanced level of
expertise and physical conditioning is necessary for even the "easiest" of the routes
described. Proper clothing and equipment are essential. Failure to have the necessary knowledge, equipment, and conditioning will subject you to extreme physical danger, injury, or
death. Some routes have changed and others will change; avalanche hazards may have
expanded or new hazards may have formed since this book's publication.

Blue Clover Press

For orders, new author guidelines, discount sales and other product information contact mgardner@aol.com
719.473.5456 / Voice

Cover photo of Mount Sneffels (Routes 3.4.7, East Couloir, and 3.4.5, North Buttress)
from Cirque Mountain, by Spence Swanger
All other photos by Louis W. Dawson II unless otherwise credited.

Colorado Fourteeners Initiative
A Partnership for Preservation

The Colorado Fourteeners Initiative is a multi-year, private-public partnership between private
organizations and individuals concerned with preservation of the Fourteeners. The goal of the initiative is to mitigate the hiking/climbing impact on the Fourteeners, thereby preserving the
peaks' natural integrity and the quality of the Fourteeners' hiking/climbing experience. The initiative provides for the study of hiking/climbing impacts, on site mitigation work, and user education. The Colorado Fourteeners Initiative partnership presently includes: the Rocky Mountain
Field Institute, Colorado Mountain Club, Colorado Outward Bound, Volunteers for Outdoor
Colorado, and the US Forest Service.

*Blue Clover Press donates a portion of the proceeds from the sale of this book to
support the Colorado Fourteeners Initiative.*

Library of Congress Catalog Card Number: 94-71273
ISBN 0-9628867-2-6

Printed in the United States of America

ACKNOWLEDGMENTS

The contributions of many people made this book possible. I should mention my first fourteener climb, an ascent of Pyramid Peak in the capable hands of an Ashcrofters Mountain School instructor. After Pyramid, our group went on to a memorable train and backpack trip to Chicago Basin where we climbed Windom Peak. That was more than 30 years ago. I've forgotten our instructor's name, but I thank him. In the 1960s Dave Farney gave many young mountain men a start through the Ashcrofters. My wife Lisa did valuable work on the maps, and kept our household together. John Quinn joined me for many memorable weeks of small town motels, 1:00 AM alarms, and wonderful summits. Indeed, it was his idea to produce this book! Michael Kennedy contributed invaluable editing, advice, and enthusiasm as the idea germinated. Jon Waterman deserves double thanks for advice and encouragement—not to mention friendship throughout the years. Miller and Tua supplied me with excellent skis. Glen Randall lent his awesome photography and mountaineering skills during the completion of my "ski the fourteeners project." Kim Miller of Black Diamond has given me terrific support, both with encouragement and gear. I heartily thank Mountain Smith Packs for their continued help as an equipment sponsor. A mountaineer has to eat, and my favorite snack is the *Fxtreme* Energy Nutrition Bar, the best endurance food I've ever used. Mark Synnott put in many hours assisting with editing and field research. Thanks to Jeff Hollenbaugh for his hard work on the maps, and the same thanks to Chad Hilliard. Thanks also to Bob Pearlmutter for his companionship and enthusiasm. Ascension Enterprises kept me supplied with their excellent climbing skins. Special thanks in this volume go to Steve Cheyney for his input on Pikes Peak and to Gary Neptune, who provided invaluable information on several obscure routes.

My special gratitude goes out to Ken Ward, who accompanied me on more than a dozen fourteener climbs and ski descents, and an equal number of reconnaissance missions and failed attempts. He deserves special mention for doing most of the driving while I tickled my laptop computer. A big thanks to physical therapist Karen Church for her help repairing my wheels—and the same thanks to Dr. Michael Berkley. Jim Gilchrist gave me valuable help with several route descriptions.

Moreover, I must acknowledge you, the user of this guide book. After publication you give it the acid test. Without a doubt you'll find mistakes and inconsistencies. That's the nature of an information-intensive project done on a limited budget, with the constraints of time, weather, and the author's physical abilities—not to mention dated signs and place names. Thus, I'd like to thank in advance those people who take the time to report corrections to me. I can be reached care of Blue Clover Press. Naturally, all such details will be verified and included in future editions. Also, I welcome any reports of fourteener "firsts," especially rock climbs, ski descents, and snow routes.

Finally, thanks also to others too numerous to mention here.

Berg Heil,
Louis W. Dawson II
Carbondale, Colorado

TO LISA

*For all we've shared
in our adventure together*

"I am fain to confess a deplorable weakness in my character. No sooner have I ascended a peak than it becomes a friend, and delightful as it may be to seek "fresh woods and pastures new," in my heart of hearts I long for the slopes of which I know every wrinkle, and on which each crag awakens memories of mirth and laughter and of the friends of long ago. As a consequence of this terrible weakness, I have been no less than seven times on the top of the Matterhorn."

—A. F. Mummery, 1874

TABLE OF CONTENTS

CHAPTER 1: PIKES PEAK

CHAPTER 2: SANGRE DE CRISTO MOUNTAINS

CHAPTER 3: NORTH SAN JUAN MOUNTAINS

CHAPTER 4: SOUTH SAN JUAN MOUNTAINS

Topping out on the Ellingwood Arete, Crestone Needle. Humboldt Peak in background. (Summer)

FOREWORD

by Michael Kennedy

For many of us, a particular mountain assumes a significance beyond what we've achieved on it, although it is often only in retrospect that we understand the nature of our relationship. So it has been for me with Capitol Peak, a mountain close to home and close to heart.

My introduction to the perverse pleasures of winter climbing came in January 1974, when Lou Dawson and I made the second winter ascent of Capitol's North Face, during which I bagged my first new route, first gearless bivouac, and first near-death experience when, on the descent, I slid a hundred feet on steep snow before being stopped by a rock. Over the next four years I climbed the North Face three more times, twice in summer and once again in winter, and after each of these climbs we'd come down Capitol's Knife-edge Ridge. Although only a mildly technical scramble, it's still one of the hardest standard routes on a Colorado Fourteener. I'd always wanted to make a one-day winter-conditions ascent, and at the end of March 1991 decided that now was the time , even though I'd miss calendar winter by a week.

Spontaneity breeds simplicity. Skis for the approach, ice axe and crampons for the ridge, stove and food to keep the fire burning. Lightweight gear and years of experience had bred a certain efficiency and confidence. A chilly 4:30 a.m. saw me gliding along a well-frozen crust, hoarfrost sparkling in the headlamp's beam. Slow and steady, I wandered up through pine and aspen as the sky brightened from purple to pink to blue. The dense forest gradually gave way to frozen lakes, windscoured snow, and rocky ridges against an electrically clear sky.

Five thousand feet from the valley floor, I stepped out of ski bindings and donned crampons. After a delicate scramble across the blade-like section of ridge the route is named for, I plodded deliberately up the last half mile of funky snow to the top. I gazed out over the familiar snowy landscape, thinking of other mountains beyond the horizon. Satisfied, I headed down. Almost too soon I was back at the car, bone-tired and thirsty, but full of the simple animal pleasure of 12 hours and 28 miles alone on a peak that had meant so much to me over so many years.

Lou Dawson and I have shared many adventures since 1974, from big-wall climbing in Yosemite and Alaska to long weekends in local huts with our wives and children, but for me that first climb on Capitol remains both a gift and an inspiration for all that has followed. Despite my fascination with the remote peaks of Alaska and the Himalaya, I've always come home to the mountains of Colorado

Lou has never really left. No one understands the Colorado Rockies better or has a more intimate feel for their secrets, the kind of hard-won knowledge only gained from three decades of backcountry travel in all seasons. Thankfully, Lou continues to explore and learn, and thus to inspire climbers in their travels in our magical backyard wilderness. May he do so for another 30 years.

PREFACE

In 1987, my friend John Quinn suggested I write a fourteener guide book. We'd been struggling that spring with a lack of information, but had been amazing ourselves as we snow climbed and skied dozens of classic lines on Colorado fourteeners. Like children on the first day of summer, a world of discovery fell in our laps. The climbing was exciting but relatively safe; the skiing as good as you

In American Basin near Handies Peak.

could wish for; and the backcountry we saw lured us like sailors coming home to port.

Since then I've climbed, skied, hiked, biked—even driven—fourteeners until anyone would think I'd gotten my fill. Not so. Around every corner, on every face, below every summit, I find a new bowl of snow, an elegant arete, or a classic couloir. Indeed, on these 54 mountains you can find several lifetimes of adventure.

The questions I'm most often asked are: "what's your favorite peak?" and "what's your favorite ski descent?" My favorite fourteener is Mount Sneffels. I'm always astounded by Sneffels' combination of access, interesting climbing, and the magnificent stature of this noble arete. My favorite ski line? I'd have to categorize that. For extreme skiing, I'd pick the east face of Wetterhorn Peak. Grab your binoculars, pick a clear morning, drive to the top of Slumgullion Pass outside of Lake City, and see if Wetterhorn pulls you. Then go ski it and let me know what you think. For easier skiing with good access, my favorite line is Handies Peak from American Basin. For true wilderness skiing, I'd pick Snowmass Peak from Snowmass Lake. Spring snowcamping at Snowmass Lake, in the middle of a vast wilderness, is an experience you'll never forget.

I should note that, while most of the peaks in this guide are "official" fourteeners included in the famous fifty-four, I have added several peaks. These extra mountains have aesthetics, interest, and beautiful routes that easily qualify them as separate summits. I have no wish to argue, however, with the classic count of fifty-four Colorado fourteeners. Goals and standards are part of being human, and checking 54 peaks off a list is a fun and worthy challenge. The official peaks are listed in Appendix 7, and unofficial peaks are described as such in the route description. One unofficial fourteener I included is Challenger Point (14,120', called Challenger Peak herein) in the northern Sangre De Cristo mountains on the west ridge of Kit Carson Mountain. Challenger can be climbed and skied via beautiful routes separate from those for Kit Carson Peak.

Moreover, due to its commemoration of the Challenger Space Shuttle astronauts, Challenger Peak has a special feel. Look down at Challenger from the summit of Kit Carson, however, and you'll be hard pressed to call it a separate mountain. Go figure. Another added fourteener is North Eolus Peak in the South San Juan Mountains. This beautiful summit, with its sublime east-facing ski bowl and good view to the north, gets status in this book. Also, it should be noted that El Diente Peak, if you apply a standard of a 300' saddle drop, doesn't count as a separate peak. I beg your pardon! For most people El Diente counts just because it looks right—and climbing it is a worthy challenge. Many other peaks could also qualify for guide book space; I'm open to suggestions.

While numbers and names are fun, what is mountaineering really about? It's not math. It's not how steep you can ski or what grade rock you can climb—or how many peaks you tick. Mountaineering is adventure. It's a new pitch just around the corner; a new breathtaking view from a hard-won summit; a route that required masterful navigation. And mountaineering is utterly human. It's a social voyage that cements friendships—or reduces us to the raw basics of negotiation, leadership, and conflict. When you solo, mountaineering puts you in touch with your unique feral intelligence. Mountains teach us about ourselves and about life, with joy in the learning. They've done that for me, and still do. I wish the same for you, and intend this book as a helpmate.

Lou Dawson, 1996

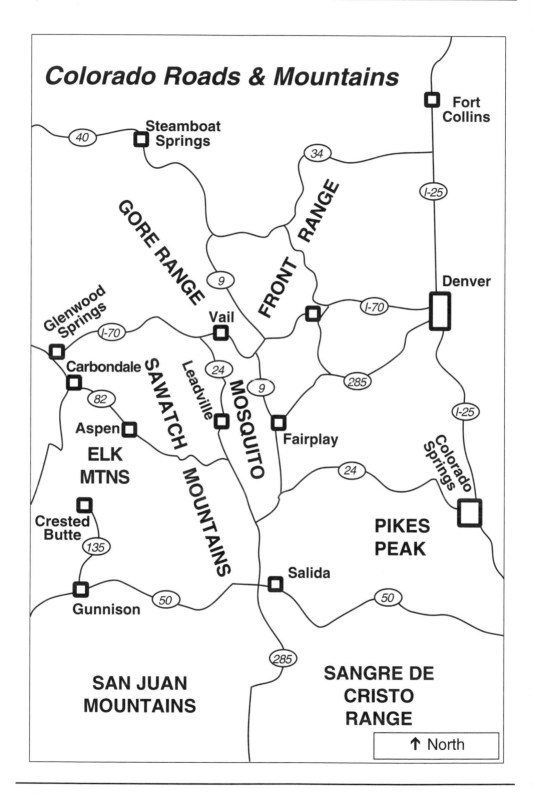

Colorado Roads & Mountains

Fort Collins

Steamboat Springs

40

34

I-25

GORE RANGE

FRONT RANGE

9

Denver

Glenwood Springs

I-70

Vail

I-70

285

I-25

Carbondale

SAWATCH

Leadville

24

MOSQUITO

9

82

Aspen

Fairplay

Colorado Springs

ELK MTNS

24

Crested Butte

135

PIKES PEAK

Salida

Gunnison

50

50

285

SAN JUAN MOUNTAINS

SANGRE DE CRISTO RANGE

↑ North

INTRODUCTION PART 1

HOW TO USE THIS BOOK

The peaks covered in this guide are contained in several mountain ranges which subdivide the south and central Colorado Rockies. The map on the previous page shows these ranges, and the chapters are ordered according to them. These ranges have their gray areas, as do most manmade definitions. But such divisions organize a guide book and help identify departure points for doing several routes during one trip. Most routes are described in their entirety—with little cross referencing. This results in redundancy but saves page turning. At the beginning of each route description you will find a data block similar to the following one:

1.1.1	**Pikes Peak via Barr Trail**	
Ratings:	Summer Climb—Novice	Ski Descent—N.R
	Snow Climb—Novice	
Season:	Summer or Spring	Winter
RT Data:	15 hours, 26 miles, 7,429'↑	Overnight, 26 miles, 7,429'↑
Start:	Barr Trail Trailhead	Barr Trail Trailhead
	6,680'	6,680'
1 Day from Rd:	Summer or Late Spring	Winter
	Yes, but use high camp	No
Map:	pg. 43	
Photo:	pg. 45	

ROUTE NUMBER

The routes are described and numbered consecutively. Referencing is by number. The number is a combination of chapter number, section, and route. For example, in chapter 3, section 4, the second route in the section is numbered 3.4.2.

PEAK NAME AND ROUTE NAME

Fourteener names are those used on official USGS maps. Route names are those in common usage, including generic designations such as "northwest face." Some mountains have been named by locals or mountaineers, but the names are not shown on the USGS maps. These colloquial names are used whenever possible. When peaks have similar names, a range or direction indicator is added, e.g. North and South Wilson.

SUMMER CLIMB RATING

The Summer Climb rating is for the route after the late spring snow melt-off. If in doubt about snow cover, use the Snow Climb Rating. From a purely physical standpoint, many fourteener climbs are mere hikes, but even routes rated as Novice are still a mountaineering endeavor. Consider sudden weather extremes, afternoon lightning, and the effects of exertion at altitude, as well as "trails" that pass close to dangerous cliffs and gullies. Indeed, no fourteener route is just a hike, though it might feel that way to a fit climber on a perfect summer day.

Consider the Novice rating as a caveat, not a license for carelessness. In other words, a Novice rated summer route usually requires no "hand and foot" climbing, but you should still know your mountain craft. You won't find any "beginner" routes in this book. Beginners (people with little or no experience) should hire a guide or climb with experienced friends.

Old tram tower, Silver Pick Basin, San Juan Mountains.

An Intermediate rated summer climb will have harder route finding and might bring you closer to hazards like cliffs, loose rock, or steep summer snow. For an Intermediate route, you should have climbed other fourteeners, have some knowledge of safe movement on steep, loose rock, and know how to judge the safety of a snow slope. If need be, you should know how to use a rope, crampons and ice axe.

Advanced rated summer climbs require astute route finding and complete knowledge of mountain craft. If you tackle an Advanced route, you should have climbed many other fourteeners at the Novice and Intermediate levels (or Advanced level with a guide or expert friend). You should know how to use a rope for 5th class climbing of rock and ice, and you must be expert with crampons and ice axe. In short, a climber on an Advanced route should be a seasoned mountaineer or an intermediate level climber accompanied by a guide or experienced friend.

Several climbs in this book involve technical rock climbing. These are rated with the Yosemite decimal system familiar to rock climbers. For example, the Ellingwood Arete on Crestone Needle has a 5.7 rating. Climbs that are easier than 5.0, but still require a rope, are known to many climbers as "4th Class." This "class" system is highly informative for mountaineers. A simple hike on a trail would be rated 1st Class, a harder hike with steep ground would be rated 2nd Class. Starting with 3rd Class, mountaineers should be aware of fall potential; 4th Class involves difficult scrambling, with real fall potential—you may need a rope. Technical rock climbing is 5th Class and is the foundation for the Yosemite decimal system (YDS). This system is open-ended; starting with 5.0, while 5.14 rates the hardest rock climb existing today. In this book all 4th and 5th Class climbs are rated Advanced, and the need for rope work is covered in the text, as is the exact YDS rating.

SNOW CLIMB RATING

On a Novice rated snow route you will need an ice axe in hand. You should carry crampons and know how to use them—though they may not be necessary. You must have practiced the ice axe self arrest, and know its method and limitations. A rope and related gear are unnecessary, but you should have enough knowledge to recognize and avoid terrain where you might need such equipment.

For an Intermediate rated snow route you must be expert with ice axe and crampons. Use of a rope probably won't be necessary, but you should carry one and know how to use it; it can get you out of some touchy situations. Only experienced snow climbers should climb Intermediate rated routes. An Intermediate route has more fall potential than a Novice route.

If you take on an Advanced rated snow climb, you should be expert with varied crampon techniques and the use of two hand-tools. A rope and climbing hardware may be necessary and should always be carried. Only expert mountaineers will be able to handle an Advanced snow route safely and efficiently. Several snow routes are rated Extreme. This rating is reserved for routes with problems such as heavy rockfall danger, mixed climbing (snow, ice, and rock), or formidable route finding.

While most fourteener snow climbs are dry by mid-summer, some gradually become ice climbs. Such climbs require more skill and equipment than their rating indicates.

SKI RATING

A Novice rated ski route is skiable for mountaineers who can do a solid stem turn and traverse kick turn. Nearby terrain may be steeper and more dangerous. Thus, if you tackle a Novice route, you must be able to distinguish between appropriate terrain and that which could get you into trouble. If you tackle a Novice route as a learning experience, consider traveling with a more experienced friend, or hire a guide.

An Intermediate rated fourteener ski route is serious business for any ability level. To do an Intermediate route safely you must have experience with high altitude camping and emergency bivouacs. Your skiing skills should be solid intermediate to expert, with experience in poor snow conditions and survival skiing. Some map reading skill is necessary, and you should have a fair degree of mountaineering judgment. Even if you are an experienced ski tourer, for skiing an Intermediate fourteener you should have done several routes with a Novice ski rating.

For safe enjoyment of an Advanced ski route, you must have a high degree of skill in all aspects of ski mountaineering, including high-angle snow climbing. Some Advanced routes may require belayed rock climbing, especially if you fail to find the best route. Again, if you have never done a fourteener, try a few with easier ratings before you do an Advanced route; that way you'll get a sense of the rating curve.

For an Extreme ski route you must be highly skilled in extreme skiing and technical climbing. Extreme routes are inherently dangerous because of cliffs and steep snow that may exceed 45 degrees. Nevertheless, the Extreme rated routes in this guide can be done safely by experienced mountaineers, provided they possess the skill, equipment, and knowledge necessary to tackle the route when the snow and rock are in proper condition. Do not attempt routes rated as Extreme unless you are an elite ski mountaineer.

RECOMMENDED SEASON

This is the season or seasons recommended for climbing the route described. Reasons for recommendations vary. A route with high avalanche exposure might only be recommended for summer after snow melt-off. A route with a rough scree gully might only be recommended as a spring snow climb or ski descent.

ROUND TRIP TIME, DISTANCE, AND ELEVATION GAIN

The time and distance are estimates; use them as a general guide. In most cases these estimates assume the descent was made by downclimbing. A ski descent—if it goes smoothly—can shorten the time. Distance varies because of road closures, snow conditions, and individual navigation decisions. A number of routes have long "backpack" approaches.

Nonetheless, many of these routes can be done without an overnight by experienced, fit climbers. Such routes often have no defined start other than the trailhead. For these reasons, most routes in this guide, even in the case of those with a backpack approach, are figured from the trailhead. When necessary, additional data is given in the body of the route description.

Elevation gain is figured by subtraction, with additional gain factored in when the route makes more ups and downs. For climbing, elevation gain gives the best estimate of how long a route will take you. After a few peaks you'll have a rough idea of how long it takes you to climb each thousand vertical feet. With this information, you can use simple math for surprisingly accurate time estimates. To begin, try figuring 1,000 vertical feet an hour while you're actually climbing. For travel on low-angled terrain, use two mph in the spring and one mph in the winter. These figures include rest stops.

START, TRAILHEAD

The trailheads are marked on all the maps and are described in the section introductions. You can reach most trailheads in an average passenger car, but low-slung cars could have problems on even the best dirt roads. If you need a tougher vehicle than a passenger car, the text reminds you that you need either "high clearance 2-wheel-drive" or "4-wheel-drive." In the former case, a pickup truck, van, or passenger car with plenty of clearance will suffice. In the case of 4-wheel-drive, you need at least a stock 4-wheel-drive off-road vehicle—not the "all wheel drive" type vehicle; these don't have low enough gearing or high enough clearance for crawling up a rough jeep trail. Extreme 4-wheel-drive routes are also noted. These require skilled driving and are not recommended for novice " 'wheelers."

Finding your trailhead is often the crux of fourteener success. Signs may be absent or confusing; roads change; trails are renamed; snow closure varies; roads are gated to prevent erosion. Moreover, guide book information, by nature, is dated. If you plan a one-day ascent with an early start, it's wise to check the trailhead the day before you start, perhaps by camping nearby. Though you'll have to figure most trailhead changes out for yourself, a stop by the local Forest Service office, map in hand, can save you grief. For snow closure information do the same, and call the county's road maintenance division (see Appendix 3). In the latter case, you'll need to know the county road number and name (if any).

The mileage data in the trailhead descriptions was measured by car odometer. Don't panic if the turnoff doesn't appear at the exact tenth—car odometers differ and are inexact. When mileage is described from a town, assume that your starting point is the center of the town, unless otherwise noted.

If you're short on time, or short on strength for an overnight pack, consider vehicle access. Indeed, climbers with medical problems or disabilities will find that Colorado's copious road access allows them to enjoy many peaks that would otherwise be out of reach. After melt-off, many high trailheads are accessible with a 4-wheel-drive vehicle or bicycle. During snow season these same roads are often popular snowmobile trails. Local snowmobile clubs and guide services can help with snowmobile transport on these routes—or you can use skis or snowshoes and take advantage of the machine-packed trail. Later in the spring, motorcycles and bicycles work well for roads that are dry but still gated.

Parking your vehicle at a remote roadhead can tempt criminals. At the very least, do not leave valuables in your car. More than one luckless mountaineer has returned from a nice climb only to find a broken car window and a subsequent monthly bill tracing a trail of check and credit card purchases across the continent!

ONE DAY FROM ROAD

You can climb many fourteeners in one day from parking. Nonetheless, winter and late spring ascents often involve more than one night out, especially when snow closure forces a long approach. Also, a number of fourteeners require backpack approaches. These factors are noted in this part of the data block.

MAPS

In most cases, the maps in this guide are all you'll need for field navigation. But some complex routes might require a full-size USGS topographic map. In this case, use the book map for reference and buy USGS topo maps according to the list at the head of each section. Routes on the text maps are marked with a dark line and a reference number corresponding to the route number in the text.

For road navigation use text maps or 7.5 minute topos in conjunction with the Forest Service Visitor maps and Colorado state road maps. The National Forest maps are updated more often and cover larger areas. Thus, they are outstanding for the big picture, but poor for backcountry navigation. All these maps are available at mountaineering stores and Forest Service regional offices. You can buy USGS maps via mail order from the United States Geological Survey, or at the USGS map outlet at gate 5 of the Denver Federal Center (see Appendix 7).

PHOTOGRAPHS

The Colorado Rockies have a split personality. For about four months a year they rise as gray monoliths through the summer haze. In winter, spring, and early summer, the same peaks sparkle with snow. With variation like this, no photograph can reflect the true nature of a route—it only shows how it was for a moment. With the type of photo reproduction used here, it's much easier to see terrain variations defined by snow. Thus many of the photos show the mountains with their white mantle. This should pose no problem for summer climbers, since it's easy to imagine the mountain with no snow.

ROUTE DESCRIPTIONS

Used with this book's maps, the route descriptions give you plenty of information, but they are not an inch-by-inch account. You will find enough detail for you to enjoy the routes in the traditional mountaineering sense—that is, a feeling of adventure combined with enough safety to ensure your being able to enjoy the mountains another day. One important warning: our mountains are a dynamic and ever-changing land. Though great pains were taken to verify the accuracy of facts in this guide, trails close, landslides occur, signs deteriorate. Take time to verify the written description with your map, talk to locals about your route, and stay aware of your surroundings—safe mountaineering is impossible with a connect-the-dots attitude.

SAFETY NOTES

This section mentions any safety problems specific to the route, as well as general reminders. The latter may be repetitive, but bear repeating. Included in the Safety Notes is information about "sunhit." This is roughly the time the sun hits the top of the route, an essential factor for safe spring season snow work or for early summer starts to avoid lightning. For more on timing your start, see the appendices.

PLACE NAMES AND NAME CONVENTIONS

Place names add interest to a map, give us a sense of history, and allow precise communication about routes. Where possible, traditional common usage names are used in lieu of commemorative names that often appear only on the map. Unnamed points are referred to by their marked elevation, e.g. Point 12,380'. Variations from "official" names are clarified on the text map (see the Peak Name section above for more information). On occasion, a name is used that was either suggested to the author by other climbers or used in other publications. Readers are encouraged to correct these names or suggest alternatives.

Note the abbreviations used in this book. United States Forest Service is shortened to USFS. Compass directions are abbreviated when they describe direction of travel. For example, you would head "E" up the "north" side of the creek.

APPENDICES

The appendices are an essential aid for your planning. They include listings of routes by difficulty, recommended routes, a sunrise table with tips on starting times, map lists, and other useful information. To some climbers, the recommended routes are the most valuable part of this guide. For those who'd like to ski all the peaks, do their "grand slam," or just pick the best route for their ability, these lists are the ticket.

FOR THE BEGINNER

This is not a "how-to" book. It is simply a guide book for mountaineers who like to climb and ski the finest peaks in Colorado. If you like the idea of climbing and skiing the high peaks but lack the skill, do not hesitate to contact the excellent guide services and mountaineering schools listed in the appendices. Above all, while you are using this book, remember that a guide book cannot take the place of knowledge and judgment; it is only a supplement.

On the West Ridge, Mount Lindsey, Sierra Blanca.

INTRODUCTION PART 2

FOURTEENER CRAFT

Mountain climbing is a craft. If you're a novice, the learning process can be overwhelming. Some information is obvious, but you can bog down in detail. Still other parts of the craft are best learned from a teacher. The process can be frustrating. Thus, many people give up learning after they master the basics; then they substitute a dilatory attitude that can cause the "didn't have to happen" accident. With a dangerous craft like climbing, a continued quest for knowledge will give you a balance between risk and reward—a balance that tips the scales in your favor.

If you're new to mountain climbing, a good way to learn quickly and safely is from guides, climbing schools and friends. A caveat about friends: often you'll end up simply following them, with little learning. Your friend should be a willing mentor. With such training you can gain adequate skill in three or four seasons—so long as you keep enough modesty to "know what you don't know."

Are you an expert? If so, can you boast equal skill in route finding, weather prediction, avalanche hazard evaluation, first aid, skiing, snow and rock climbing, and general knowledge of the alpine world? The sad fact is that many expert mountaineers learn the basics, then plateau where their skill level is "good enough." Often, they mistake their conquests as a sign of great skill, while luck may play a more vital role than they realize. Pluck and luck only go so far—a craftsman must be skilled. Following is a brief sketch of Colorado mountain craft. Novices can use this as a basic outline; experts can check for any voids in their know-how.

ROCKFALL DANGER

The fourteeners were formed by a variety of processes. The most important was a huge uplift of the land that began 70 million years ago. As the land rose, it was attacked by water erosion, and in more recent geologic time, the glaciers of the Ice Ages. The uplifted rock of sedimentary origin, as well as much of the igneous rock in the Rockies, is fractured and loose. Climbing such rock can be like tailgating a gravel truck—only more lethal. The only fourteeners solid enough to keep rock climbers happy are Longs Peak and parts of the Crestones. Yet even these peaks have their share of incontinence.

To travel safely in loose rock terrain, NEVER CLIMB ABOVE ANOTHER CLIMBER. Always move side by side or one at a time. Take care not to stray onto steeper loose rock. Even with utmost care you may still find yourself on rock that gets steeper and looser by the step. In this case don't force your route. Backtrack immediately and look for a safer line; a short traverse will often lead around a steeper area. Wear a helmet for all but the easiest hike routes. If you do dislodge a rock, loudly yell *rock!* to warn climbers who might be below you.

Beware of spontaneous rockfall in gullies. Loose rock stabilized by a freezing night will fall at first sunhit—another reason to start early. Snow climbers may encounter less rockfall danger, but it's amazing how fast rocks roll down a couloir full of frozen spring snow.

MOUNTAIN WEATHER

Lightning, hypothermia, poor visibility, snow avalanches—nothing causes more accidents than weather.

Summer weather—as we usually think of it—never occurs above 13,000' in Colorado. It does stop snowing, however, and you can sometimes climb in a t-shirt. But your t-shirt will often stay in your pack. Indeed, you can have full winter conditions on the fourteeners during any month. One common story is of a party climbing on a sunny "summer" day; a storm moves in, and in minutes the mountain is covered with a thin layer of treacherous ice. What's more, every summer you hear reports of exposure accidents and near misses during cold and windy rain storms. Dressing properly, timing your trip, and using good judgment are all ways

Powder in American Basin, San Juan Mountains.

to avoid problems from inclement weather.

Unseasonable cold is a grim prospect. But heat can also be a problem—summer or winter. To prevent overheating, start hydrated and stay that way (carry at least a quart of water and drink several cups each hour), wear clothing that's easy to ventilate and shed, and do so as soon (or before) you break a sweat. Heat exhaustion or heat stroke can ruin a trip just as effectively as a lightning bolt.

Be prepared for wind. Strong jet stream winds have hit 193 mph on the fourteeners, and it's common to encounter winds strong enough to knock you off your feet, or at least compromise visibility and make it hard to stay warm. Remember that when the air temperature is at freezing or below, high winds may cause instant frostbite on exposed skin. Climbers in high winds, with improper dress, may become hypothermic in minutes. Ski goggles and a balaclava that covers your face are essential for climbing in high winds, and wearing nylon shell garments helps keep you warm. Most importantly, turn back if you encounter winds that are knocking you off balance, if you feel you don't have the right equipment, or if the wind is increasing.

High altitude sunlight, with less atmospheric filtration, will injure your skin. You can sunburn in less than an hour, and cumulative damage can cause skin cancer. Moreover, thinning of the earth's ozone layer has increased this danger. Fortunately, skin protection is easy: at least every two hours, slather full block sunscreen (SPF 16 or more) on your exposed skin. Don't forget the backs of your hands, your neck and your ears. For added protection wear a long-brimmed hat (add a piece of cloth to the back of your hat for ear and neck protection). Remember sunglasses and carry backup eyewear.

Lightning is a common weather hazard on the fourteeners, and even strikes in the winter (though this is rare). In summer, avoid lightning by starting your trip early in the morning—you must be off the summit before the afternoon thunder clouds build. A good rule of thumb is to leave exposed ridges or summits by noon.

If you're on a high point when thunder booms or electricity crackles, quickly move down so that you aren't the highest object around. You should be at least several hundred feet below ridge crests and summits, preferably lower. While you wait out a storm squat with your feet together as protection against ground bolts. Deep caves offer good protection, but stay out of shallow overhangs where a ground-bolt could use you as a connection between the overhang and ground below. If you have time, stash your metal equipment (such as skis or climbing hardware) away from your huddle. Remember, lightning is a hazard like the avalanche: an encounter will most likely leave you on the losing end.

Winter temperatures in Colorado can drop below -40° Fahrenheit. Combined with ubiquitous wind, this makes frostbite and hypothermia real dangers. On a winter ascent of Pikes Peak, climbers reported a temperature of -30° F, with 50 mph winds—a wind chill of more than 100° below zero! During some winters little snow falls. Depth hoar crystals form within these thin snowpacks, causing extreme avalanche danger (see Early Winter Subseason below). Conversely, such drought winters have the best weather for climbing: cold but clear.

During heavy winters, strong storms move through the mountains one after the other, sometimes up to three a week. Climbing during these winters can mean many aborted trips. Slide danger can be dreadful, and trail-breaking is almost impossible in the loose deep snow. Yet every winter has a bit of everything: sparse snow periods and periods of constant storm. So take heart; some climbing is possible during even the heaviest winters.

A fourteener winter ascent can be a splendid experience. The keys to safety and success (and enjoyment) are timing and perseverance.

Ideally, start your trip on short notice. This allows you to catch the snowpack in the window 24 hours after the last storm (for avalanche stability), but before the next. Short notice starts are hard if you have an inflexible job, or you're from out-of-state. In this case begin your trip, but have an alternate plan in case your chosen time falls during a storm. For options, take a valley tour or ski at a resort. Above all, don't let time limits force you into weather you'd otherwise avoid. If you can, wait for good weather; remember—most Colorado storms last only several days. It's likely you'll get a few days of good weather between storms.

In Colorado, snowshoes or skis are necessary for almost all winter climbing. While most climbers use skis, snowshoes are used by non-skiers or climbers on technical routes where carrying skis would be awkward.

TIPS FOR FORECASTING
ROCKY MOUNTAIN WEATHER

1. Use your altimeter to check the barometric pressure: steadily falling pressure usually indicates an approaching storm; steadily rising barometric pressure usually indicates clearing weather.
2. Precipitation has little chance of continuing when the barometric pressure is more than 30.10 (again, use your altimeter).
3. When the temperature during a storm drops to less than 5° F, snowfall will rapidly diminish.
4. Cirrus clouds can precede a storm by 24 hours or more. (A ring around the moon is caused by thin cirrus.)
5. Thickening and lowering clouds (usually approaching from the west) indicate an approaching storm.
6. Thickening mountain wave clouds indicate increasing moisture, increasing winds aloft, and a possible approaching storm.
7. Mountain wave clouds and snow plumes on ridges indicate high winds at mountain top levels.

Climbing for a spring ski descent.

8. Thinning and lifting clouds indicate clearing weather. The end of a storm is often indicated by the lowest point of the barometric pressure curve (see tip 1), a wind shift, and the sudden appearance of ice coated snow crystals or graupel (snow that looks like small styrofoam pellets).
9. Current weather reports on radio, especially NOAA Weather Radio (VHF band), are your best sources for accurate forecasts while mountaineering.

STREAM CROSSING

If you climb mountains in Colorado, you must cross open streams—during any season. Stream crossing is tricky. You can slip on icy or wet logs; you can break through snow bridges. During spring you'll confront streams in spate with snow melt.

If you're on a summer trail, look for a log crossing or foot bridge. During snow season, you might find a snow or ice bridge. In spring most snow bridges melt, but you might find a bridge formed by avalanche debris. Be certain such bridges are sturdy, especially later in the day when the snow softens. If all else fails, you'll have to wade or rock-hop across. During spring, plan for the daily flood cycle. At higher elevations, streams will be at their lowest in the early morning, then become a raging torrent by late afternoon.

Rock hopping is tough. Stream rocks are often slick and may have a coating of morning ice (or ice all day in winter). Thus, you might end up wading anyway. Wading is unpleasant, but safe if you do it right. Wear your boots with no socks or inner boot. Leather boots will absorb a little water. Even so, they won't end up much wetter than they would from a normal day's sweat. If you wear plastic boots the water will be even less of a problem—just pour it out when you're done. If you're wading in the winter, take care that your feet are warm and your circulation is good before continuing on the trail.

Wading deep fast streams is perilous. Belaying the wader can lessen the danger. But belaying must be done properly—people have drowned while tied to the end of a rope. The proper method is to use two lines. Set one as far as possible upstream above the wader, the other on the bank where he starts across. The upper line keeps him from being washed down the stream; the lower line is used to pull him in if he gets in trouble. It is easy to set up this system with two belayers, but tricky with one. For the one belayer method, station yourself on the bank where the wader starts. The upstream rope goes from you, upstream through an anchored carabiner, then back downstream to the wader. The lateral rope goes from you directly to the wader. Use a belay brake on the upstream rope; the force of moving water can outdo the strongest belay hand. Roped stream crossing works well on smaller streams—in "big water" a person in trouble will drown before you can haul them in.

A ski pole self arrest may work, but an ice axe is better.

SAFETY ON STEEP SNOW:
SNOW CLIMBING AND MOUNTAIN SKIING

Climbers and skiers die every year from sliding falls on snow. Thus, no discussion of safe snow climbing and steep skiing would be complete without a review of the self arrest—the time honored method for stopping such falls.

For snow climbers and mountain skiers the self arrest has four forms. These depend on gear. Climbers should learn to use their ice axe. Skiers can use specialized self arrest grips on their ski poles. These are less effective than an ice axe, yet skiing while holding an ice axe is dangerous and awkward, so arrest grips can be useful. If you have ski poles, but no arrest grips or ice axe, you can perform a self arrest with your pole tips. This is awkward and ineffective. Lastly, if you have nothing, you can try to arrest with your hands and boot toes. This is bogus—but good to practice so you know why you need a tool for an effective arrest.

A successful self arrest is a skilled acrobatic maneuver. You must practice until it becomes instinct. If you're new to the game, a snow climbing course is your best bet for learning. If you're an expert, you should still practice periodically.

Self arrest has one other important aspect: whether you're climbing or skiing, wear non-skid clothing. Slick nylon can turn a small slip into a deadly sliding fall. Wool blend knickers and ski pants are nonskid, as is pile fabric. Cordura nylon is better than slicker nylons. Experienced snow climbers and backcountry skiers have a name for slick nylon shell pants: "death pants."

SKI SAFETY

Most backcountry skiing accidents are the result of skiing out of control and without regard for hidden obstacles. In general, to ski safely in the wilderness you should "survival ski." To survival ski means to ski in control. You must anticipate hazards, fall as little as possible, and if a fall is inevitable, do it in a way that makes the consequences less serious. Practice survival skiing at the ski resort, then use it in the backcountry.

Backcountry skiing on the fourteeners adds a few wrinkles to ski safety: mainly steep snow. The danger in skiing steep snow is that a fall will result in the dangerous sliding fall mentioned above under self arrest. You can't evaluate this danger by slope angle alone. A 38 ° powder slope might present no danger of a fall, but the same slope covered with frozen spring snow could be deadly. Even low-angled slopes can be dangerous given certain conditions, such as rain glaze.

Learning to judge "fall potential" is hard. Plainly, you can not gain experience on the slopes in question. Again, what you must do is practice your self arrest on slopes with safe runouts. Lots of self arrest practice, on slopes with different angles and snow conditions, will give you the background you need for judgment—and for correcting your mistakes!

Skiing steep terrain requires special techniques. Speed control is the key, and extreme skiers use several types of turns to bring their skis around quickly and prevent "unwanted acceleration" down their chosen couloir. A simple jump turn is popular since it's relatively easy to master. The key with jump turns is to minimize flailing and use finesse—"hop" might be a better term than "jump."

Extreme technicians improve the jump turn with the pedal hop turn. This involves using both skis independently, is hard to master, and best learned from a teacher. Many other factors are crucial to safe extreme skiing and should be considered by all aspirants. Among these are pole and ski length, how skis are tuned, and mental preparation. Detailing these subjects is beyond the scope of this introduction.

SNOW CLIMBING

Most of the safety aspects of steep snow are covered above under Ski Safety, yet steep snow climbing has its own set of problems. Foremost is the question of rope use. Many snow climbers are convinced that connecting their group with a rope increases their safety. The theory is that if one person slips, the others can drop into a self arrest and stop the fall. In reality this technique may not work. If the fall happens when the party is inattentive, they'll be jerked off their feet and fall in a tangle of bouncing packs, people, and ropes. Climbing literature abounds with accounts of such falls.

All things considered, snow climbers should only tie together while using anchored belays, moving through a crevasse area on a glacier, or negotiating a corniced ridge. In other rare situations climbers might travel "in coils" to save the time of tying in and untying (time saved can greatly increase safety). If you must safeguard novice climbers on steep snow, you can make roped travel safer with fixed ropes. Used quite often by Outward Bound, and in the past by mountain clubs in the Northwest, fixed ropes provide almost fail-safe protection. For example, a group of 4 climbers could carry several 165′ ropes. All party members are equipped with a climbing harness and ascending device. When they reach steeper terrain, they tie all the ropes together (if need be), and the best climber in the group climbs the snow while on belay from the bottom. He can protect himself with rock or snow anchors if needed (in that case the ropes would be used for individual pitches rather than being tied together). When he reaches his destination (or runs out of rope), he anchors the rope, and the party climbs together while protecting themselves with their ascenders. The beauty of this system is that it averts the danger of unanchored roped travel without sacrificing the huge amounts of time to belay climbers one at a time.

The routes in this book seldom require rope work. Nevertheless, unusual snow or ice conditions or a sick partner can change the easiest climb into a technical problem. So on all but the easiest routes, carry a lightweight rope. If you do carry a rope, be sure you know the fundamentals of belaying and rappelling. Indeed, a rope can get you out of hairy situations, but like any tool a rope is only as good as its user.

Also, don't hesitate to set anchors and belay your skiing in steep terrain. A belayed ski descent is a legitimate application of mountain craft. Purists might scoff—you cannot argue the beauty of an individual challenging a mountain solo, with nothing but skis, axe, and crampons—but most of us would forgo the "edge" in favor of many years of mountain enjoyment—protected by the safety of a rope.

It's immeasurably safer and more efficient to climb snow with crampons and ice axe. Make these items a standard in your kit if snow climbing is remotely possible. The same goes for the excellent ski crampons available for alpine touring ski bindings. Crampon technique for snow is simple. Walk with a normal gait for low-angle work. Steeper terrain requires more technique: balancing on your front points or using a series of traverses to keep your feet flat or a combination of the above. "Snow school" with a guide service is a good way to learn snow climbing.

Crampons give you security, but conversely they also cause falls. One noxious occurrence, known as "snow balling," happens when snow sticks to your boot soles. It gets so thick that your crampon points won't bite. Some models of crampons have a plastic sheet that helps prevent snow balling. Silicon spray helps, too. Sometimes nothing works and you must whack the snow off your crampons before every step. A sharp rap with your axe works well. The other common trip-up occurs when your crampon catches your other leg's clothing or crampon strap. Prevent this with a careful gait and heavy fabric gaiters which a crampon point is less likely to penetrate. Many snow climbers dull their crampons slightly to make them less likely to catch on clothing, but this makes them less sure on ice.

THE SNOW AVALANCHE

In fourteener country, snow blankets the ground from fall to late spring—a span that can cover more than 6 months! During that time, avalanche danger is always possible. Snow slides are a terribly fickle phenomenon. Great strides have been made in avalanche prediction, but experts are still "dead wrong" much too often. Yet you can reduce avalanche risk to an acceptable level, chiefly by choosing times and routes for your climbing that will expose you to less hazard. This is done by the practices of "hazard evaluation" and "hazard avoidance."

In "hazard avoidance," your first step is to carefully determine which routes to avoid, and whenever possible, travel in areas which are not exposed to slides. Such navigation seems basic: for avalanche terrain you need a slope of 25° or more—and snow. But route finding in slide terrain is as subtle as celestial navigation, and just as hard to master. You must put in hours of book study (see bibliography)—and many days in the mountains. The subtleties arise because of slight terrain variations that make the difference between safe and dangerous routes.

To make sense of the terrain, subtle or not, you must evaluate snow stability: this is "hazard evaluation." Again, the key is education. If you are a novice, begin your study with books, advice from others, and perhaps a session with an avalanche school. Combine your study with practice. Indeed, "experience is the best teacher"—but you must temper your experience with caution. With practice you'll be able to pinpoint times when your intended routes are an acceptable risk.

The best way to be safe from snow slides is to stay off avalanche slopes and out of run-out zones. Below timberline, heavily timbered terrain can give you these danger-free routes. Just remember: light timber is no insurance against slides. As the saying goes, "if the trees are close enough together to make you cuss, they're safe." Above timberline, rock ribs and ridges provide safe lines to the fourteener summits.

In many situations skirting a runout or not crossing a slope are impractical choices. If your hazard evaluation skills are good, you may make a decision to expose your party to minimal hazard. Above all, don't let summit fever cloud your judgment. You can come back another day—the mountain will still be there.

RULES OF THUMB FOR AVALANCHE SAFETY

1. **At home:**
   - Call the Forest Service avalanche information number.
   - Check your group for essential items and knowledge: Survival gear, avalanche transceivers, shovels, self-rescue skills, and knowledge of snow and avalanches.
   - Know previous weather, current weather, and forecast.
   - Know the regional history of your snowpack.
   - Check your map and guide book for your route's avalanche exposure.
   - Set your group goals and accepted level of risk—talk about it.
   - Never travel alone in avalanche terrain.
2. **At your trailhead:**
   - Look, listen, feel for avalanche danger signs such as recent heavy snowfall, settling snow, or recent avalanches.
   - Check all transceivers.
   - Review your group's style and goals.
3. **Identify terrain while you travel:**
   - Refer to your map often.
   - Identify every avalanche path (including runouts).
   - Exercise constant vigilance.
4. **Make extra efforts to find and use 0-hazard routes:**
   -Areas with no snow (wind or sun).
   -Early morning frozen snow (in spring).
   -Heavy timber.
   -Slope angle below 26° or over 50°.
   -Ridges.
   -Valley floor (with an eye for danger above you).

IF YOU MUST TRAVEL OVER OR BELOW AVALANCHE SLOPES

5. **Be willing to turn back; evaluate slide probability via:**
   - Snow pit study.
   - Recent snow accumulation (wind or precipitation).
   - Sunrise time and nighttime low temperature (spring season).
   - Slide activity on other slopes.
   - Knowledge of past avalanche cycles.
   - Remember Forest Service avalanche forecast.
6. **Travel one at a time over lowest-angled portion of the path.**
7. **If you must enter the path at a high-point, do so from as high as possible.**
8. **Identify and travel between islands of safety.**
9. **Avoid starting zones.**
10. **If you carry a rope, use an anchored belay while crossing smaller slopes.**

Avalanche!

HOW TO REDUCE AVALANCHE RISK

1. Wind

Year around in the Rockies, wind hammers the lands above timberline. Areas where the wind scours or packs the snow may be avenues of safety. Areas with no snow are obvious, while wind-packed snow is less distinct. Look for patches of vegetation and ground to get an idea of how deep the pack is, and keep an eye out for sastrugi (means "frozen ocean," see photo) patterns more than several inches deep. These indicate major wind erosion and compaction.

Wind-scoured areas present several problems. First, they are uncommon below timberline, so you can't count on wind scour for a safe approach. Second, if wind has been strong, snow may have been transported from scoured areas and deposited as a dangerous hair-trigger slab on other slide paths above timberline. Most experts get real careful when they deal with paths of this sort. Yet down in the trees, many of the same people blithely cross horrendous slide runouts without thought of the snow above. To prevent this mistake, include all the snow above you in your "sphere of awareness." Third, because wind-deposited snow varies so greatly by exposure, climbers can easily traverse from a safe scoured area to an unsafe slab that is literally inches away. For the reasons above, careful route finding should go hand in hand with crystal-ball guesses about snow stability at high altitudes.

2. Timing

Snow is most likely to slide within 24 hours after it is deposited (by wind or storm) at a rate of 1 inch an hour or more for 9 hours or more. Thus, by using this simple rule of thumb you can better your odds: wait at least 24 hours (or better 48 hours) to expose yourself to avalanche slopes that have been newly loaded. Avalanches may still fall after this period—but they are less likely. Even with less loading than that described above, this 24 or 48 hour rule is

Deep hard sastrugi such as this may indicate stable, wind-compacted snow.

still a good standard.

The cyclic nature of slide danger can help you in another way: simply pick a route that has already avalanched. If no other slides are possible, either from more snow in tributary paths or from a collection area above the path, climb it. Bed surface snow (that which remains after an avalanche) has been known to slide on rare occasions, but only when it is a thick slab over another sliding surface—an easy thing to check with a quick snow pit.

3. Seasons of the Colorado Snowpack

Colorado avalanche danger varies by four subseasons: early winter, mid-to-late winter, spring, and summer. You can use qualities unique to these seasons for help with your safety decisions.

Snowpack/Early Winter: During this subseason the Colorado peaks have a thin snowpack, weak sunlight, and very cold temperatures. Almost every year an unstable layer of temperature gradient snow crystals (depth hoar) forms in the snowpack. This depth hoar layer is so loose that it's hard to climb or ski, and it forms a perfect trigger and sliding surface for avalanches. During most years many avalanches run during the early winter season.

Nonetheless, the early winter season can be safer in two scenarios. First, every few years the early winter season is cut out by heavy snow falls. In that situation the snowpack mimics mid-to-late winter season snow—without the dangerous depth hoar layers. In the second scenario, at the start of a normal early winter season you can find fairly safe snow before the depth hoar forms. This snow, however, is usually thin and infirm, making for laborious climbing and dangerous skiing because of hidden obstacles. Perhaps the safest early winter seasons are those with little or no snowfall. In this event skiers will weep, but you can climb fourteeners on foot and snowshoe via their summer routes with no avalanche danger.

For the expert mountaineer early winter can be a bittersweet time on the fourteeners. It's always cold and slide danger is often extreme. Yet the short days with their longer dusks and dawns have a subtle beauty that's worth enjoying. With proper hazard evaluation and avoidance, you can climb and ski the fourteeners in the early winter. But only experts should venture; less experienced winter mountaineers should stick to safer valley excursions.

Snowpack/Mid-to-Late Winter: In this subseason, usually between January and early March, warmer temperatures and deep snow retard the depth-hoar formation that makes early winter snow so dangerous. Like a fallen cake, the thick snowpack collapses under its own weight. It either stabilizes by virtue of the snow crystals adhering to each other (sintering) or avalanches with the new snow's weight as a trigger.

If the snow slides to the ground (a "climax avalanche") stability may result if the slide cleans out the depth-hoar and new snow builds up fast enough and thick enough to sinter and not develop more depth-hoar. What's troublesome is that climax avalanches during the mid-to-late winter season often lead to "repeater" slides. In this event, a layer of depth hoar crystals is either left on the slide path after the slide, or new snow isn't deposited quickly enough to halt the formation of new depth hoar. Danger develops again as soon as new snow is deposited over the depth hoar.

You can climb and ski safely during many days in the mid-to-late winter season. Some days, however, are extremely dangerous. During these periods skiers are even killed during "safe" valley tours when gigantic slides fall from above. To travel safely in this season, you must practice your hazard evaluation and avoidance and take avalanche hazard reports seriously. If hazard in your area is rated as extreme, or an avalanche warning is in effect, stay away from all avalanche terrain. If you lack the skill to identify such terrain, travel with someone who can.

Snowpack/Spring: During the spring subseason, a period of 12 to 16 weeks between late March and July, the snowpack begins to thaw and compact. This process is contingent on elevation, aspect, and weather. Thus, one slope can still have a mid-winter snowpack while another has a spring snowpack.

The outstanding attribute of spring snowpack is that avalanche danger is almost totally predictable—and thus avoidable. This is a marked contrast to Colorado's deserved reputation as a winter slide trap. Spring snow is predictable because spring avalanches are almost always one of two types: the wet snow slide and the direct action slide.

Direct action slides are those that happen during or just after storms when new snow slides off of the older snow underneath. They are common in the spring because frozen spring snow makes a good sliding surface. Direct action slides are easy to avoid: simply stay out of avalanche terrain during and shortly after spring storms.

Wet snow slides are possible only when most of the snowpack is thawed and saturated with water. Fortunately the thawing process follows a daily cycle, freezing by night and melting by day. While the snow has a solid frozen shell it will not avalanche (for total safety ski or climb under these conditions). In the morning, as soon as the sun hits, this shell begins to thaw. In the afternoon thawing takes place in earnest and avalanches are common. Keep in mind you are dealing with slopes of varied aspect, so the morning sun hits them at different times. A north or west slope will warm much later than a south or east slope. See the appendices for sunrise times and a detailed treatise on timing a snow climb or ski descent.

Beware of one "gotcha": after a warm or cloudy night only a thin shell of snow will freeze—or not freeze at all. Either occurrence makes the snow unsafe. You can test for the freeze by digging and probing. While the whole snowpack will not freeze, it should have a solid frozen shell that's too thick to kick a boot through. Also, check the air temperature when you get up in the morning. If you're at a high camp, the temperature must be in the low thirties for a proper freeze. Yet the air temperature need not drop to freezing for the snow surface to freeze; radiant cooling also helps the freezing process—hence the need for a clear night. At lower elevations it is hard to use temperature to evaluate the snow above. Try adding 2° to 31° for every thousand feet below 11,000'. If the morning temperature is warmer than that, take time to carefully evaluate the snow as you climb. (Take similar precautions after a night with cloudy skies.) Don't hesitate to leave earlier in the morning if you doubt your timing—you can always lounge on the summit if it's too dark to descend. As one climber said, "you can never start too early for a real adventure."

One caveat about the spring season: sometime, usually in May, a major slide cycle occurs when the snow from 10,000 feet on up finally gets saturated with water. You don't want to be traveling during this time, since whole valley sides may run. You can avoid this cycle by paying attention to Forest Service avalanche reports, as well as making your own observations while driving over passes and into the higher valleys. Look for consecutive warm days and nights combined with a deep snowpack from heavy March storms or a heavy winter.

For a fabulous alpine holiday, time your skiing or snow climbing to coincide with the spring season. You'll find the perfect crampon surface on the frozen morning snow. Often you'll find a layer of "corn snow" covering the snowpack. Corn is so fun to ski that some mountain skiers seek out the stuff like pilgrims.

Snowpack/Summer: Eventually the freezing, thawing, and compaction described above leads to a dense snowpack that is almost free of avalanche danger. You'll find this mature snow at high altitude in late spring and summer. Fourteeners have a lot of it. Mature snow only slides when it undergoes rapid melting, such as several inches of warm rain or unusually hot weather. It is decent for skiing, but usually has lots of embedded rocks and sun cups. If you climb or ski in mid-summer, this is the snow you will find. Cramponing mature snow is delightful. It's also the only way you can safely climb such snow. Indeed, many climbers are hurt or killed climbing on mature snow without proper gear and technique.

BE FOREWARNED:
THESE SUBSEASONS MAY OVERSIMPLIFY THE PROBLEM

After a winter with a "bad" snowpack (a snowpack with many dangerous weak layers), the potential for slab avalanches can persist through spring and into summer. Moreover, snow can fall during any month. Since most late spring or summer slide danger is caused by thawing snow, you can avoid hazard by starting your climb early. For example, in June of 1992, two people were killed in a slab avalanche in an east-facing couloir on South Maroon Peak. They were climbing during late morning. Several other people had climbed the same snow earlier in the morning—those people are still alive.

Many nonseasonal factors alter snowpack stability. Suncrust layers, surface hoarfrost, and wind loading are a few examples. What's more, pinpointing these snow subseasons is complicated by many things. Their durations vary from year to year and by exposure. For example, a mountain could have spring-season snow on a south face, while the north face snow still behaves like a mid-to-late winter pack. To identify snow subseasons study the descriptions above. Keep a record, perhaps a journal or just a good memory, of the winter's crucial avalanche factors. These include snowfall, wind activity, thaws, and slide cycles. Supplement your field experiences with this information. To get a sense of conditions, speak with mountaineers who have recently traveled in the area. Ski patrol snow safety people, who deal with slide danger every day, are another good information source, as are highway department avalanche safety people. Finally, make regular calls to the local Forest Service avalanche information number (see directory in the appendices). This number provides information on seasonal trends, and also gives a general hazard rating.

It is impossible to be one hundred percent sure about any avalanche slope. Your best defense is total defense: avoid avalanche slopes whenever possible and turn back at the slightest provocation.

During winter, most backcountry deaths in the Rockies result from avalanches. Nevertheless, many snow-season backcountry accidents and medical emergencies result from causes other than snow slides. Mountaineers should take care not to be blinded from these hazards by avalanche paranoia.

IF YOU GET INTO TROUBLE: EMERGENCY PROCEDURE

The mountains are a dangerous place for us fragile humans, and no matter how careful we are, human error or "acts of God" can strike. Thus, you must be prepared to handle an emergency. To do so, you should be skilled in first aid or emergency medicine. Often, you'll need to move an accident victim to a safe bivouac or helicopter landing area. If you're a snow climber or skier, you should know how to move an injured person on snow. Gain these skills by taking courses and studying books. Practice. These techniques look easy on paper but are hard in the field.

Carry a simple first aid kit with plenty of athletic tape, a large elastic bandage, a few sterile compresses, and comfort items such as pain killers and blister dressings.

A well-planned and expedient rescue begins in the field with the victim and companions. In the case of an avalanche burial or severe medical emergency, self rescue and "self treatment" are the only ways you have of saving an accident victim's life. If you carry out the initial rescue properly, the mountain rescue team can follow through efficiently.

In the Colorado Rockies, most people with serious medical problems are evacuated by helicopter. Now and then, a rescue group will use horses, snowmobiles, a human carried litter, or a ski patrol sled. Whatever method you use, your sequence of action should look like this:

1. Before you leave for a climb, be sure someone in civilization knows of your route and schedule. This person should notify the county sheriff if you are overdue (see directory in the appendices for county phone numbers). Even with this arrangement, you cannot count on rescuers appearing when things go wrong. You need to take other steps.

2. Your first step is to do the proper first aid, or in the case of an avalanche, extrication then first aid. After that, move the person to a safe bivouac.

3. If you decide you need a rescue, send someone out for help. If there are only two of you, be sure your companion is safe and comfortable before you leave. His location should be well-marked.

4. People who go for help should have a map clearly marked with the location of the victim. A description of the accident and injuries (or illness) should be written on the back of the map. Those going for help should travel with care and reserve enough energy for simple communication once they get to civilization. They might even need to fly back in and help locate the victim. To notify the authorities, call the sheriff of the county where the victim is.

5. If the sheriff decides you need a rescue, he may authorize a helicopter. Choppers are subject to the whims of weather and landing sites, so you might have a wait if the weather is shaky. Thus, it's good to bivouac as close as you can to the most likely landing site. The land-

If you need a chopper, use proper procedures.

ing site should be clear and level—a rule of thumb for landing site size is 200' by 200'. Some ships require more room, and some can squeeze into a smaller area. Room like this is hard to find on a mountain. In the case of poor landing options, the trend is to use a sling and hoist and not to land the craft. In this event, or in a situation with fall potential, the victim should be wearing a climbing harness and helmet.

6. You should make an effort to be close to likely landing sites, but the pilot will select his own. So put your energy into a survivable and well-marked bivouac. Marking can be hard. On the side of a mountain, your only choice might be waving, or flashing a light if it's dusk or night. If waving is your only choice, try to wear clothing that contrasts with your surroundings. If you have snow to work with, stamp out a large figure. An SOS, X, or an arrow pointing to your exact location will do fine. Down in the timber, a smoky fire can help by acting as a signal and showing wind direction. But do not depend on this alone, and do not build it in the middle of a possible landing site! You can use brightly colored gear to show your location. Anchor such gear to withstand the hurricane winds of helicopter rotors. Any objects sucked up into the rotors will cause a major mishap. If you're on flat ground, but you haven't had time to construct good markers, you'll have to signal the aircraft with your body. To do so, wear bright clothing, lie down in an open area, and wave your arms. It's surprisingly hard to spot a person from the air.

After a helicopter lands, do not run to the ship in your joy. Wait for the rotors to stop, or for the pilot to gesture to you. Before approaching an operating copter, secure all your loose clothing, and carry skis at hip level horizontal to the ground. When you're around this kind of machinery, think before you act. A simple mistake can easily compound an already serious rescue.

7. Remember that the more threatening the situation, the more important your calm attitude is for a successful resolution.

ROUTE FINDING ON THE FOURTEENERS
Orienteering

Orienteering means finding exact locations—and navigating between them. When climbing and skiing on the fourteeners, you use orienteering mostly on your approach to the peak. Intricate routes, such as those on Pyramid Peak, may require orienteering during the actual climb.

The essentials for effective orienteering in the Colorado Rockies are topographic maps (those reproduced here will suffice for all but the most complex routes; such routes are noted in the text), a quality altimeter, a compass, and skill. The former items can be purchased at any mountaineering store. Skill requires practice. Treat each of your backcountry trips, no matter how simple, as route finding exercises. Start with simple routes such as Handies Peak from American Basin, then graduate slowly to complex routes. Above all, know your limits. If you doubt your abilities to follow a route, hire a guide or climb with a friend who knows the route. Have patience—learning this skill requires a long apprenticeship.

The importance of your altimeter is paramount. It, a compass, and a map are the only tools that allow you to safely navigate low-visibility conditions. The trick to using your altimeter is to keep it calibrated. An altimeter reads air pressure, and weather constantly changes air pressure. To counteract this you must recalibrate at every chance. Calibration is simple but takes discipline: each time you reach a location with a known elevation, check your altimeter and set it to the known elevation if it deviates. Mountain tops, passes, huts, stream confluences and trail heads are good places for recalibration.

Once your altimeter is calibrated, you can identify your exact progress up a valley, along a mountain side, or along a ridge. Do so by map-plotting the intersection of your route with your elevation. For flawless route finding, use your compass as well and estimate how far you traveled (based on a known travel speed from other trips).

Though compass work is often secondary to map and altimeter, it can be invaluable. This is especially true in poor visibility when you have no clearly defined drainages or ridges to follow. This situation is quite common in the alpine bowls of the Rockies. Another use of your compass is for low altitude travel in darkness. Snow climbers and skiers are often in this situation.

Use a compass with a flat see-through base and rotating needle housing. Usually, you use your compass to "orient" your map. This means positioning the map to match the land surrounding you so you can visualize your route and navigate from an oriented map.

What you must remember about compass orientation is that two "norths" confuse the issue: magnetic north and geographic north. The vertical borders of the map line up close to geographic north—but your compass shows magnetic north. This is known as *declination.* The simple way around this problem is to use the direction rays on your map. Rotate your compass needle housing until the north-south lines are parallel to the long edges of the compass base. Next, line up the edge of the compass base with the magnetic north line on the direction rays, then rotate the map and compass until the compass needle is pointing to the N on the needle housing. Your map is now oriented. Take heed: orienting by compass is easy, but an oriented map is no help unless you know your location and can identify surrounding terrain. In other words, use your map before you get lost!

On rare occasions when you encounter dense timber, fog, or white-out snow, you will utterly depend on your compass. This demanding form of compass use is called "following a bearing." Simply put, by combining map and compass (and compensating for declination) you figure out your direction of travel. You then use your compass needle and dial to spot a landmark that marks your travel direction, and you travel towards your landmark. In situations with limited visibility use nearby landmarks, and repeat the process each time you reach a landmark. With complete lack of visibility, such as in fog, you may have to use a companion as a marker. Using your compass, you direct her movements as she walks, then have her stop while she is still in sight. You then move to your "human landmark" and repeat the process. This is an effective, albeit tedious, method. One problem is that you must follow a straight line—a hard task if you need to avoid avalanche slopes and such. What do you do with complete lack of sight, such as during night travel? Hold your compass in front of you and check it every couple of minutes—it's surprising how quickly you'll walk a circle when you have no points of reference.

A high-tech navigation device known by the generic term "GPS" (Global Positioning System) is now available. These small handheld units use a system of satellite signals to calculate your longitude, latitude, and elevation. A GPS is quite useful in locating your position on the global grid and will record your route from a position so you can follow it back (thus useful for hunting, mountain rescue, and other activities that involve marking and returning to exact locations). Nonetheless, the GPS altimeter function is not accurate enough for most mountain navigation, and the units are expensive and may be complicated to use. Moreover, while knowing your exact longitude and latitude is certainly useful for ocean or desert navigation, it's not essential in Colorado mountain orienteering where you rarely follow a straight line and locations have more to do with terrain features than points on a grid.

SNOW SEASON CLIMBING
Trail Breaking

At most times in winter, as well as spring afternoons, skiers and snow climbers sink down into the snow with every step. If you're on foot this is fondly termed *post holing,* and can be one of the most strenuous things you'll ever do. Share the labor by changing leads often. With a party of five, for example, change lead about every ten minutes. By doing so, you'll only break trail for a short period once an hour. While breaking trail, use a rhythmic pace at your endurance level of exertion. You can tell you are at your endurance level by being able to converse; if you are gasping too hard to talk, you won't last long. Remember to eat and drink regularly—about once an hour is a good schedule. After doing your stint at the front, drop to the end of the line, sit on your pack, pull out your water bottle, and take in the peaceful beauty around you. With the rest of your party moving at the slow breaker's pace, you'll catch up quickly—refreshed and ready for another turn at the helm.

Summiting Mount Lindsey, Sierra Blanca.

Finding Good Snow

The fourteeners never have a total snow cover. Wind and sun strip various exposures, and from year to year different ranges have more or less snow depending on storm tracks. Nevertheless, from late October to July, climbable and skiable snow exists in the Rockies. If you suspect problems with snow cover, try to check out your intended route from a road. Dedicated ski mountaineers have also been known to recon from an airplane before committing to a hidden fourteener.

In the winter, more skiers are stymied by trap crust than any other snow condition. This variety of breakable crust sucks your skis down under the surface and prevents them from turning. But you can ski trap crust—and even have fun in the process. Most skiers handle trap crust with rebound turns. These are jump turns that use the springboard effect of your skis to pop you up out of the snow. Regular jump turns use wild leaps to do the same, but take more energy and provide less control. To do a rebound turn, first commit yourself to the fall line using proper anticipation; then, when completing your first turn, aggressively press your skis into the snow with a little extra leg extension. Let your skis snap back, and as they do pull them out of the snow with a leg retraction. While your skis are still above the snow, change their direction just enough to make them keep turning when they are back in the snow. A smooth but aggressive rhythm helps with rebound turns. So does practice.

Another desperate snow condition is the bottomless unconsolidated pack during winters with thin snow and cold temperatures. This snow "rots" as it undergoes temperature gradient metamorphism and changes to "Colorado sugar," or "depth hoar." Rotten snow is hard to ski. Conventional telemark or parallel turns will often mean dropping to your waist in a "hoar pond," coming to a rapid stop, and likely going ass over teakettle. Your best bet for skiing bottomless depth hoar on regular-width skis is to keep excess weight on your tails by sitting and leaning far back, then making pseudo turns by slight knee rotations to the left and right. A better way to handle this snow is to use fat skis that float. Conventional alpine width is better than the skinny telemark width, and even fatter helps.

In the spring and summer, finding good snow is a question of daily timing and slope aspect. In general, you'll find the least reliable spring snow on eastern slopes. These slopes get warmth from the morning sun, then continue to gain warmth later in the day from the warm afternoon air; this process heats eastern aspects more than other exposures. In the early spring look for good skiing on south facing slopes, and in the late spring and summer look for turns on the northern exposures (see appendices). Another factor is that Colorado's winter storms follow three different tracks: north, middle, and south. Each year one or two of these regions will have more snow than the others. A few phone calls to Forest Service regional offices (see appendices) will give you an idea of where the snow is the deepest and at what elevation snow cover begins.

A CLIMBER'S RESPONSIBILITIES

We climb, hike and ski the backcountry for many reasons—with feelings of freedom and well-being at the top of most lists. You can't beat a crampon climb up a swooping snow gully to a summit, then launching off for a long ski run. Or watching the sunrise from a fourteener. Or hiking a long ridge high above the timber.

Yet the grim fact is that all mountaineering has risks, and occasionally a mountaineer must be rescued. This costs money—sometimes a lot of money. Most county sheriff departments are mandated to rescue those in need, no matter what the cost. Such rescues may cause financial problems. For example, during the winter of 1986-1987, Summit County Colorado used up its whole emergency budget digging out avalanche victims.

Thus, the politics of rescue have boiled down to economics and led to proposals that limit or ban our use of the backcountry. Fortunately, a fair solution to this problem exists. In 1987 a Colorado law was enacted that places a portion of every hunting and fishing license fee into a state rescue fund. In 1992, this was expanded to include snowmobile and all-terrain-vehicle registrations, and broadened still further in 1993 when the state began selling a "backcountry rescue certificate" that anyone who uses the backcountry can buy, including mountaineers. If you don't already buy a credential that includes the rescue surcharge, you can buy the $1.00 rescue certificate wherever fishing licenses are sold.

Safe mountaineering on the fourteeners is a complex craft; at times it is tedious, most often it is spectacular, and it is always rewarding. Surely, one of the lures of climbing is the feeling of well-executed craft. A responsible commitment to safe mountain travel will let you take that feeling home time after time. Enjoy our glorious mountains—but enjoy them with care.

INTRODUCTION PART 3

EQUIPMENT

Today's mountaineering equipment is lightweight, durable, and well designed. Nevertheless, at times the demands of summer mountain climbing, ski mountaineering and snow climbing cause even today's equipment to fall short. Thus, choosing the right gear for your style of mountaineering is a key to enjoying the fourteeners. The following is intended only as a brief equipment primer. For up-to-date information, refer to magazine equipment reviews and shop employees.

Clothing

Though mankind was brought naked into the world, Eden was not at 14,000' elevation. In any season, you should dress with care for a climb on the Colorado fourteeners. A warm day in July might see you in shorts and t-shirt. But let the clouds roll in and you'll be reaching for more clothing. It's in your pack, yes?

The key to dressing for mountain climbing is "layering." This simply means wearing several thin garments rather than fewer thicker ones. Layering allows precise temperature control and gives you efficient insulation by virtue of trapped air pockets.

For spring and summer climbs carry (or wear) synthetic fabric shorts or hiking pants, long-sleeved shirt, and sun hat. Avoid cotton; its propensity for holding moisture, and subsequent evaporation cooling, can quickly chill you to the point of danger. People have died in the mountains because they wore cotton. When the temperature drops, remove damp clothing and dress in a light turtleneck and tights, both made from any of the excellent synthetic fibers. Colder still, dig out your jacket made of acrylic "fleece" fiber and another pair of thicker tights. Lastly, for wind or wet put on your "shell garment." Your shell should be pants and jacket made from a waterproof/breathable fabric. Carry gloves and a warm hat for "full" conditions.

Earlier, I covered the importance of non-skid clothing for snow climbing and steep skiing. Several companies make excellent climbing pants and jackets made from rough twill-like fabrics with good friction. Many mountaineers have found that traditional stretch wool ski pants, combined with gaiters (or with built-in gaiters), make good outer wear for snow or ice climbing.

Skiers will want attire suitable for their specialized movements. Wool/lycra blend ski pants with padded knees make good leg covering and have the added benefit of higher friction if you take a sliding fall. Special ski gloves help your grip, and shell jackets and pants cut for ski motion help you move.

In winter stick with the layering concept, just carry more layers. During the coldest days even waterproof/breathable shell fabrics may trap too much moisture. In this case use non-waterproof breathable nylon shells, known as "wind shirts" or "wind suits." One-piece suits, shell garments that combine jacket and pants, are terrific for winter climbing. Some of those designed for alpine skiing use breathable uncoated fabric, and are perfect for extreme cold. Others are made from waterproof/breathable fabrics and work well for all but the coldest times. Women, and perhaps both sexes, should consider having a full crotch zipper installed in their shells (some are sold with this included). Indeed, obeying nature's call in a blizzard can be dangerous if you must partially undress.

Footwear

Your footwear should suit your style. If you're bagging peaks during a dry summer day, lightweight fabric hiking shoes might be your choice. For rougher climbs and backpack approaches mid-weight boots, usually made from leather, are better. For snow or mixed snow and rock, your best choice is a pair of modern plastic mountain boots. Use gaiters whatever your choice in footwear. See below for information on ski boots.

Sun Protection

The sun's ultraviolet (UV) radiation will ruin unprotected eyes and skin. Use sunglasses with certified 100% UV filtration. On spring snow use side shields on your sunglasses or add a small flap of tape for the same effect. Skiers, winter climbers, and even spring snow climbers should carry goggles. Modern ski goggles, with double layer lenses, are good. Again, be sure these are certified to filter the dangerous UV rays. Another advantage of carrying sunglasses *and* goggles is that you're covered if you lose either.

As mentioned in Mountain Weather, pages 20-23, high altitude sunlight will injure your skin. Consult these pages for more details.

Light

Carry an artificial light source whenever you climb. If you're serious about safety, you'll start many of your climbs in the dark. Also, you never know when your or someone else's problems will require you to be out at night. The best light source is a lightweight battery operated headlamp. Carry a spare bulb and batteries. Winter climbers should note: Nicad and lithium cells give the best performance in the cold. Rechargeable Nicads also save money and cause less pollution. Handheld flashlights are useless for climbing.

Water Container

Hydration is crucial for mountaineers. Summer or winter, your lowly canteen takes on new meaning. Wide-mouth plastic bottles make the best water jars. Most hold about a quart—perhaps carry two on longer climbs. In summer you can save weight by filtering or treating water from streams. Don't drink untreated stream water. During the colder winter months, frozen water can be an acute problem—sucking on a block of ice is no way to stay hydrated. To keep your water from freezing, fill your bottle up in the morning with hot water or tea, wrap the bottle in extra clothing, and stow it in your pack as close to your back as possible. Some people carry an unbreakable thermos or one of the insulated jars available in mountaineering stores. The latter will cool sooner than a real thermos, but they never freeze. Another good method is to carry one of the new collapsible bladders in your pack near your back with a tube to your mouth. These resist freezing, and you sip water at a constant rate; thus you consume it more efficiently.

Climbing Equipment

When you pick technical climbing gear for most fourteener climbing, make weight as much a gear criterion as anything else. If your gear is too bulky and heavy, it will probably be left behind. Only a few routes in this guide require more than lightweight twelve-point crampons, a short lightweight ice axe, and a small diameter 150-foot rope. If you use stiff boots, consider crampons with a simple latch-binding rather than straps. Wear a helmet in snow gullies, on the steeper climbs such as those in the Crestones, and while you extreme ski. Carry minimal anchoring gear ("protection") on the more technical routes. Details for technical gear are covered in the route descriptions. Usually, a few slings, carabiners, and nuts will suffice. Of course, routes exist that require more equipment, such as the climbs on the east face of Longs Peak. High-angle wall climbs such as those are not covered in this book (see bibliography).

Ski Equipment

Ski mountaineering gear has evolved rapidly in the past decade; mountaineers now use everything from nordic racing skis to alpine gear with non-lift bindings. Two pivotal changes stand out. The first is the development of ski equipment that enables mountain skiers to make turns without latching down their heels. This gear is sometimes called "telemark" equipment, and is termed "free heel" ski equipment in this guide. Free heel skiing is harder than using a latched heel. But it has its place. For tours that involve a lot of distance, or much hiking, the lighter weight free heel rigs offer simplicity and walking comfort. Heavier weight free heel gear is available that mimics the performance of fixed heel alpine equipment, but offers no weight or comfort benefit. Most free heel ski boots are poor for snow, rock and ice climbing. Moreover, the inherent limits of free heel downhill skiing make steep descents in difficult snow the province of an elite group of skiers: those willing to spend hundreds of days a year perfecting their technique.

If you don't qualify for that select group of free heel skiers, the other exciting change in equipment is the evolution of incredibly light, warm, versatile, and durable alpine touring (AT) ski equipment. These set-ups consist of alpine width skis, specially designed plastic boots, and safety bindings that latch down your heel for downhill skiing—but unlatch for vertical heel movement while walking.

Modern AT equipment works well for any ski touring other than flat terrain or track skiing, and it has many advantages over free heel gear for mountain skiing. Intermediate level alpine skiers can click into AT skis and enjoy ski descents that would be impossible for them with a free heel set up. Additionally, AT boots are designed to double as climbing boots. They work well for snow and ice climbing, are adequate for moves on easy rock, and are warm and dry. For those who tackle hairy ski descents, AT equipment gives a level of safety through control that is not possible with a free heel. Many folks choose free heel gear because they think it is lighter than AT equipment. In reality you can get AT boots that weigh less than free heel boots, and AT skis weigh about the same as free heel skis. AT bindings add weight, but very little—and at least one AT binding is as light as a telemark cable binding! In the balance, the added efficiency of skiing downhill on AT gear more than makes up for any slight increase in weight you'll climb with. The fourteeners are a good place for AT ski equipment.

Whatever type of ski gear you use, climbing skins are a must. Mohair skins are the light-

Touching up the wax before a descent.

est in weight, but mountaineers have found that the durability and extra grip of synthetic nylon skins more than makes up for the slight weight increase. If you use AT gear, buy bindings with detachable ski crampons—these are a godsend. Any good quality ski pole will work for mountaineering. Of late, the super-lightweight carbon fiber poles have gained popularity. Adjustable length ski poles are useful: for steep terrain tune them for your own style of skiing, or on a long traverse adjust them to different lengths for comfort. Most adjustable poles clamp together to make a long avalanche probe which can double as a snow depth tester for shelter building. One caveat about adjustable poles: they add another layer of mechanical complexity to your system. In extreme conditions, such as winter fourteener ascents, adjustable poles have been known to collapse or break.

Some ski poles have optional self arrest grips. These are an obvious choice for extreme skiers. Yet snow climbers should consider them as well, since it is efficient to use ski poles for low-angle snow climbing. In doing so, it's nice to have something more in your hands than ski pole grips. Another warning: for performing a self arrest, ski pole arrest grips are half as effective as an ice axe , so use them thoughtfully.

Even today's superb gear can break. Analyze the frailty in your equipment and carry a well-thought-out emergency repair kit that includes essential spare parts and tools, fire starting items, and clothing repair items. Two things every repair kit should have are malleable wire and duct tape, known as "god on a roll."

"Gear does not the climber make." Be realistic about your skills and the limits of your equipment. Pick appropriate routes using the ratings in this book. Gradually escalate the difficulty of your climbs—in a learning curve you can stay alive with.

Skiing the Y Couloir, Pikes Peak, spring.

1 PIKES PEAK

SECTION 1.1

Pikes Peak (14,109′)

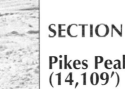

Pikes Peak dominates views from summits all over southeastern Colorado. Back in 1806, the peak attracted the first fourteener bagger when Zebulon Pike attempted to climb his eponymous mountain. Though he failed to reach the summit, Pike started the "fourteener obsession" that drives many climbers through years of alpine vistas and enjoyable rambles. The first non-native climb of Pikes was done in 1820 by Dr. Edwin James and several companions.

While Pikes Peak is relatively inaccessible in the winter, just before Memorial Day each year the Pikes Peak Toll Road and Cog Railway are opened to the summit. Both provide good access for skiing off the summit in most directions, making Pikes the easiest fourteener to ski, as well as one of the best for spring snow climbs. If you prefer less mechanized climbing, the traditional "bottom of the mountain" is the start of the Barr Trail near Manitou Springs. Many people, however, consider Pikes Peak climbed when they spend time on alpine hikes or ski tours near the summit. As is the case with most mountaineering standards, what makes a "climb" is in the eye of the climber. This is especially true for the frail or disabled, for whom Pikes Peak makes a terrific first fourteener.

ROADS AND TRAILHEADS

USGS Maps: Pikes Peak, Manitou Springs, Woodland Park, Cripple Creek N
USFS Forest Visitors Map: Pike NF

Pikes Peak Toll Road

The Pikes Peak Toll Road climbs 20 miles to the summit of Pikes Peak, where tourists mill like skittish deer. It's especially fun to walk over to the Bottomless Pit Cirque (routes 1.1.3, 1.1.4) with your skis on your shoulder, then disappear—oh to be a fly on the wall of the over-look. Usually opening around Memorial Day, with winter closure in the Glen Cove area (11,500'), the highway can be a boon to skiers and climbers but with certain unfortunate con-straints. The road doesn't open until 9:30 AM, which makes an early morning same-day start impossible unless you spend the night. A bivouac is problematic because no overnight parking on the road is allowed. You have to be dropped off to bivouac at the base of your route, then be picked up at the summit. For the spring skier who wants to tackle something less ambitious than a whole mountain, a series of switchbacks on the road (12,000' level) serve as access for several good ski runs. Walking and hitchhiking are both illegal on the toll road. Instead, use a car shuttle or walk at least 50 feet from the road. Food and a place to get warm are available at the summit house. If spaces are available (certain only on non-holiday weekdays), you can buy a downride on the Cog Railway.

The Pikes Peak Toll Road turns S off Highway 24 at Cascade, 10 miles W of Colorado Springs. The turn off has good signs.

Barr Trail Trailhead

From Colorado Springs, drive W to Manitou Springs via Highway 24. Follow obvious signs in Manitou Springs to the Cog Railroad Depot on Ruxton Avenue and park a few hun-dred yards past the depot (follow signs) in an obvious parking area at the Barr Trail Trailhead (6,650'). Though the parking lot is large, space can be in short supply during weekends and holidays. Get there early. The trail is well-signed and begins with a series of steps.

Crags Campground Trailhead

After snow closes the Pikes Peak Toll Road, the Crags Campground gives you the best access for winter climbing and ski touring on Pikes Peak. Moreover, climbing from the Crags keeps you away from the crowds on the Barr Trail and saves your knees because there's less elevation gain and loss. To reach the Crags Campground Trailhead, drive Highway 24 to the town of Divide. (Divide is 25 miles W from Colorado Springs or 72 miles E from Buena Vista.) From Divide, turn S off Highway 24 on to Highway 67. Drive 67 for 4.2 miles and take a hard-to-spot left (E) turn on Teller County Road 62, which leads 3 miles to the Crags Campground. The obvious trailhead parking area is on the east side of the campground (10,150'). During winter and early spring, snow closure may be near the Mennonite Camp at about 9,600' ele-vation, 2 miles below the Crags Campground.

1.1.1	Pikes Peak via Barr Trail	
Ratings:	Summer Climb—Novice	Ski Descent—N.R
	Snow Climb—Novice	
Season:	Summer or Spring	Winter
RT Data:	15 hours, 26 miles, 7,459'↑	Overnight, 26 miles, 7,459'↑
Start:	Barr Trail Trailhead	Barr Trail Trailhead
	6,650'	6,650'
1 Day from Rd:	Summer or Late Spring	Winter
	Yes, but use high camp	No
Map:	Pikes Peak East, pg. 43	
Photo:	pg. 45	

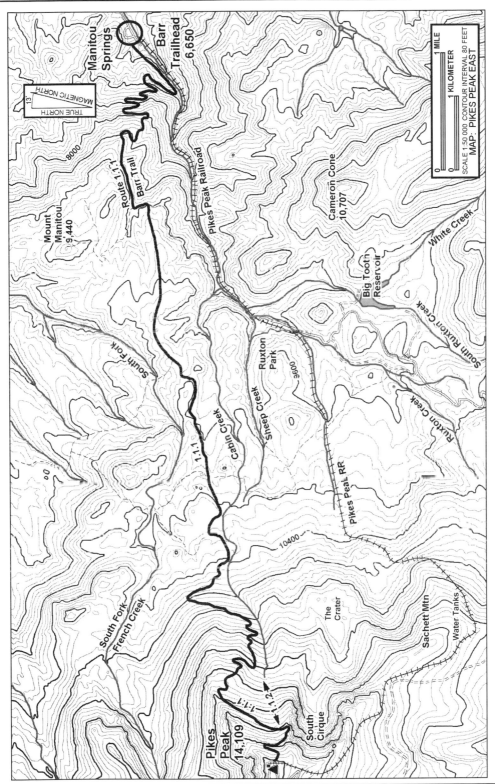

This arduous route includes more than 7,000' of thigh-scourging vertical. Adding insult to us mortals, the same trail is used for the Pikes Peak Marathon, in which runners with iron lungs and the legs of gazelles do the complete trip—up and back—in less than 4 hours. Unlike the route from the Crags Campground (1.1.7), the Barr Trail avoids climbing near the Pikes Peak Toll Road. You can use the Barr Trail as a winter route, but the Crags Campground route (1.1.7) is probably a better choice. When the road and railway are open, climbers who need knee preservation should consider climbing the trail and riding the Cog Railway back down, or having a ride waiting at the summit. For railway information inquire at the Cog Railway office near the Barr Trail Trailhead. See the section introduction for information about the toll road.

Summer after snow melt-off: With a trail as old and beaten as the Barr, route-finding is easy. Study your maps anyway. One point of confusion is a trail junction just as you cross the south fork of French Creek at 9,920', and some sections above timberline could be confusing with the trail obscured by snow. If you do the trip as an overnight, camp at an area known as Barr Camp (9,800'), or bivouac higher.

From the trailhead, the trail climbs steeply out of Englemann Canyon, then follows a long timbered ridge to the mountain's east flank, breaking timberline at about 11,000'. From the last timber, you make a spectacular series of traverses across a broad open area to the summit. The relentless switchbacks don't quit until you step over the last track of the cog railway and confront the crowds at the summit. As you climb this last section, stop for a sip of water as you enjoy the views of Colorado's noble eastern plains.

Spring snow season: Due to windscour and minimal snowfall, it's rare to find much snow climbing on this route.

Winter: It's a long trip, but doable. Plan on at least one night out.

Safety notes: Be aware of this route's length, and don't let the civilized summit lull you into complacency. Whether you're a world-class trail runner or a casual hiker, carry food, extra clothing and water. This climbing route is a backcountry adventure until you hit the summit house. For sunhit, subtract an hour from standard sunrise.

1.1.2	Pikes Peak—East Face Snow Route	
Ratings:	Ski Descent—Advanced Snow Climb—Advanced	
Season:	Snow route, Spring	
RT Data:	15 hours, 26 miles, 7,459' ↑	
Start:	Barr Trail Trailhead, 6,650'	
1 Day from Rd:	Yes, but long	
Map:	Pikes Peak East, pg. 43	
Photo:	pg. 45	

Study Pikes Peak from Colorado Springs and, with a winter or spring snow cover, an obvious terrain feature resembling a shallow curved gully or stripe of snow drops from the south summit ridge, then bends to the right (N), eventually reaching the trees at the head of Cabin Creek (12,000'). For a snow climb or ski alternative to the Barr Trail, this is a good choice. After a heavy winter, it's possible to find good snow here as late as June.

You can reach this east face snow route two ways: For a spring ski descent, simply drive the Pikes Peak Toll Road (section introduction) to the summit, then locate the route by walking a bit south and down from the summit railroad depot. Don't go too far or you'll end up in the cliffy South Cirque. Bring light hiking shoes for the walk out on the Barr Trail (1.1.1) and have a car waiting at the Barr Trail Trailhead (section introduction). To ascend the route, leave from the Barr Trail Trailhead and arrange a ride from the summit, or do the purist routine and descend your route. At any rate, to reach the Barr Trail from the gully (or the reverse), traverse a short distance N at 12,000' elevation.

PIKES PEAK
14,109 FT

EAST
FACE
SNOW
1.1.2

BARR
TRAIL
1.1.1

12,000 FT

SOUTH
CIRQUE

ENGLEMANN
CANYON

TO BARR
TRAILHEAD
& MANITOU
SPRINGS

N

East Face of Pikes Peak, spring.

Safety notes: While this is not extreme snow, you could still take a nasty slide if it's icy. Use an early sunhit time since the sun rises from a negative horizon on the eastern plain.

1.1.3	Pikes Peak—Y Couloir	
Ratings:	Ski Descent—Extreme,	Snow Climb—Advanced
Season:	Snow Route, Spring	
RT Data:	6 hours, 2.5 miles, 2,409'↑	
Start:	Bottomless Pit Cirque, 11,700'	
1 Day from Rd:	Yes, when Toll Road is open	
Map:	Pikes Peak West, pg. 47	
Photo:	pg. 48	

Climbing or skiing the North Face of Pikes Peak via the Bottomless Pit Couloirs is one of Colorado's terrific mountain adventures. Part of this area's appeal is due to the aesthetic nature of Pikes Peak's North Face, but it's also a result of the convenient Pikes Peak Toll Road (section introduction). Combined with a bit of down-scrambling, the road gives climbers easy access to the bottom of Pikes Peak's North Face. Skiers are better off climbing their route before they ski it, but the toll road is only open later in the morning, and it closes at night. Consequently, most people will probably opt for driving to the summit, skiing down the couloir as early as possible, then hiking back up to the road. Thus, keep in mind that the "trailhead" for this route could be the summit of the peak! If you opt to ski these couloirs without climbing them, remember that your intended route might be blocked by steeper terrain, ice bulges, unskiable snow, or cliff bands.

In detail, to scramble from the Pikes Peak Highway to the base of the North Face, get dropped off on the Highway at 13,100', on the south side of Point 13,363. Head N across a sandy flat, skirt a bump on its left (W) side, then scramble down a long rocky ridge known as

Rumdoodle Ridge to a saddle above and to the north of the Bottomless Pit Cirque. Scramble S from the saddle to the low-angled area at the base of the Bottomless Pit Cirque. If you ski, simply scramble back to the road by reversing the directions above. Allow a few hours for the climb and just about the same for a descent.

The face gives a choice of two main couloirs: To climber's left, a lower-angled and wider gully know as the

The civilized summit of Pikes Peak, summer.

Railroad Couloir (1.1.4) leads to the left (E) of the summit; to climber's right, a narrow cleft leads to just right (W) of the summit via two main arms that form the top of a "Y." You'll also notice several other smaller, but no less couloir-like, arms. This is the Y Couloir.

Summer or spring snow season: A snow climb of the Y Couloir is exciting and aesthetic. For this adventure, get a dropoff on the road the afternoon before your climb, then hike down the Rumdoodle Ridge descent route described above, bivouac in the Bottomless Pit, and do your climb early in the morning on safe frozen snow. The Y Couloir routes are obvious (see photo pg. 42). Taking the right branch may lead you to a nice ice bulge. The left branch may

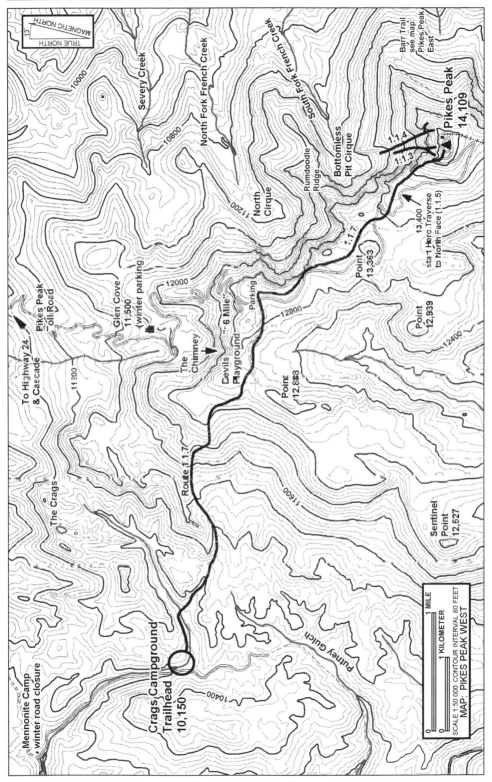

Pikes Peak, Bottomless Pit Cirque, spring.

be blocked by a small rock band, depending on snow cover.

For a ski descent of the Y Couloir, leave from the summit house and walk over to the North Face, staying to the west of the huge concrete Olympic Memorial. Walk W along the top of the face and you'll be at the top of the Y's left (east) arm. This is one choice for a ski route, though you may have to scramble 20 or 30 feet down windblown rocks before you click in. The gully drops steadily at just under 45° to a steeper section with one short portion at about 50°. The way may be blocked by a rock band which you can climb around or rappel.

To reach the western arm of the Y Couloir, which may be a better ski descent, walk a bit farther W from the Olympic Memorial, and find a couloir that starts from the edge of the road. This couloir starts out at about 45°, then steepens considerably at an ice bulge. You could take a serious fall in the upper gully, but the hardest skiing is just above the final runout, making a fall here less of a concern. Bold extreme skiers can jump the bulge, but it's easy to option out by downclimbing the bulge or traversing right (sans skis) across rocks to the east arm of the Y, which then leads to the bottom of the face.

Safety notes: These are classic high altitude couloirs. Most often, avalanche danger is minimized by snow sloughing before it can accumulate enough for a slab avalanche. Beware of situations where this does not happen, and a thick slab of unstable snow has built up in the couloir. If you suspect this situation, start skiing with a belay, and be cautious about climbing from below. Ideally, ski on compacted spring snow. Summer climbers should be prepared for technical ice climbing. Both skiers and climbers should check snow coverage by viewing the face from surrounding highways. Another safety problem, sadly of human origin, is that tourists love throwing rocks down the Bottomless Pit. Use standard precautions such as sheltering to the side of the couloir when you're not skiing, and having a spotter watch above you while you are. Wear a helmet if you're so inclined.

If you opt for descending Rumdoodle Ridge, take great care with route finding, since you can get blocked by cliffs if you blunder.

Since these couloirs are on the deeply cut North Face, they get a late sunhit. After a cold spring night, you may find firm snow till afternoon.

Spring skiing in the Bottomless Pit Cirque, Pikes Peak.

1.1.4	**Pikes Peak—Railroad Couloir**	
Ratings:	Ski Descent—Advanced	Snow Climb—Advanced
Season:	Snow Route, Spring	
RT Data:	6 hours, 2.5 miles, 2,409'↑	
Start:	Bottomless Pit Cirque, 11,700'	
1 Day from Rd:	Yes, when Toll Road is open	
Map:	Pikes Peak West, pg. 47	
Photo:	pg. 48	

The Railroad Couloir in the Bottomless Pit Cirque, so named because the top is near the Pikes Peak Railroad terminus, is the main line (but not the most direct line) in the Bottomless Pit Cirque. The top of the Railroad Couloir has several branches: The central branch, which drops from the rocks near the end of the railroad tracks, is steep and classic. Another branch, starting from a small saddle about 100 feet down the ridge NE from the tracks, may be a slightly easier way in and out (depending on snow cover.) Continue along the ridge and you'll come to the eastern and most direct branch, which you can easily look down to check conditions.

A few feet to the west of the summit house, several fingers drop from the summit and intersect the main couloir several hundred feet down. These are good snow or ice climbs, but may be too intermittent for classic extreme skiing. During late summer you may find alpine ice in branches of the Railroad Couloir, but reaching these can involve unpleasant talus climbing from below, and rockfall is prevalent.

Spring or early summer snow: To climb or ski the Railroad Couloir, use the directions in route 1.1.3 (Y Couloir) for the Bottomless Pit Cirque. If you're skiing, the tops of the couloir's branches are easy to find using the railroad track terminus as your starting point. The whole thing is obvious from the bottom. It's common to ski, then ascend back to the road via Rumdoodle Ridge. Another egress method is to ski the couloir, then climb back up to your car at the summit house "trailhead." In doing so, you not only get a ski descent, but log a summit climb as well!

Safety notes: See route 1.1.3. Sunhit will be slightly later than for the Y Couloir.

1.1.5	**Pikes Peak—North Face Mixed Climbing**	
Ratings:	Ski Descent—N.R.	Snow Climb—Extreme
Season:	Snow Route, Spring	
RT Data:	Moderate Day, depends on route	
Start:	Bottomless Pit Cirque via Hero Traverse or Rumdoodle Ridge	
1 Day from Rd:	Yes, when Toll Road is open	
Map:	Pikes Peak West, pg. 47	
Photo:	pg. 48	

You don't have to travel to Chamonix, France for legendary mixed snow and rock climbing. Try Pikes Peak instead. The North Face of Pikes Peak, basically the upper third of the Bottomless Pit Cirque, is composed of a solid granite split with hundreds of interesting couloirs. During a spring or early summer morning, with the loose rock cemented by the nightly freeze, you can wander out on the face and enjoy all manner of alpine challenge. The word is "pick your route," since it's often possible to switch lines on the broken face, thus creating a route according to your ability.

The main features of the face are the Railroad Couloir and Y Couloir (see routes 1.1.4 & 1.1.3) and a large pale rock buttress to the right (W) of the Y Couloir known as the Corinthian Column. A popular mixed route known as Total Abandon (5.9 & technical ice) takes the right side of the Corinthian Column; another route known as Blind Assumption takes the left side. Between Blind Assumption and the Y Couloir, a good snow-climb takes the narrow and steep Guides Couloir. Still another route takes the buttress between Guides Couloir and Y Couloir. Other mixed climbs take rock and ice in just about every area of the upper face. Go explore.

The simple way to reach the face, especially for the uninitiated, is to scramble down Rumdoodle Ridge (see route 1.1.3), then climb up one of several obvious couloirs to the base of the rock buttresses. In late spring or early summer, these couloirs melt out to heinous talus. Then, a better approach might be the "Hero Traverse," a lateral scramble from the Pikes Peak Highway out into the Bottomless Pit Cirque. While the Hero Traverse is best done with someone who has previous experience, the following directions may suffice for astute navigators: Start from the Pikes Peak Highway at 13,400' elevation. Park where the road curves through a very flat area just several hundred yards from the Bottomless Pit Cirque. Walk east (perpendicular from the road), then take a slightly dropping traverse east into the Bottomless Pit Cirque, eventually reaching the bottom of the Corinthian Column. Once you know the Hero Traverse, it's also a good way to reach easy skiing in the lower sections of several couloirs.

Safety notes: Other than extreme skiing, mixed climbing is the highest form of alpincraft. Don't attempt any such climbing in the Bottomless Pit Cirque unless you're an elite alpine climber or accompanied by an expert companion or guide. Use standard sunrise for approximate sunhit.

1.1.6 Pikes Peak—Road Access Hiking and Skiing

Ratings:	Ski Descent—Intermediate to Extreme Snow Climb—Novice
Season:	All
RT Data:	Moderate Day, gain varies with route
Start:	Pikes Peak Toll Road
1 Day from Rd:	Yes, When Toll Road is open
Map:	Pikes Peak West, pg. 47

Summer after snow melt-off: Just about anywhere off the Pikes Peak Toll Road (section introduction) you can find fine hiking, wildlife viewing and picnicking. Perhaps of most interest to those of the alpine persuasion will be the vast area of tundra and talus above timberline. Countless hikes are possible in this area, but remember the constraints with parking and walking near the road (see section introduction).

Spring and early summer snow season: After heavy spring snowfalls, you may find delightful skiing in the upper portion of the drainage west of the Pikes Peak summit. Take the Pikes Peak Toll Road (section introduction) to the summit. Drop SW off the summit and enjoy varied terrain down to 13,000'; this run is known as the West Ridge. The drainage below here steepens considerably and may be avalanche-prone, so take a climbing traverse N to regain the road at 13,100', perhaps near Devils Playground.

Other popular ski runs take the slopes near switchbacks at the 12,500' level, where the Pikes Peak Toll Road tops timberline via a series of switchbacks known as the "W." Skiers call this area "16-Mile." The most popular run, the Bowl, is the tempting slope closest to the road. West of the Bowl, extreme skiers often tackle the couloirs of "The Three Little Pigs." These are the obvious slots that attract your attention as soon as they come into view as you drive from Glen Cove. The eastern (skier's right) Pigs are the easiest, but may still have a 6-foot mandatory jump to exit the bottom. The western Pig, a long improbable looking finger, is harder to ski, but doable for the expert extremist. Moving still farther to the west, you can access a long and wider couloir known as the Chimney. Then the runs become wider, with the farthest west run down a corniced bowl known simply as Cornice. To access these runs, park near or at the Devils Playground parking area (16 miles from Cascade). For the Bowl, simply ski from the road. To access the other runs, hike to the top of a rocky knob a few hundred yards west of the road. This is part of Devils Playground. From the top of the knob, you can descend directly to the Pigs, or traverse W to the easier (but still Expert rated) slopes.

Safety notes: The west side of Pikes Peak is usually wind-blasted, with continuous snow a rarity. Search out the quality sections and do laps with either car or foot transport. Get an early start and be sure the snow froze tight the night before. Be aware that spring snowfall can recreate winter conditions. Because of varied aspects, use standard sunrise for an average sun-hit time.

1.1.7	Pikes Peak from the Crags Campground	
Ratings:	Summer Climb—Novice	Ski Descent—N.R.
	Snow Climb—Novice	
Season:	Summer or Spring	Winter
RT Data:	10 hours, 12 miles, 3,959′↑	10+ hours, 12+ miles, 4,509′↑
Start:	Crags Campground 10,150′	Crags Campground, 9,600′
1 Day from Rd:	Yes	Yes, but long day with snow closure
Map:	Pikes Peak West, pg. 47	
Photo:	pg. 54	

This is perhaps the best backcountry route for Pikes Peak and is probably your best choice for a winter climb. It's not a terrific ski route, but snow season climbers may want skis or snowshoes for the lower sections and for the long "flats" from 13,000′ to the summit.

Summer after snow melt-off: Park at the Crags Campground (see section introduction). Find the well-signed trailhead for the "Crags," and follow the Crags Trail for a short 250 paces. Look for three steel pipes to the left of the trail. Continue up the Crags Trail for 50 more paces past the pipes, then turn right off the trail, cross a creek, and find a rocky trail (an old road usually marked with cairns) that leads uphill. The creek you crossed will be on your left, with another creek on your right. Follow the old road as it climbs through beautiful forest, crosses the stream at 10,360′, then becomes more of a trail at 10,650′, where you'll see your first good view of the rock crags to your left.

Continue up the well-defined trail which crosses a stream again at 10,860′ (again, the trail resembles an old road). Stick with the obvious trail as it angles left and climbs to 11,130′, where it peters out in an old logging area. But not all is lost. Look sharp, and you'll see an obvious foot trail that heads right (E).

This well-defined path takes several switchbacks and breaks timberline on a pristine, rock-studded shoulder (11,800′). Stick with the trail as it swings right along a short level section into the upper reaches of a tundra-blanketed bowl. The trail gets fainter but still navigable and climbs to a saddle (12,730′) where you get your first view of Pikes summit. Make an effort to use the cairned trail in this alpine section, thus preventing trail braiding and erosion.

At the saddle you'll see the summit looming in the distance, and the switchbacks of the Pikes Peak Highway give you a civilized message. Walk a well-defined dirt road left (NE) from the saddle, then E for 1/2 mile to intersect the Pikes Peak Highway at a large parking area. Walk the left (E) side of the road (staying 50 to 100 feet from the road) for 3/4 mile to intersect the road again at an overlook (12,920′).

Continue paralleling the left side of the road from the overlook for about ¹/2 mile, then depart from the road and hike around the north side of Point 13,363. Intersect the road again on the south side of the point, climb up between several switchbacks, then leave the road for good and climb the final north shoulder to the summit. This last pitch has a few hundred feet of scrambling over large boulders.

Descend the same route. Or if your knees creak, ride the railway down or have a friend pick you up. Remember that walking on the road or road shoulder is illegal, and the road is heavily patrolled.

Spring snow season: While you won't find much skiing on this route, it's certainly a fine choice for a spring climb. With good snow cover it's worth carrying skis for a scoot back down from the summit. To determine snow conditions, check the Peak from Highway 24 while you're driving to Divide.

Winter: This is a good choice for a winter ascent of Pikes. The upper reaches are often wind-scoured, and the road access is good. (The winter access road may be closed several miles below the Crags Campground; see section introduction). Follow the summer route, with variations to avoid avalanche slopes.

Safety notes: This route has many miles of alpine terrain. Summer climbers should consider lightning hazard. Winter wanderers could be trapped by high winds. Though the first part of this trail faces west, the upper portions of Pikes Peak get early sun. Base your starting time on standard sunrise.

When climbing Pikes Peak from the Crags Campground, you'll arrive at this saddle with a good view of road and summit.

2 SANGRE DE CRISTO MOUNTAINS

A summer climb of Mount Lindsey's west ridge.

USFS Forest Visitor Maps: Rio Grande National Forest, San Isabel National Forest

Steep, dry, remote—stupendous in their beauty. Those words do scant justice to the Sangre De Cristo Mountains. The most southerly fourteeners in Colorado, the Sangres are bordered on the west by the vast San Luis Valley, including the huge sand mountains of the Great Sand Dunes National Monument. The east side of the range is bordered by more prairie and high ground, including the strikingly beautiful Wet Valley with its vast irrigated ranchlands.

As a mountain range, the Sangres form a clean 120-mile spine that snakes south from Salida, Colorado, to the New Mexico border. The Sangre fourteeners can be divided into two subgroups: the Sierra Blanca to the south and the Crestones to the north. Because the range is rarely more than one or two mountains wide, summer access is easy via a multitude of roads and trails. One caveat: when they say 4-wheel-drive in these mountains, they mean it! Sangre 4x4 roads are steep, loose, and studded with "baby-heads"—rocks just large enough to cause endless misery to your suspension. Not just any 4x4 will do. You need a rig with vast clearance, body work that can stand a few scratches, and running boards that can take the occasional rock impact. If you do not own such a truck, plan on extra walking.

In the winter and early spring, road closures are far from the peaks, necessitating multi-day expeditions or snowmobile transport. The latter can be arranged via local snowmobile clubs and businesses (see directory). As for seasons, because the Sangres are so dry, and so far south, the spring snowpack matures early. As soon as March, snow climbers and skiers may find a reliable melt-freeze snowpack on all but northern exposures.

Another aspect unique to the Sangres is the amount of private land you must deal with. During Colorado's formative years, huge blocks of land in and around the Sangre De Cristo were given into private ownership as land grants. Several fourteener summits are covered by such land, and it complicates access to many mountains. Sadly, this has curtailed exploration of routes on peaks such as Mount Lindsey and Culebra Peak. Mountaineers with a yen for exploration should try for permission to cross private land if need be. Please do not trespass—there is no surer way to jeopardize access.

SECTION 2.1
The Crestones: Crestone Peak (14,294'), Crestone Needle (14,197'), Humboldt Peak (14,064'), Kit Carson Mountain (14,165'), Challenger Peak (14,080')

Like a medieval rampart, the cold gray rock of the Crestone Peaks rises west from the Wet Valley and east from the San Luis Valley. The jagged summits of Crestone Peak and Crestone Needle have awed mountaineers for years. In contrast to fourteener climbing on the "humps" in the Front Range and Sawatch, climbers in the Crestones find that they must use their hands as well as their feet, and even tie into a rope on occasion! Indeed, some of Colorado's finest alpine rock climbing can be found on the Crestones.

As you can guess, peaks with this kind of climbing are hard to ski. With the exception of Humboldt's classic southeast flank (2.1.2), every summit ski in the Crestones is rated Extreme. Nonetheless, skiers of all abilities can enjoy the Crestones—provided they set realistic goals. For example, few people should attempt skiing off the summit of Crestone Needle; but you can catch superb skiing on either side of Broken Hand Pass.

ROADS AND TRAILHEADS

USGS Maps: Crestone, Beck Mountain, Crestone Peak

South Colony Lake Trailhead

Anyone headed for South Colony Lakes should make a pit stop in the town of Westcliff. In this pleasantly quaint farm community, the tallest objects around are the steeple of the Lutheran Church—and the Crestone Peaks. Clean looking motels and cafes, ranch pickups parked in front, lend a rural feel. You reach Westcliff via either of two state highways that plow relentlessly through Colorado's eastern plains and foothills: 96 from the east, or 69 from the north and south. Driving these roads is a treat. A new view unfolds every few minutes, and with luck, you'll see a sunrise or sunset you will remember forever.

To reach the South Colony Lakes Trailheads, from the main street of Westcliff take the well-signed turn S onto Highway 69. Drive 69 for 4 1/2 miles to the well-signed Colfax Lane (Custer County 119). Turn onto Colfax and drive 6 miles south on Colfax to a T intersection. This is the snowplow turn in the winter.

In the summer, take a right (W) on to the well-signed South Colony Lakes Road (Custer County 120). All but the lowest slung cars can make it up about 3 miles to 2-wheel-drive parking (9,600'). From this point, any short wheel-base 4x4, driven well, can handle the track. Doing so (or walking) will take you 4 miles to 11,040'.

Two trails lead from the road to the lakes. The first (well-signed) is used more by people who are walking the road. It leaves the road at 11,040' and heads up W through evergreen forest 1 mile to the lakes. For the other trail (also obvious and well-traveled), simply walk up the valley from the road closure.

In mid-May, snow closure is around 9,500', or somewhat higher after a light winter (inquire locally). The road is well-used by snowmobiles in the winter, as well as a snowcat which travels the road once a month to measure the snowpack water content. In the winter, it's common for climbers to get a pull to the wilderness boundary from local snowmobilers (see directory). For snow work and skiing, a high camp at the Lakes is helpful, but not a necessity.

Willow Lake Trailhead

This is the west side access for climbs on the north side of Challenger and Kit Carson Peaks. Willow Lake Trailhead is in a remote location, and climbs from here involve a long hike to a high camp. However, if you want to enjoy Kit Carson and Challenger without the crowds of the South Colony Lakes, or you want to ski, this is the best approach. Another plus for this approach is that you get to see the vast San Luis Valley, replete with the Great Sand Dunes National Monument.

You reach the Willow Lake Trailhead via the town of Crestone, a quaint hamlet nestled in the hills at the base of the Sangres. For Crestone, drive Colorado Highway 17 from the N or S to a well-marked turnoff just S of Moffat. Turn E here and drive the obvious road 12.5 miles to Crestone. Stay on the main road (Alder Street) as it leads you into the heart of the town. At the post office (a nondescript building on the east side of the road) turn right (E) on Galena Avenue. Follow Galena Avenue (which becomes South Crestone Road No. 949) 2.3 miles to an obvious turn-around/parking area at 9,070' elevation. This road is rough, but passable with high clearance two-wheel-drive when it is dry. The South Crestone road may be unsigned in Crestone. Look carefully for the Post Office and use it as your landmark. If you plan an early morning start, it might be a good idea to recon this trailhead the day before. Also, the trails and roads in this area can change because of private land concerns.

Trailhead parking is poorly signed, but it's clear where you stop driving. You'll pass some specific signs a few hundred yards up the foot trail. One points to the right and says "Willow Creek Trail." This is the trail to Willow Lakes.

Spanish Creek Trailhead and Cottonwood Creek Trailhead

These trailheads are on private land with no deeded public access. They may be officially closed, though it may be possible to obtain permission to use them. To gain permission, make inquires in the town of Crestone. Respect private land. To reach the trailheads, follow the directions above in the Willow Creek Trailhead description for the town of Crestone. About 1/4 mile before Crestone, turn right (S) off the main road onto the private Baca Road. A sign here says "Baca Grande" (a large residential development). For Spanish Creek drive 3.6 miles to parking at an obvious bridge (8,270'). To reach Cottonwood Creek continue another 1.7 miles miles to an obvious water tower on the left side of the road. Park here (8,420'). Cottonwood Creek passes under the road through a culvert. A faint trail stays north of the creek and becomes harder to find the higher you get. This road and trailhead are on private land with no deeded public access. Thus, for current access policy you should make inquiries in Crestone. Permission may be required. Please respect private land.

Skiing down to South Colony Lakes from Crestone Peak, spring.

2.1.1	**Humboldt Peak—West Ridge**	
Ratings:	Summer Climb—Novice Ski Descent—Intermediate Snow Climb—Novice	
Season:	Summer or Spring	Winter
RT Data:	10 hours, 14 miles, 4,464' ↑	overnight, 16 miles, 5,464' ↑
Start:	South Colony Trailhead 9,600'	South Colony Trailhead 8,600'
1 Day ***from Rd:***	Summer or Spring Yes	Winter No
Map:	Crestone Peak, pg. 66	
Photo:	pg. 60	

This is the standard hike route for the summit of Humboldt Peak. It is one of the simplest routes on the fourteeners and is highly recommended as a beginner summer fourteener climb.

Summer after snow melt-off: From upper South Colony Lake (section introduction), hike N up grass and scree to the saddle on the west ridge of Humboldt (Humboldt Saddle, 12,850'). From here, stick to the ridge and follow grass, scree and the occasional boulder pile to the summit.

Spring snow season: Because of windscouring, the upper portion of this route is often devoid of snow. The slope from South Colony Lakes up to Humboldt Saddle is often bare as well. Consequently, spring snow season climbs of Humboldt via this route are often little different than summer climbs.

Winter: Winter climbers will find this route to be straightforward with minimal avalanche danger. Use windscoured ribs for a safe line to Humboldt Saddle.

Safety notes: Though this route is an easy hike, the north face of Humboldt has plenty of cliffs and steep couloirs that could trap the unwary. Use standard sunrise for sunhit.

2.1.2	**Humboldt Peak—Southeast Flank Snow Route**
Ratings:	Ski Descent—Intermediate Snow Climb—Intermediate
Season:	Spring snow season
RT Data:	4 hours, 2.5 miles, 4,464' ↑
Start:	South Colony Trailhead (2X2), 9,600'
1 Day ***from Rd:***	Yes
Map:	Crestone Peak, pg. 66

This is a beautiful ski descent, and unlike most other snow climbs and ski descents in the Sangres it's rated Intermediate. If you're learning snow climbing and mountain skiing, you should put it on your short-list. Skiers with fourteener descents as a goal should be aware that this is the only slope on Humboldt that consistently holds enough snow for a summit ski descent. Also, remember that spring comes early to the Sangres—especially to south facing slopes such as this.

Spring snow season: As with Humboldt's standard climb (2.1.1), this route is simple. From 10,880' on the South Colony Road (section introduction), head N through dense timber, working up then gradually E to intersect a drainage with an intermittent stream. Follow the snow-filled stream course, then obvious slopes, to the summit.

Safety notes: Snow season mountaineers should note that this is an active avalanche

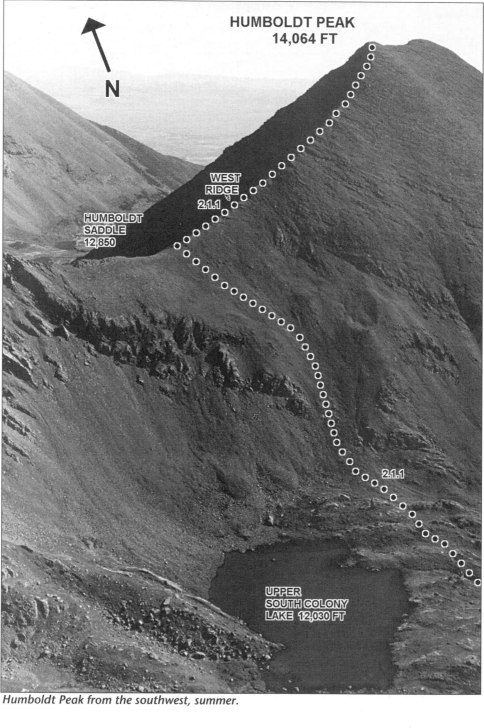

Humboldt Peak from the southwest, summer.

path. Thus, it should only be climbed and skied on a firm spring snowpack. Subtract 1 hour from standard sunrise for sunhit due to the negative horizon to the east.

2.1.3	Crestone Needle—South Ridge and South Couloir	
Ratings:	Summer Climb—Advanced	Ski Descent—Extreme
	Snow Climb—Advanced	
Season:	Summer or Spring	Winter
RT Data:	14 hours, 15 miles, 4,597'↑	Multi-day, 18 miles, 5,597'↑
Start:	South Colony Trailhead (2X2)	South Colony Trailhead
	9,600'	8,600'
1 Day	Yes with 4X4	Winter
from Rd:	Long day with 2X2	No
Map:	Crestone Peak, pg. 66	
Photo:	pg. 62	

This enjoyable summer scramble route is the choice of most climbers bagging "The Needle." Of all the fourteener trade routes, this one has the longest sections of real hand and foot climbing. With that in mind, many novice mountaineers leave Crestone Needle for one of their last goals. In reality, fourteeners such as Pyramid Peak and North Maroon Peak, with their loose rock and treacherous snow fields, require the most skill for safe climbing. Nonetheless, Crestone Needle is hard; this is not the place to learn rock climbing. Novices should travel with a more experienced partner or commercial guide.

With snowcover, the south side of Crestone Needle is transformed into an alluring maze of icy couloirs. After a winter with normal snowfall, fine snow climbing abounds here. As for skiing, this is the only route on the Needle that is skiable from the summit. Even so, it is steep and dangerous and must be in perfect condition for safe skiing.

Summer after snow melt-off: Park at either the South Colony 2-wheel-drive or 4-wheel-drive trailheads. Hike to lower South Colony Lake (section introduction). From the lake, your first goal is Broken Hand Pass (12,900')—the notch between Broken Hand Peak and Crestone Needle. To reach Broken Hand Pass from the lower (east) end of the lake, climb SW up a long traverse (cairned, with many sections of well-worn trail) into the small bowl on the north side of the pass. Keep climbing up scree towards the pass, contouring to the left of a small pinnacle barring the way, then up more scree and steep grass to the pass.

From Broken Hand Pass, ascend a climbing traverse on well-worn paths NW towards the summit of the Needle, eventually intersecting a major couloir. Climb this couloir until it steepens into a corner. To avoid this steep section, climb left (W) over a small rib into another narrower couloir. Follow this couloir to just below the summit, and continue to the summit on easy ground. Descend your ascent route, or continue and traverse the ridge to Crestone Peak (2.1.5).

Spring snow season: Use the route above. At the steep corner you may want to continue up rather than switch couloirs. For a ski descent use the main couloir; the steep crux is at the corner mentioned in the ascent description. It's short, narrow, and steep at 55°. It may be too narrow to ski for about 30 feet, but it is easy to downclimb—just remove your skis before your tips and tails are hanging on the rock! An ice bulge below the steep corner may also bar the way. With enough snow, it's possible to ski around this by connecting a series of snow covered ledges to skier's left. With less snow, a rappel down the ice may be a better solution.

Winter: The crux of winter climbing on this route lies in avoiding avalanche danger on the climb from lower South Colony Lake to Broken Hand Pass. A few rock ribs and shelves help with one-at-a-time travel through exposed areas, but no route allows complete avalanche avoidance. Thus, astute stability evaluation is a must. The south-facing couloirs are usually wind-scoured, and even in the winter the snow may be sun-hardened. If you encounter loose

At Broken Hand Pass, contemplating a winter ascent of Crestone Needle.

snow, get your rope out—even a small avalanche could take you down the couloirs and over cliffs.

Safety notes: Due to the popularity of this route, human-generated rockfall is a concern. Wear a helmet and keep to the sides of couloirs. Use standard sunrise for sunhit.

2.1.4	**Crestone Needle—Ellingwood Arete**	
Ratings:	Ski Descent—N.R. Snow Climb—N.R.	
	Summer Climb—Advanced	
Season:	Summer	
RT Data:	10 hours, 4 miles, 4,597′↑	
Start:	South Colony Trailhead (2X2), 9,600′	
1 Day from Rd:	Yes, but long day with 2X2	
Map:	Crestone Peak, pg. 66	
Photo:	pg. 64, 68	

Without doubt this is one of the classic fourteener rock climbs. This magnificent ridge is easy by today's standards (5.7) but still requires good judgment and a fair amount of skill. If you get butterflies thinking about the airy pitches ahead, remember that the arete was first climbed in 1920 by Albert Ellingwood.

Summer after snow melt-off: Park at the South Colony Trailhead and hike to lower South Colony Lake (see section introduction). Viewed from the lower lake, the Ellingwood Arete is the breathtaking ridge that drops to the right from the summit of Crestone Needle. Simply put, the route follows the ridge line.

In detail: Hike around the left (S) side of lower South Colony Lake, then hike talus to the broad apron at the base of the Ellingwood Arete. Begin climbing to the left of the ridge-proper, then gradually work your way right to intersect the ridge crest at about 12,600′. The climbing to this point is very easy. Once on the ridge, climb several pitches on mostly easy ground to the crux section where things get considerably steeper at an obvious headwall.

Set a belay at the base of the headwall. The first headwall pitch heads right up an angled crack system. The second pitch, the crux, takes a 5.7 crack head-on. Above the crack the angle eases off again, and easy ground leads to a rubble-filled gully below the summit. To avoid rock fall, climb a pleasant pitch to the right of the gully. Descend route 2.1.3, and take care with your route finding on the way down.

Safety notes: The most serious safety problem on this route is the potential for rockfall started by climbers above. Wear a helmet. Holidays and weekends are crowded. Use standard sunrise for sunhit.

At South Colony Lakes, looking at Crestone Needle, summer.

2.1.5	**Crestone Needle to Crestone Peak via Connecting Ridge**	
Ratings:	Summer Climb—Advanced	Ski Descent—N.R.
	Snow Climb—Advanced	
Season:	Summer or Spring	Winter
RT Data:	16 hours, 15 miles, 5,394'↑	Multi-day, 18 miles, 6,394'↑
Start:	South Colony Trailhead (2X2)	South Colony Trailhead
	9,600'	8,600'
1 Day	Summer	Winter
from Rd:	Yes with 4X4	No
Map:	Crestone Peak, pg. 66	
Photos:	pg. 68, 72	

If you love a day in the sky, make this exciting rock climb a priority. This is a 4th class and possibly lower 5th class (depending on exact route) technical route, and should only be attempted by experienced rock climbers or guided parties.

Summer after snow melt-off: Park at the South Colony Trailhead. Take the South Couloir route (2.1.3) to the summit of Crestone Needle. Get a good rest and enjoy the view—you won't have much idle time for several hours. While you relax, examine the ridge ahead. Notice the Red Couloir, an obvious reddish chute dropping down the south side of the ridge. Also notice the hope-bashing false summit (14,040'), just east of Crestone Peak's true apex.

For the most fun, immediately follow the ridge about 100 feet from the summit of the Needle. You'll soon arrive at the obvious first dropoff. Head a few feet N here, then rappel or do belayed downclimbing to the base of this steep section. Next, begin to move along the ridge towards Crestone Peak, and as soon as you can, drop from the crest of the ridge into the couloirs on the south side. Traverse towards Crestone Peak while staying as high as you can in the couloirs.

Skirt the false summit on the south side. Next, climb the Red Couloir to the saddle on the ridge. Make note of this location for your descent, as this is the entry to the North Couloir. From the Red Saddle, follow the left (S) side of the ridge to the summit.

Your work is not yet done. For the descent, head back down to the Red Saddle, and work your way down the North Couloir (2.1.6) to about 13,000'. At this point, exit the couloir to the right (NE) and traverse easy ledges to the north ridge of the peak. Follow the north ridge to the broad flat area at 13,120', known as the Bears Playground. Head SE from the Bear's Playground and downclimb one of several couloirs in the headwall of the South Colony cirque. Several of these couloirs have cliff bands. You can see all the way down the correct couloir, so take your time to check things out before you start down.

Spring snow season: Use the summer route above. Carry crampons and axe.

Winter: Winter strategy for this route is complex. Starting from the Cottonwood Creek Trailhead avoids the north facing slopes on Broken Hand Pass, but you still have to contend with your descent of Crestone Peak. During times of low avalanche hazard, a descent of Crestone Peak's South Couloir (2.1.8) is the most logical, but a wrong guess about slide danger could exact a stiff penalty.

Safety notes: Summer climbers should remember that this route is more ambitious than most fourteener climbs. You'll be in places with fall-potential, and the rock is funky in sections. In winter, avalanche problems are compounded by the need to return to South Colony Lakes via the North Couloir on Crestone Peak, as well as the slopes dropping from the Bears Playground. Thus, snow season climbs of this route should only be attempted during periods of utmost stability. Use standard sunrise for sunhit.

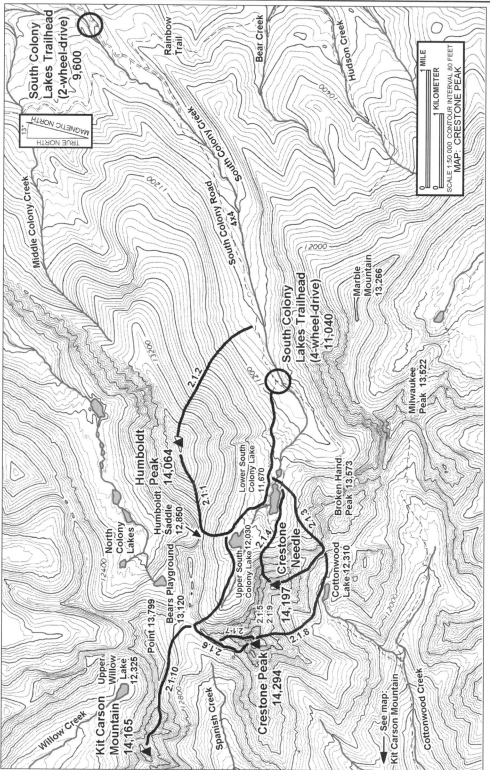

2.1.6   Crestone Peak—North Couloir

Ratings:	Ski Descent—Extreme Snow Climb—Advanced
	Summer Climb—Intermediate
Season:	Spring snow or Summer
RT Data:	6 hours, 3 miles, 4,694'↑
Start:	South Colony Trailhead (2X2), 9,600'
1 Day from Rd:	Yes with 4X4, use high camp if road closed by snow
Map:	Crestone Peak, pg. 66
Photo:	pg. 68

From South Colony Lakes, the North Couloir is the most direct route to the summit of Crestone Peak. With a solid spring snowpack this route can be an enjoyable crampon cruise. Yet in the dry and windy Sangres, couloirs are often devoid of snow. Climbing the North Couloir when it is dry is unpleasant at best—dangerous at worst. With no snow, you will be greeted by loose rock and dirt—and perhaps a little ice to keep things interesting. If you encounter these conditions, consider taking the North Buttress (2.1.7) to climber's left of the Couloir. As for skiing, if this couloir ever filled up with snow it could be a classic, at least down to the cliffs.

Summer after snow melt-off: This route is slightly more involved than most couloirs because the face the couloir splits is not in the South Colony drainage. From upper South Colony Lake, gain the west rim of the South Colony cirque via any one of several obvious couloirs. Spring snow climbers may want to use the left (S) most couloir, since it gains the ridge in a good place to traverse into the North Couloir. If all these couloirs look unattractive, you can also begin this route from Humboldt Saddle, although this involves quite a bit more time and distance.

At the 13,000' level on the ridge, traverse an obvious ledge system SW into the main North Couloir of Crestone Peak. Be sure you enter the couloir above the cliff bands that start just below 13,000'. Climb the couloir to the Red Saddle (14,000'), an obvious low point on the east ridge of Crestone Peak, between the peak's two summits. Be sure to stay in the main couloir—there are several offshoots up and to the right that could attract the unwary. From Red Saddle follow the ridge SW to the summit. Descend your ascent route with careful downclimbing. Or for a double bagger, take the long and hard traverse to Crestone Needle (2.1.9).

Spring snow season: Because of unpleasant scree and loose rock after the North Couloir is dry, some climbers feel the only time to climb this route is as a spring snow climb. Cliff bands make the North Couloir an ugly ski route.

Safety notes: This is not recommended as a winter climb, and should only be climbed on a very stable snowpack. Dirt, mud and ice patches can make this couloir quite miserable when it's melted out. To avoid rockfall danger, climb while no climbers are above you. Climbing on a weekday will make this more likely. Use standard sunrise for sunhit, since the Bears Playground couloirs have easterly aspects, and the climb finishes on a southeasterly face.

Later during the summer climbing season, the North Couloir on Crestone Peak (2.1.6) becomes a heinous shooting gallery filled with loose gravel and patches of ice. The North Buttress is a good way to avoid the North Couloir—provided you're capable of safe movement over steep rock. The climbing is rated as "4th Class," which means that most experienced rock climbers will still want a rope, but may not need much hardware for protection. Even so, on routes such as this, it's easy to get lost and wander onto tougher terrain. With that in mind, bring a reasonable selection of rock hardware.

Crestone Needle and Crestone Peak from the north, winter.

2.1.7	**Crestone Peak—North Buttress**	
Ratings:	Ski Descent—N.R. Summer climb—Advanced Snow Climb—N.R.	
Season:	Summer	
RT Data:	12 hours, 14.5 miles, 4,694'↑	
Start:	South Colony Trailhead (2X2), 9,600'	
1 Day from Rd:	Yes, best with 4X4	
Map:	Crestone Peak, pg. 66	
Photo:	pgs. 68	

The route is straightforward. To begin, follow the directions in route (2.1.6)) to Bears Playground, then follow the traverse SW that would eventually lead to Crestone Peak's North Couloir. About halfway along the traverse, simply start easy hand-and-foot climbing towards the buttress that looms above you. Continue up the buttress. The climbing varies from enjoyable to a bit of loose stuff now and then. You'll first summit on an arete (14,240') near the true summits of Crestone Peak. Downclimb the west side of this pinnacle (rope may be appreciated here), then dance across a slabby traverse to Red Saddle, the cleft between Crestone Peak's two summits. Take easy ground from the saddle to the west summit. Descending this route is not recommended. Use the North Couloir (at least you didn't have to climb it), or continue to Crestone Needle (2.1.9) then descend the Needle's South Couloir (2.1.3).

Safety notes: This is a more sustained technical route than most others in this guide. Though 4th Class rock climbing is a modest grade by today's standards, remember that this is rock climbing at high altitude with the potential of bad weather, rockfall, and problems with route finding. Use standard sunrise for sunhit.

2.1.8	**Crestone Peak—South Couloir**	
Ratings:	Ski Descent—Extreme Snow Climb—Advanced	
	Summer Climb—N.R.	
Season:	Spring or Summer Snow	
RT Data:	14 hours, 15 miles, 5,894'↑	
Start:	South Colony Trailhead (2X2), 9,600'	
1 Day from Rd:	High camp recommended	
Map:	Crestone Peak, pg. 66	
Photo:	pg. 72	

When you mention skiing the fourteeners, someone always asks about Crestone Peak and Crestone Needle—they can't believe the peaks can be skied. That's understandable. Out of all the fourteeners, these two mountains are the most arete-like; their towering summit blocks say "rock climbing." Skiing appears ridiculous. Indeed, while a ski descent of the Needle is possible via route 2.1.3, it has no classic ski line, but Crestone Peak's South Couloir rivals any extreme descent for aesthetics and challenge, and also serves as a fine snow climb.

Spring snow season: Start from the South Colony Trailhead (section introduction). To do the route in one push, you'll need a very early start and enough fitness for a major epic. Otherwise use a high camp. You can also do this route from the Cottonwood Creek Trailhead (section introduction).

Skiing above South Colony Lake, spring.

From the upper end of lower South Colony Lake (11,670'), climb SW to Broken Hand Pass (12,900')—the saddle between Broken Hand Peak and Crestone Needle. Keep a sharp eye out for Bighorn Sheep in this area. The climb to the pass follows obvious snow slopes and short couloirs. Descend the SW side of Broken Hand Pass (good skiing, Advanced) to Cottonwood Lake, then do a climbing traverse W then N to 12,600' level at the base of Crestone Peak's south face. Take care to identify the peak and face, as there are many gullies and rock faces in this area.

The couloir is an obvious cleft in the south face, beginning with several steep steps (maximum 46°) and with a small cliff band about ²/₃ of the way up. Turn this cliff band on the right. The South Couloir leads to Red Saddle—the small col at the head of the North Couloir (2.1.7). To stay on snow to the summit, traverse climber's left and take the southern face from the saddle to the summit.

For a ski descent, click in on the southern face several feet below the summit, then make a few traversing turns back to a point below the saddle. From here, ski the fall line to the first small rock outcrop blocking the couloir. This outcrop is fairly obvious, but pay attention. On good snow years, you may find skiable snow on skier's left, but you may need to remove your skis and downclimb a few feet. Finally, as you near the end of the couloir, break left and traverse into the bowl at the base of the face. This traverse avoids questionable terrain lower in the couloir.

Safety notes: The top portion of this route gets an early sunhit.

2.1.9	**Crestone Peak to Crestone Needle via Connecting Ridge**	
Ratings:	Summer Climb—Advanced	Ski Descent—N.R.
	Snow Climb—Advanced	
Season:	Summer or Spring	Winter
RT Data:	16 hours, 15 miles, 5,294'↑	Multi-day, 18 miles, 6,294'↑
Start:	South Colony Trailhead (2X2) 9,600'	South Colony Trailhead 8,600'
1 Day from Rdl	Yes, with 4X4 or use high camp at South Colony Lakes	
Map:	Crestone Peak, pg. 66	
Photo:	pg. 72	

While it's debatable which direction is best for running the ridge between Crestone Peak and Crestone Needle, Peak-to-Needle might be the more attractive alternative. You finish closer to the trailhead, and the descent of Crestone Needle is a little easier than that of Crestone Peak. Nonetheless, either way you tackle it, this is a 4th class technical rock climb.

Summer after snow melt-off: Park at the South Colony Trailhead. For one-day ascents, use a 4-wheel-drive vehicle and drive the South Colony Road to road closure. Climb Crestone Peak via the North Couloir (2.1.6), or North Buttress (2.1.7). Reverse the summit ridge portion of the North Couloir route back to the Red Saddle (at the top of the North and South Couloirs). Climb down the South Couloir (2.1.8) about 200 vertical feet, then head southeast well below the ridge crest. Continue on ledges and scramble terrain most of the way across the traverse, eventually crossing 250' below the Black Gendarme—the northern companion of three gendarmes near Crestone Needle's summit.

Now the real climbing begins. Your goal is the notch between the two gendarmes on the summit-side of the Black Gendarme. Scramble to the notch, traverse around the base of the gendarme towards the summit, then take more 3rd class terrain to the ridge. One more 4th class pitch leads up the ridge crest to the summit. If you haven't broken out your rope yet, you may want it here. Descend Crestone Needle to Broken Hand Pass (2.1.3), and continue down to your parking.

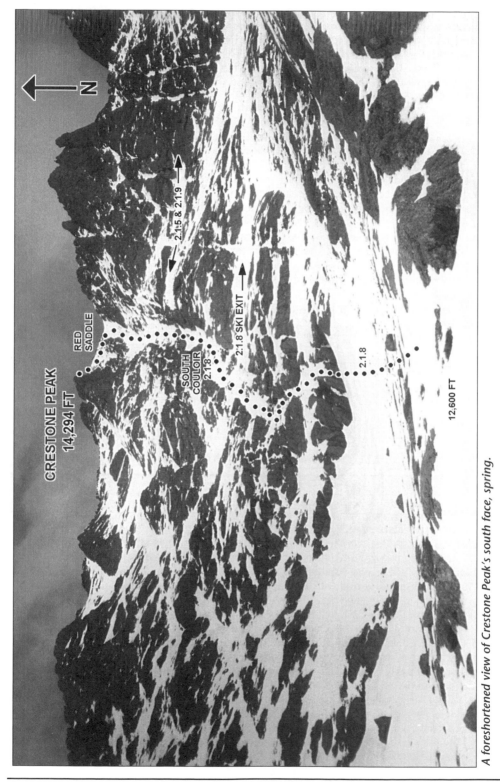

A foreshortened view of Crestone Peak's south face, spring.

Spring snow season: Use the summer route described above. Start early and carry your axe and crampons.

Winter: Connecting Crestone Needle and Crestone Peak in winter is a major endeavor. You need a spell of good weather, low avalanche danger, and the ability to climb 4th and 5th class terrain with sketchy protection and snow-covered holds. To avoid north-facing avalanche slopes, the best strategy is probably to climb from the Cottonwood Creek Trailhead, then summit Crestone Peak via the South Couloir (2.1.8). After that, use the summer route as described above.

Safety notes: Carry a rope and know how to use it. In spring, beware of problems with thawing afternoon snow. Winter climbers should be aware they are undertaking a world-class climbing challenge. Use standard sunrise for sunhit.

2.1.10	Kit Carson Mountain—East Ridge from South Colony Lakes	
Ratings:	Summer Climb—Intermediate	Ski Descent—N.R.
	Snow Climb—Intermediate	
Season:	Summer or Spring	Winter
RT Data:	Overnight, 17 miles, 5,415'↑	Multi-day, 20 miles, 6,415'↑
Start:	South Colony Trailhead (2X2)	South Colony Trailhead
	9,600'	8,600'
1 Day	Summer	Winter
from Rd:	Yes with 4X4	No
Map:	Crestone Peak, pg. 66	
Photos:	pg. 74, 79, 83	

Kit Carson Mountain is a huge monolith and getting to the summit from South Colony Lakes is a major effort. This ridge route is the most reliable and popular, and is a fine summer climb. As a winter route for Kit Carson this is probably the best line, although it has a few tricky sections. Since Kit Carson is often done in conjunction with other peaks, or from a high camp at lower South Colony Lakes, the data above is figured for lower South Colony Lake.

Summer after snow melt off: From the right (N) side of Lower South Colony Lake (section introduction), climb an indefinite trail N then W about 1/2 mile and 360 vertical feet to Upper South Colony Lake (12,030'). Stop here and examine the upper part of the cirque to the west. The saddle which forms the obvious rim of the cirque is known as the Bears Playground. Your next project is to hike W from the lake to the head of the cirque, then climb to the Bears Playground (a huge flat saddle, 13,120') via one of several gullies. Without snow, the gullies to the left are a bit shorter, while the ones to the right make better snow climbs.

Hike N across the Bears Playground, then climb W to your first high point (13,799')—this looks like a mountain but it's only a false summit. Downclimb the west ridge of the false summit into a discouraging notch, then continue up the ridge to what looks like the summit. Nip over this jagged false summit, downclimb some hand-and-foot terrain into a daunting notch, then climb 470 vertical feet W to the true summit. Return via the same route.

Spring snow season: Use the summer route above. Carry ice axe and crampons.

Winter: You have two bad avalanche slopes to contend with on this route. The first is your gully to the Bears Playground. Avoid these gullies by climbing windblown slopes to the Humboldt Saddle (on the West Ridge of Humboldt, see route 2.1.1), then stick with the ridge W to the Bears Playground. The second problem is avoiding slide danger while climbing from the first notch to the false summit. This snowface is visible from the Bears Playground (it looks like the summit). There is no way around this face, and the snow often extends across the face and blends with a cornice at the ridge. Thus, it's hard to find a safe ridge line. Perhaps the only way to climb this with any avalanche safety is via a series of roped pitches that stick as close to

On Kit Carson's east ridge, approaching the false summit, winter.

the ridge as possible (with anchors on rock outcrops).

Safety notes: This climb keeps you at high elevation for many hours. Be in shape and start early. Winter climbers should be willing to turn back if they encounter unavoidable avalanche slopes. Use standard sunrise for sunhit.

2.1.11	**Kit Carson Mountain—North Ridge**		
Ratings:	Ski Descent—N.R.	Snow Climb—N.R.	Summer Climb—Advanced
Season:	Summer		
RT Data:	14 hours, 12 miles, 5,095'↑		
Start:	WIllow Lake Trailhead, 9,070'		
1 Day from Rd:	Yes, for the fit, high camp recommended		
Map:	Kit Carson, pg. 76		
Photo:	pg. 83		

One of the best lines in the Crestones, this relatively easy technical climb takes an airy ridge. While the climbing is certainly of the hand-and-foot variety, it's almost all easy 4th Class. Bring a rope and a light selection of rock climbing hardware.

Summer after snow melt-off. Park at the Willow Creek Trailhead (section introduction). Hike the Willow Creek Trail as it follows a north-facing hillside for about ³/₄ mile, then stays on the south side of the Willow Creek drainage for several miles to 11,000', where it crosses to the south side of the valley in the midst of a headwall studded with cliffs and ledges.

Once past the first headwall, stay in the drainage to Lower Willow Creek Lake. Follow the north shore of the lake, then climb up and around another headwall. Continue up the drainage to 12,000'. The bulky north ridge of Kit Carson will now be almost directly south. Swing south, and hike ¹/₄ mile up the low-angled valley side to the base of the ridge. Start just to climber's left of a notched couloir. Don't mistake this for the Outward Bound Couloir (2.1.12). For your descent, downclimb from the summit to Challenger Peak (2.1.15), then descend Challenger's North Face (2.1.17).

Safety notes: All but elite climbers should have previously climbed their chosen descent route. While this is not a 5th class climb, you could run into such terrain. Start early, and use standard sunrise for sunhit.

2.1.12	**Kit Carson Mountain—O.B. (North) Couloir**		
Ratings:	Ski Descent—Extreme		Snow Climb—Advanced
Season:	Spring or Summer Snow		
RT Data:	14 hours, 13 miles, 5,095'↑		
Start:	WIllow Lake Trailhead, 9,070'		
1 Day from Rd:	No		
Map:	Kit Carson, pg. 76		
Photo:	pg. 83		

Used by Outward Bound as a training climb, this couloir is a fine way to climb Kit Carson Mountain from the north (Willow Creek drainage). The climb is only recommended as a snow route. It also makes a good Extreme ski descent. The late Stuart Mace, musher and pioneer from Ashcroft, Colorado, described a near deadly fall down this couloir during his climbing days in the early 1950's. He said, "it gets pretty icy." Take heed.

Spring snow season: Since an early start is a must for any snow route, backpack in to Willow Lake and set a high camp. Start at the Willow Lake Trailhead (section introduction).

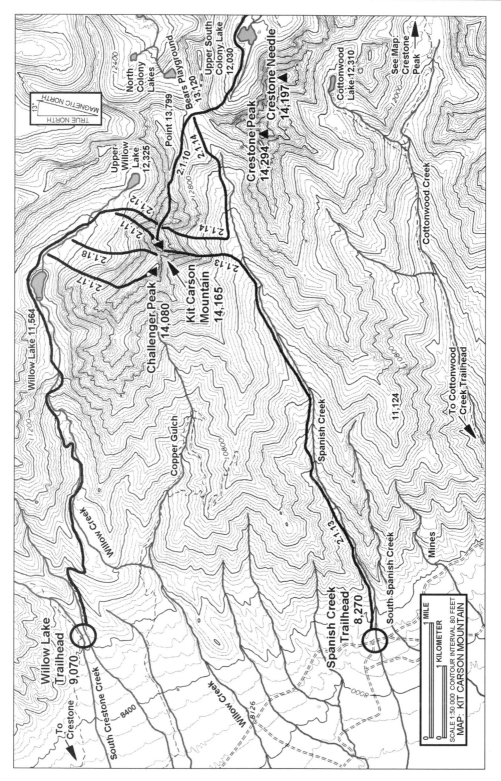

Take the trail as it follows a north-facing hillside for about 3/4 mile (still small snowdrifts here in early April), then stays on the south side of the Willow Creek drainage for several miles to 11,000', where it crosses to the south side of the valley in the midst of a headwall studded with cliffs and ledges. The trail in this area is improperly marked on the USGS Crestone and Crestone Peak maps (it stays on the north side for slightly longer until crossing the valley). In the summer, this is no problem since the trail is an obvious horse path. But with snow cover, it's important to remember that the route traverses the transition between the lower, more jumbled cliffs, and the upper unbroken vertical ramparts. Early season hikers and skiers should beware of ice falling from the upper cliffs.

Once past the first headwall, stay in the drainage to Lower Willow Creek Lake. With good snow cover, follow the the south shore of the lake, then climb S up and around another headwall, where you finally cross timberline. You can also get around the lake on its north side, and this option might be better with consolidated spring snow cover, since it's a little more direct. Once past Lower Willow Lake, continue up the drainage to 12,240' (about 1/4 mile

Kit Carson Mountain, Outward Bound Couloir. Exit after a spring storm.

below upper Willow Lake). Leave the valley here and climb directly SW towards the notch that divides the true Kit Carson summit from the east false summit. The couloir leads to the notch, and becomes deeper and more pronounced the higher you get. Descend your ascent route.

Safety notes: When dry, this couloir is filled with dangerous loose rock and patches of alpine ice. This deeply notched couloir has a late sunhit, but the route above the couloir gets early sun. Skiers may find the top portion is too steep and icy for safe turns.

2.1.13 Kit Carson Mountain—The South Prow

Ratings:	Ski Descent—Extreme		Snow Climb—Advanced
Season:	Late Spring or Summer (No Snow)		
RT Data:	16 hours, 11 miles, 5,895'↑		
Start:	Spanish Creek Trailhead 8,270'		
1 Day from Rd:	High camp recommended		
Map:	Kit Carson, pg. 76		
Photo:	pg. 79		

A classic alpine rock route that follows an elegant line, Kit Carson's South Prow is highly recommended for experienced rock climbers.

Summer after snow melt-off: The approach is long, so most parties use a high camp as a base for this climb. Park at the Spanish Creek Trailhead and hike up a faint trail that stays somewhat to the north of the creek, but crosses the creek many times. Camp near timberline.

The South Prow is the obvious fin-like ridge that catches your attention during the approach. Hike to the base of the Prow, then climb easy slabs to gain the ridge crest. The real climbing begins with a 5.8 overhang that gets you on the real Prow (you can avoid this by taking slabs farther to the right). After the overhang, trend right for the first few pitches (to avoid a bulge), then stick with the Prow for many awesome pitches (5.5) leading to the top of the South Prow (14,000').

There are two ways to reach Kit Carson's summit via continued technical climbing. One option is to head N across the Prow/Carson saddle (13,920'), then work your way across an easy ledge system to the Challenger/Kit Carson saddle. This ledge system is known as Kit Carson Avenue because of its size. From the saddle, climb several easy 5th class pitches to Kit Carson's summit. The other option—one that offers better but harder (5.7) climbing—is to simply continue up the south arete to the summit.

To avoid the above technical finishes, you can traverse Kit Carson Avenue E from the top of the Prow and intersect an obvious gully on the east side of Kit Carson's summit. Follow the gully to the summit. This is the same finish you use for climbing Kit Carson from Challenger Peak (2.1.15).

For your descent, use the South Couloir (2.1.14), or take the East Ridge (2.1.10) to Bears Playground, then drop back down Spanish Creek.

Safety notes: Consider the time-consuming nature of technical climbing. Develop a descent strategy based on snow conditions, your climbing ability, and your knowledge of other routes. Use standard sunrise for sunhit.

2.1.14	Kit Carson Mountain—South Couloir (Cole's Couloir)	
Ratings:	Ski Descent—Advanced Snow Climb—Intermediate	
Season:	Spring or Summer Snow	
RT Data:	Overnight, 4,565'↑	
Start:	South Colony Trailhead (2X2) 9,600'	
1 Day from Rd:	No	
Map:	Kit Carson, pg. 76	
Photos:	pg. 79	

Kit Carson's South Couloir, located in a curious, deep-cut slot on the south side of Kit Carson Mountain, is a terrific climb and ski descent. Access problems, however, preclude calling this a classic. The route has been done in a marathon 15 hour day from parking on the South Colony Road, but a push such as that requires fanatical attention to the weather, and above average endurance. Also, an extremely early start is essential for a one day bid—around 1:00 AM. Good 24 hour weather forecasts are available for Alamosa and vicinity, but longer forecasts are not. Looking at the map, Spanish Creek is the obvious approach (see section introduction). But Spanish Creek has a poor trail and thick brush (and possible access problems due to private property.)

Nonetheless, people do climb Kit Carson via Spanish Creek. If you're fit and can find the faint trail, it's actually a decent day-trip, but a high camp is probably better for your first time—just in case you waste a few hours finding the best trail. Incidentally, the summit of Kit Carson is likely on private property, but local tradition has always allowed unlimited climbing.

Spring snow season: Probably the best strategy for Cole's Couloir (but one that involves more uncertainty with weather because of the lack of long range forecasts) is to

FITZ/PFEIFFER COLLECTION

POINT
13,799

2.1.10

N

SPANISH CREEK VALLEY

KIT CARSON MOUNTAIN
14,165 FT

SOUTH COULOIR
2.1.14

SOUTH PROW
2.1.13

Kit Carson Mountain from the south, winter.

spend your first morning establishing high camp at the upper South Colony Lake (12,030'). The next day, a normal alpine start should allow you to nip over Bears Playground into Spanish Creek, climb Cole's Couloir, then reverse back to camp. You will need to accomplish this all *before* the snow becomes dangerously thawed.

Looking up valley from Upper South Colony Lake, the saddle known as the Bears Playground (13,120') forms the obvious rim of the cirque. Your first crux of the route, and the steepest snow you'll encounter, is to climb to the Bears Playground via any one of the obvious gullies. In most cases the right hand gullies will have firmer snow because of more sun action. Beware of cornices at the top of the gullies.

Once at the Bears Playground, descend the Spanish Creek drainage to 12,000'. Break left around steep rocky areas midway down, but as you approach 12,000', work your way over to the north side of the valley. Skis are efficient for this. As you descend, do careful map reading to identify Cole's Couloir, since the couloir itself is hidden from view unless you drop too far into Spanish Creek. The trick is to identify Point 13,799, then locate the first rocky high point to the west, which you can mistake for the true summit. Cole's Couloir separates this false summit from Kit Carson's true summit. Remember, Cole's Couloir is a deep hidden notch, not a wide, obvious line like the couloir that drops from the false summit.

Starting Cole's Couloir is deceptive since the actual couloir does not drop to the valley floor. Climb likely looking snow in a low-angled rocky bowl that leads up into the area between the two summits—the couloir will become obvious. The climb is fun and straightforward (maximum angle 45° with most of the narrow couloir at 40°).

Near the top of Cole's Couloir (a few hundred feet below the notch between the real and false summits) obvious snow leads out of the couloir (left) up to the Kit Carson Summit (steepest 45°). Descend and return via the same route.

Safety notes: This route involves more distance and vertical than most, so beware of thawing snow—get that early start. If you reach the top of the Bears Playground couloirs and they're dangerously thawed, you can hike the ridge E to the Humboldt saddle and descend dry slopes into South Colony. Because the deeply-notched couloir is so shaded, it takes at least 48 hours for new snow to consolidate—even in late spring. New snow in the section from the summit down to the couloir will harden in 24 hours during clear spring weather. The upper portion of this route is east-facing and gets sun from sunrise on. The deep part of the couloir, however, does not get full sun until at least 4 hours after sunrise.

2.1.15	**Kit Carson Mountain from Challenger Peak**	
Ratings:	Ski Descent—Advanced	Snow Climb—Advanced
	Summer Climb—Intermediate	
Season:	Spring Snow or Summer	
RT Data:	12 hours, 11 miles, 5,170'↑	
Start:	WIllow Lake Trailhead 9,070'	
1 Day from Rd:	Yes, in summer; in spring, high camp recommended	
Map:	Kit Carson, pg. 76	
Photo:	pg. 83	

With a wilderness approach on a good trail, fewer people, and a relatively direct climbing route, this is one of the better routes for Kit Carson. Portions of the route finding near the summit are slightly more intricate than on the East Ridge (2.1.10), but it goes.

Summer after snow melt-off: Park at the Willow Creek Trailhead and use Challenger Peak route 2.1.17 or 2.1.18 to reach Challenger's summit. From Challenger's summit, hike the easy ridge a few hundred yards down to the Challenger/Carson saddle (13,790'). The trick from here is to get on a ledge system known as Kit Carson Avenue. This ledge system traverses south from the Challenger/Carson saddle, then swings east to the Prow/Carson saddle (13,920', see route 2.1.13).

From the Prow/Carson saddle, continue NE along a slightly dropping traverse on the obvious ledge system which leads to the east side of the Kit Carson summit pyramid. Once to the east of the summit, take easy terrain W about 400 vertical feet to the summit.

Spring snow season: Use the summer route described above. While you can't ski most of the terrain between the two summits, both routes up Challenger Peak are good ski descents, hence this route's Advanced ski rating.

Safety notes: Though this route is technically easy, it involves more route finding than many other fourteeners. Take your time. During spring snow season beware of unstable snow on the ledge systems, especially when daily thawing commences. Before you climb the final section to the summit, be sure you have traversed well around to the east side of Kit Carson's summit.

2.1.16	Challenger Peak—East Ridge from Kit Carson Mountain	
Ratings:	Ski Descent—N.R. Snow Climb—Intermediate	
	Summer Climb—Intermediate	
Season:	Late Spring or Summer No Snow	
RT Data:	Overnight, 18 miles, 5,880'↑	
Start:	South Colony Trailhead (2X2), 9,600'	
1 Day from Rd:	No	
Map:	Kit Carson, pg. 76	
Photo:	pg. 83	

Challenger Peak (14,080') is one of those quasi-fourteeners that some folks quibble about. It was unnamed and on few climber's tick lists until the space shuttle Challenger exploded; it was then named for the shuttle, and has become a more popular goal. It's a good climb after melt-off, and provides two classic summit ski descents that are slightly less intimidating than the usual Crestone "adult" skiing. Though Challenger is certainly dubious as a truly separate mountain, it meets the aesthetic requirement when climbed from the Willow Creek Drainage.

If you like long hikes, with some intricate scrambling, this route from the summit of Kit Carson could be attractive. Other routes described here are less tedious.

Summer after snow melt-off: This is a technically easy, but long and strenuous route. You must get an early start to avoid afternoon thunderstorms. First, climb Kit Carson Peak (hikers will probably prefer using the East Ridge route for this, route 2.1.10. The remainder of the route to Challenger is simply the reverse of route 2.1.15. To begin, from the summit of Kit Carson drop E the way you climbed up for approximately 400 vertical feet, then carefully traverse the Kit Carson Avenue ledge system SW to the Carson/Prow saddle (13,920'). Swing NW here and continue along ledges to the Carson/Challenger saddle. From the saddle, climb W for 300 vertical feet up the obvious ridge (easy hike terrain) to the summit of Challenger. Return via the same route.

Spring snow season: Firm spring snow can make this route much easier, but beware the afternoon thaw.

Safety notes: This can be a reasonable winter route, provided you can get from South Colony up the couloirs to the Bears Playground (route 2.1.10) with minimal avalanche risk. However, it would be a very hard day. Use standard sunrise for sunhit.

2.1.17	**Challenger Peak—North Face**	
Ratings:	Ski Descent—Advanced Snow Climb—Advanced	
	Summer Climb—Intermediate	
Season:	Spring Snow or Summer	
RT Data:	10 hours, 9.5 miles, 5,010'↑	
Start:	WIllow Lake Trailhead 9,070'	
1 Day from Rd:	Possible in Summer, no Spring and Winter	
Map:	Kit Carson, pg. 76	
Photo:	pg. 83	

This is perhaps the best ski route for Challenger Peak (route 2.1.18 is a good bet, but harder to get from the summit), and it makes a passable summer climb as well. Dry season climbers, however, would be smart to get here in the spring to enjoy the snow climbing instead of the scree and steep slabs which you'll encounter later in the summer.

Summer after snow melt-off: The route is simple. Park at the Willow Lake Trailhead and hike up the Willow Creek Trail (see section introduction and route 2.1.11). Take a poorly maintained trail around the north side of Willow Lake, which leads to the shelf above the lake (11,800'). Climb S and a bit SW out of the drainage up scree and low-angled rock slabs. The terrain steepens below the summit but is little more than a steep hike.

Spring snow season: With a spring snowpack this route is a superb snow climb or ski descent. The snow route is similar to the summer route described above, but with good conditions it ends up being more direct. Follow the Willow Creek Trail (see routes 2.1.11 and 2.1.12) to Willow Lake, then continue around the north or south side of the lake, depending on snow conditions, to 11,800' in the drainage above the lake. Climb S and a bit SW to a well defined "one-sided" couloir on the left side of the face. The couloir is termed "one-sided" because the right side is well defined by a rock ledge, while the left side blends into the mountain. Take care here not to go too far left into a very steep, cliffy area. Follow the couloir until it peters out, then continue up to the summit ridge west of the summit. Follow the ridge to the summit. Descend your ascent route, and be careful of cliff bands.

Safety notes: Spring comes early to the Sangre De Cristo; skiing and snow climbing may soon become marginal after a normal winter's snow accumulation. Don't hesitate; snow in this couloir could be in condition as early as April. Beware of cliff bands on the north face of Challenger. Locate these during your climb so you can avoid them during your descent. As with most "non-ridge" routes, summer climbers should be aware of rockfall danger. Consider wearing a helmet. This northerly route gets a late sunhit.

2.1.18	**Challenger Peak—Kirk Couloir**	
Ratings:	Ski Descent—Extreme Snow Climb—Advanced	
	Summer Climb—N.R.	
Season:	Spring Snow	
RT Data:	10 hours, 9.5 miles, 5,010'↑	
Start:	WIllow Lake Trailhead 9,070'	
1 Day from Rd:	Yes, but high camp recommended	
Map:	Kit Carson, pg. 76	
Photo:	pg. 83	

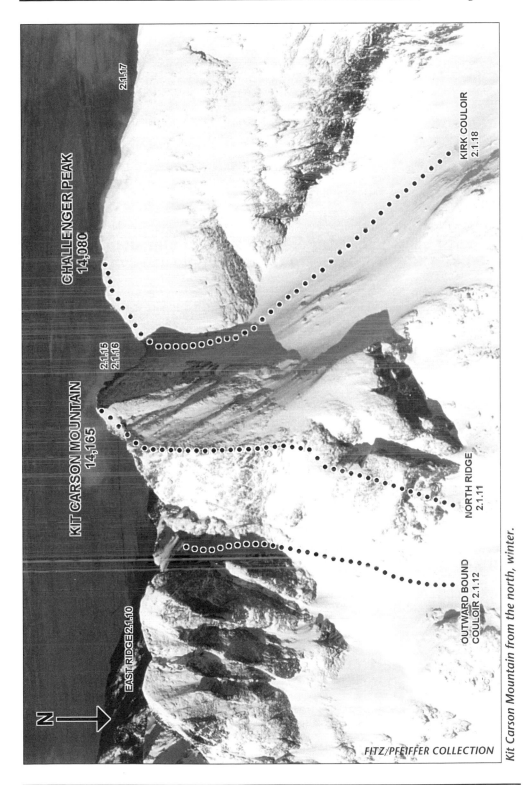

CHALLENGER PEAK
14,080 2.1.17

KIRK COULOIR
2.1.18

KIT CARSON MOUNTAIN
14,165 2.1.15
2.1.16

NORTH RIDGE
2.1.11

OUTWARD BOUND
COULOIR 2.1.12

EAST RIDGE 2.1.10

N →

Kit Carson Mountain from the north, winter.

FITZ/PFEIFFER COLLECTION

This classic line makes a superb ski descent or snow climb. The route is as clean and clear as can be.

Spring snow season: Park at the Willow Lake Trailhead and follow the Willow Creek drainage to the shelf above lower Willow Lake (see section introduction and route 2.1.12). At 12,000' in Willow Creek, climb the obvious snow bowl up and S between Challenger Peak and Kit Carson Mountain. At 13,000', the bowl steepens and narrows into a nice couloir (maximum angle 48°), which leads directly to the Kit Carson/Challenger saddle (13,790'). From the saddle, follow the ridge W for 300 vertical feet to the summit of Challenger. For your descent reverse the route. Skiers may find little snow on the summit ridge—but the couloir is always well stocked. You'll usually find the best ski snow in late April, before the snow is channeled from spring melt-off.

Safety notes: Remember, spring comes early to the Sangre De Cristo. This north and northwesterly route gets a late morning sunhit.

SECTION 2.2
The Sierra Blanca: Blanca Peak (14,345'), Ellingwood Peak (14,042'), Little Bear Peak (14,037'), Mount Lindsey (14,042')

For one of the finest mountain views in Colorado, drive into the San Luis Valley north of Alamosa, Colorado. Here, the Sierra Blanca portion of the Crestone Range (Blanca, Ellingwood and Little Bear peaks) rises more than 6,000 vertical feet from the valley floor. In addition to climbing, consider a visit to Great Sand Dunes National Monument, where huge, wind-buffeted sand dunes contrast with the alpine peaks above.

In the summer, it's common for climbers to bag Blanca and Ellingwood Peaks in one day via an easy route on the west side of the connecting ridge (2.2.3). Hearty experts sometimes add Little Bear Peak for a triple header, as the ridge connecting Blanca and Little Bear can be traversed in either direction (2.2.2). You must have technical climbing skills for this route. With a snow cover on Blanca and Ellingwood, several good ski routes and snow climbs come into condition. The ski down Blanca's west face (2.2.1), through the Crater Lake and Blue Lake basins, could be called one of the fourteener classics. Little Bear has been skied down the west face towards Little Bear Lake, but skiing on Little Bear is not recommended because of access problems.

Mount Lindsey is a fine climb (easy by Sangre standards), and a consummate skiers' mountain. The peak forms the southeastern bulwark of the Sierra Blanca. Since it sits in the midst of private land, access to Lindsey is limited. For the Lindsey approach most mountaineers use the Huerfano River drainage, where deeded public access cuts through several parcels of private land. The men who accomplished the first ski descent of Lindsey gained permission to approach the south face from the ranch lands north of Fort Garland. With permission, good 4x4 roads lead up fairly close to the mountain from this side. By most accounts, permission from the ranch is seldom granted. As of 1990 the ranch was called the Forbes Trinchera, and the phone number may be found under that listing.

ROADS AND TRAILHEADS

USGS Maps: Blanca Peak, Mosca Pass

Como Lake Trailhead
The Como Lake Trailhead is located on the Como Lake 4-wheel-drive trail. This road, if you can call it that, is arguably the roughest 4x4 trail in Colorado. Complete with a gravel hill as loose as a Maroon Bells Couloir, vertical rock steps more than 2' high, and endless sections paved with shaky "baby-heads," it could be said that driving to Lake Como is harder than climbing the peaks above! Most climbers park low and walk the hard-core part of the road.

A spring walk on the Huerfano Road.

To reach the Como Lake Road from the south, start at Alamosa. Drive E on Highway 160 for 26 miles to Highway 150. Take a left (N) on 150, and drive 3 miles and turn right (E) on to a poorly marked dirt road that heads directly towards the peaks of your dreams. This is the Como Lake Road. Drive 2-wheel-drive 2 miles to parking in the desert at 8,020'. Even this section of road is rough and rocky; high-clearance is recommended. Watch for good parking spots and quit while you're ahead—that extra bit of walking might save you the cost of car parts.

To reach this trailhead from the north, drive S on Highway 17, and follow signs to Great Sand Dunes National Monument. From the Monument, drive 14 miles south on Highway 150, and turn E at the dirt road mentioned above.

Climbers with an average 4x4 and some driving skill can get several miles past 2x2 parking to the first crux hill at 10,000'. Here you'll find a turnaround with parking for one vehicle.

You'll find good lodging in Alamosa. The lower section of the Lake Como Road has plenty of tailgate camp sites with no amenities. Do not leave valuables in your car. For a high camp, try the national forest in the basin above the private land around Lake Como.

Huerfano Valley Trailhead

Huerfano means "orphan boy" in Spanish. When you see how isolated the Huerfano Drainage is, you'll know the name fits. To reach the Huerfano Valley Trailheads from Gardner (one gas station) on CO 69, drive N a few hundred yards, then take a left (W) on to the obvious, well-signed road to Redwing. Follow the Redwing Road 6.8 miles to a major intersection. A sign here indicates REDWING to the left. Do not turn left, but continue straight ahead (W) for another 4.8 miles to the next major intersection. The signs here point left to the Huerfano Road (#580) and right to Mosca Pass. Stay left here on the Huerfano Road and continue 3.5

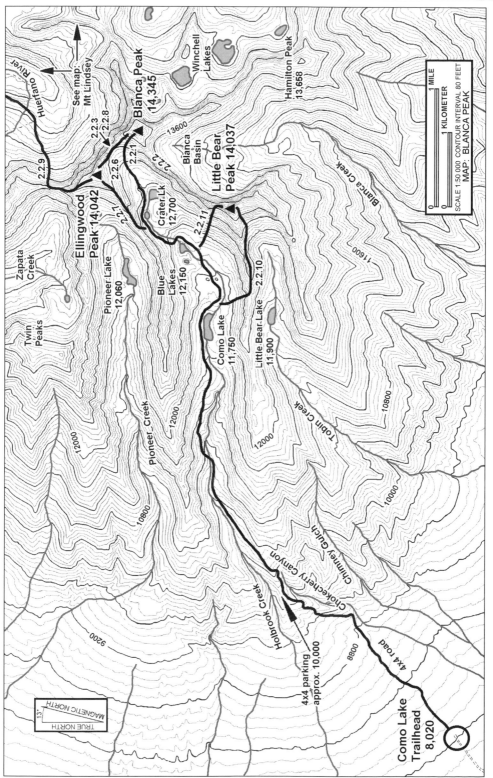

miles to the Singing River Ranch. Park here in winter (8,980').

In the summer you can drive 5.9 miles from Singing River Ranch to road closure at 10,680' (high clearance 2-wheel-drive). In spring the road melts out quickly to meadows at 10,000', and in late May or June you can drive to the summer road closure. If you camp near the road, take care to use public land (mostly at the upper end of the road). Plentiful no-trespassing signs make things clear. You'll find decent camping at the summer trailhead.

Winter parking is obvious at a turnaround near the beginning of private property in the vicinity of Singing River Ranch. Do not park at the end of the plowed road (usually 1/2 mile farther on private land). The jeep trail is used by snowmobilers, but during sparse snow years long sections of south facing road may be devoid of snow, precluding most snowmobile use and making for unpleasant skiing.

2.2.1	Blanca Peak—Northwest Face and North Ridge	
Ratings:	Ski Descent—Advanced Snow Climb—Intermediate	
	Summer Climb—Novice	
Season:	All	
RT Data:	12 hours, 9 miles, 6,325'↑	
Start:	Como Lake Trailhead (2X2) 8,020'	
1 Day from Rd:	High camp recommended	
Map:	Blanca Peak, pg. 86	
Photo:	pg. 88	

This is the standard "list ticker" route for Blanca, as well as the only ski descent.

Summer after snow melt-off: Follow the Como Lake Road (section introduction) to Como Lake (11,750'). Skirt the north side of the lake and continue on a well-defined foot trail to the two Blue Lakes, then to the north side of Crater Lake. Continue up into the basin east of Crater Lake. At about 13,000' the terrain steepens. Climb SE directly up Blanca's west face to the summit—it looks harder than it is.

Spring snow season: Use the route described above for terrific skiing and easy snow climbing. The most logical ski descent begins at a saddle a few hundred feet below and to the west of the summit. If duty calls, you can do a true summit ski by picking through the rocks on the west face just below the summit, but only after a winter with average or above average snowfall. Maximum angle here is 46°.

Winter: Winter climbs of Blanca (as well as Ellingwood and Little Bear) are not the most popular activity in the Sierra Blanca. Nevertheless, with the Como Lake Road behind them, winter mountaineers will find plenty to hold their interest. For a winter ascent of Blanca use the northwest face route described above (provided avalanche danger is minimized by wind scour). You can also avoid slide terrain by ascending the crest of the ridge connecting Blanca with Ellingwood (Blanca's North Ridge). This is rough lower down, but gets easier the closer you are to Blanca's summit. Problem is, you still have to contend with potential avalanche slopes to gain the ridge. Thus, a winter ascent of this route should only be attempted at times of low slide hazard.

Safety notes: The snow melts early in the Sierra Blanca, so most summer climbs of Blanca involve little snow or ice work. Still, the deeper couloirs and clefts may hold dangerous ice. Carry an ice axe while rambling on these peaks, and know how to use it. When this peak is dry, falling rock is a likely hazard. Wear a helmet. Start early to avoid lightning storms. If visibility is limited, be aware of the vertical faces to the north and northeast of the summit. This northerly route gets a late morning sunhit.

ELLINGWOOD PEAK
14,042 FT

N

2.2.7

2.2.6

2.2.1

Spring at Blue Lakes, the west approach to Blanca and Ellingwood Peaks.

2.2.2	**Blanca Peak From Little Bear via Connecting Ridge**	
Ratings:	Ski Descent—N.R.	Snow Climb—N.R.
	Summer Climb—Advanced	
Season:	Summer	
RT Data:	16 hours, 15 miles, 6,825'↑	
Start:	Como Lake Trailhead (2X2) 8,020'	
1 Day from Rd:	High camp recommended	
Map:	Blanca Peak, pg. 86	
Photo:	pg. 91	

While this is one of Colorado's greatest ridge runs, it involves poorly protected 5th class climbing that's only safe for experienced climbers.

Summer after snow melt-off: Start at the Como Lake trailhead, and use a high camp unless you're a fast climber. Take Little Bear Peak via the standard bagger's route (2.2.10). From the summit of Little Bear, downclimb the ridge crest N, then continue along the ridge (technical rock rated 5.2) to Bivouac Tower, a square monolith about 40' high. Pass around the tower by traversing its left (W) side. After a lengthy section of tedious ridge, you'll reach the official Blanca/Little Bear saddle (13,670'). You're now about halfway in distance, but much of the hard-core climbing is behind you.

Continue on the ridge until a major subpeak (13,860') confronts you. Turn this on the right (S), then climb up to a notch in the ridge. Stick with the crest—which includes a classic knife ridge—the remainder of the way to Blanca's summit. Downclimb Blanca via route 2.2.1.

Safety notes: To tackle this route, you must be comfortable with unroped movement over 5th class rock. Though a lightweight rope might be handy for emergencies, most of the technical moves on the ridge are in places where ropework is too time-consuming or just plain impractical. Allow yourself many hours for the climb, and beware of afternoon lightning.

2.2.3	**Blanca Peak from Ellingwood Peak**	
Ratings:	Summer Climb—Advanced	Ski Descent—N.R.
	Snow Climb—Advanced	
Season:	Summer or Spring	Winter
RT Data:	12 hours, 9.5 miles, 7,025'↑	Multi-day, 9.5 miles, 7,025'↑
Start:	Como Lake Trailhead (2X2) 8,020'	Como Lake Trailhead 8,020'
1 Day from Rd:	Summer Yes	Winter No
Map:	Blanca Peak, pg. 86	
Photo:	pg. 95	

If you'd like two summits, with Ellingwood as your first and Blanca second, take this route.

All seasons: Follow any route from Como Lake Trailhead (section introduction, routes 2.2.6 or 2.2.7) to the summit of Ellingwood Peak. Drop down the talus and rocks (or snow in winter or spring) of the south face towards Blanca Peak, then contour as high as possible to Blanca's west face. Continue up the west face to Blanca's summit. Descend Blanca's west face, then pound your knees back down to the desert and your waiting cooler. You did remember the ice?

Safety notes: See the above reference routes. Beware the demanding vertical gain this climb entails. Use standard sunrise for sunhit.

2.2.4	Blanca Peak—North Face	
Ratings:	Ski Descent—N.R. Snow Climb—Advanced	
	Summer Climb—Advanced	
Season:	Late Spring or Summer No Snow	
RT Data:	16 hours, 10 miles, 3,665′↑	
Start:	Huerfano Valley Trailhead 10,680	
1 Day from Rd:	Yes, but very long	
Map:	Mount Lindsey, pg. 100	
Photo:	pg. 92	

One of the fourteeners' few truly technical nordwands, this swooping face was first climbed in 1927 by the late Robert Ormes, the great man of Colorado mountaineering. Legend holds that a few of Ormes' pitons are still in place. Trust them? The face falls in and out of favor as the years roll by. Some parties report rock that's too loose for good climbing. Others say the route is worth your while.

While any number of routes could be made up on this broken and relatively low-angled face, consensus is that the best climbing is the Ormes Route, which follows a buttress quite a distance right (NW) of the true directisima. The route stays either on the crest of the buttress or to the left, with the crux about halfway up (5.6). You'll find much loose rock at the start of the route, but it gets cleaner the higher you go.

There is a hidden gully to the right (NW) of the Ormes Route. This could be a good climb or descent when filled with snow.

It's possible to forge a directisima up the center of the face, but this route is usually wet and has looser rock than other lines.

Safety notes: Rockfall is your gravest concern on this route. Wear a helmet and set belays in protected spots. Use standard sunrise for sunhit.

2.2.5	Blanca Peak—Gash Ridge	
Ratings:	Ski Descent—N.R. Snow Climb—N.R.	
	Summer Climb—Advanced	
Season:	Late Spring or Summer No Snow	
RT Data:	12 hours, 9 miles, 3,665′↑	
Start:	Huerfano Valley Trailhead 10,680	
1 Day from Rd:	Yes, very long	
Map:	Mount Lindsey, pg. 100	
Photo:	pg. 92	

If you've viewed Blanca Peak from Mount Lindsey, you probably noticed the sinuous arete that winds towards you from Blanca's summit. This is Gash Ridge. It's rated 4th class or

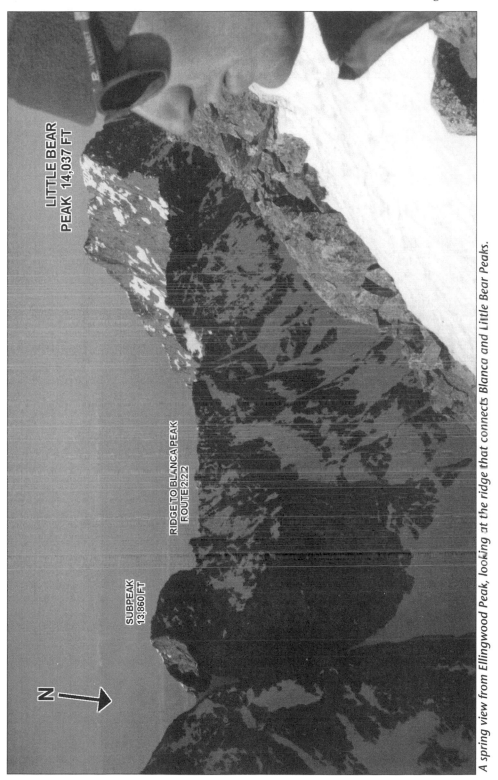

LITTLE BEAR
PEAK 14,037 FT

RIDGE TO BLANCA PEAK
ROUTE 2.2.2

SUBPEAK
13,860 FT

N →

A spring view from Ellingwood Peak, looking at the ridge that connects Blanca and Little Bear Peaks.

Blanca Peak from the east, summer.

low 5th class, and forms a technical line that's safer from rockfall than the North Face (2.2.4).

Summer after snow melt-off: To climb Gash Ridge, start at the Huerfano Creek Trailhead (section introduction). Hike the foot trail up the valley. Instead of following the Lilly Lake Trail, stay close to Huerfano Creek and follow the valley near the creek to 10,100', where Huerfano Creek bends west. Continue south here, leaving the valley and climbing a beautiful ridge south to Point 13,390 on Gash Ridge. Now the fun begins.

Head west from Point 13,390, and let yourself be drawn ever deeper into the Gash. You may need a rappel or belay here. Continue west from the Gash (more ropework), and stick with the ridge until you're just below the summit. You can

FITZ/PFEIFFER COLLECTION

A spring ski descent of Ellingwood Peak's South Face.

continue up directly to the summit or trend slightly to climber's right where you might find easier terrain.

Descending your ascent route is probably not a good idea. Instead, nip over to Ellingwood Peak (2.2.8), then descend Ellingwood's north ridge 1/2 mile down to a major saddle (route 2.2.9). Descend slabby terrain (possibly semi-technical) down into Huerfano Creek, eventually intersecting the Lilly Lake Trail at 11,600'. Stroll the Lilly Lake Trail back to the trailhead.

Safety notes: Carry a rope and know how to use it. Beware of lightning hazard. Use standard sunrise for sunhit.

2.2.6	Ellingwood Peak—South Face		
Ratings:	Summer Climb—Intermediate		Ski Descent—Advanced
	Snow Climb—Intermediate		
Season:	Summer or Spring		Winter
RT Data:	10 hours, 8.5 miles, 6,022'↑		15 hours 8.5 miles, 6,022'↑
Start:	Como Lake Trailhead		Como Lake Trailhead
	8,020'		8,020'
1 Day from Rd:	Summer or Late Spring		Winter
	Yes		No, High camp recommended
Map:	Blanca Peak, pg. 86		
Photos:	pgs. 88, 95		

The status of Ellingwood as an "official" fourteener has long been debated. Actually, this peak is beautiful, has good routes, and is considered by most baggers to be an essential score if they want to say, "I've done them all." Since an aesthetic ski descent is possible from the exact summit, the same could be said of a skier's grand slam. While a high camp is recommended for most Sierra Blanca climbs, this is one trade route where an early start and an average level of fitness can bag you a one-day summit.

Summer after snow melt-off: Park at the Como Lake Trailhead. Follow the Como Lake Road (section introduction) to Como Lake (11,750'). Skirt the north side of the lake and continue on a well-defined foot trail to the two Blue Lakes (12,150'), then to the north side of Crater Lake. Continue into the basin east of Crater Lake. At about 13,000' the terrain steepens. Pause and identify Ellingwood's summit, then climb a bit to the right where the angle eases, then swing left to the top. The route takes easy scree and talus.

Spring snow season: Snow climb a fairly direct line to the summit from 13,000', perhaps staying a bit to the right. This is a classic ski descent, but leaving from the exact summit requires a bit of interesting finagling.

Winter: Use a high camp, and pick a day in late winter with low avalanche hazard. A safer alternative might be the Southwest Ridge (2.2.7).

Safety notes: While this is a good "first teener," you should be comfortable with steep scree and talus. Use an ice axe and crampons for spring snow climbing. With unstable snow, this face could avalanche. The lower part of the face is shaded from morning sun by the Ellingwood/Blanca ridge, but snow near the summit gets sun at standard sunrise.

2.2.7	Ellingwood Ridge—Southwest Ridge	
Ratings:	Summer Climb—Intermediate	Ski Descent—N.R.
	Snow Climb—Advanced	
Season:	Summer or Spring	Winter
RT Data:	12 hours, 13 miles, 6,022'↑	Multi-day, 13 miles, 6,022'↑
Start:	Como Lake Trailhead	Como Lake Trailhead
	8,020'	8,020'
1 Day from Rd:	Summer or Spring	Winter
	Yes	No
Map:	Blanca Peak, pg. 86	
Photos:	pg. 88, 95	

If you like rock scrambling, put this route on your list.

Summer after snow melt-off, or spring snow season: Park at the Como Lake Trailhead (section introduction). Follow the Como Lake Road to Como Lake (11,750'). Skirt the north side of the lake then continue on a well-defined foot trail to the two Blue Lakes (12,150'), then to 12,540'. Leave the valley here and climb N several hundred vertical feet to the ridge crest. Continue on a clean ridge run to the summit. The difficulty never reaches 4th or 5th class, but it comes close.

Winter: This is the best route for avoiding avalanches on Ellingwood Peak, but the climbing involves hand-and-foot rock climbing with the potential for fatal falls. Remember that snowcovered rock will be several times harder to climb than when it's dry; you should have highly developed alpine climbing skill for a winter climb of this route.

Safety notes: Climbers on this route should be comfortable with unroped movement on steep, exposed rock. Add several hours to standard sunrise for sunhit.

ELLINGWOOD PEAK 14,042 FT

N

22.7

22.3 & 22.8

22.6

TO CRATER LAKE

13,000 FT

2.2.8	**Ellingwood Peak From Blanca Peak**	
Ratings:	Summer Climb—Intermediate Ski Descent—N.R. Snow Climb—Advanced	
Season:	Summer or Spring	Winter
RT Data:	12 hours, 13 miles, 6,725'↑	Multi-day, 13 miles, 6,725'↑
Start:	Como Lake Trailhead 8,020'	Como Lake Trailhead 8,020'
1 Day from Rd:	Summer or Late Spring Yes	Winter Yes, but multi-day
Map:	Blanca Peak, pg. 86	
Photo:	pg. 95	

This simple connecting route takes the west side of the ridge between Ellingwood Peak and Blanca Peak.

Start at the Como Lake Trailhead (section introduction), and take Blanca's standard route to the summit (2.2.1). Drop down Blanca's west face (trend towards Ellingwood while doing so), contour below the ridgeline at about 13,600', then climb Ellingwood via its south face (2.2.6). Descend Ellingwood's south face, then follow the trail and road back to your car.

Safety notes: Remember how many vertical feet you're doing. Be fit. Eat and drink frequently. Use standard sunrise for sunhit.

2.2.9	**Ellingwood Peak—North Ridge from Huerfano Valley**
Ratings:	Ski Descent—N.R. Snow Climb—Advanced
Season:	Late Spring or Summer (no snow)
RT Data:	9 hours, 8 miles, 3,362'↑
Start:	Huerfano Valley Trailhead (summer) (10,680')
1 Day from Rd:	Yes
Map:	Blanca Peak, pg. 86; Mount Lindsey,100
Photo:	pg. 92

Use this route as an alternate to the ever-crowded Como Lake routes. As a bonus, it also has fewer vertical feet of climbing.

Start at the Huerfano Valley Trailhead (section introduction) and hike the Lilly Lake Trail to a switchback at 11,600'. Leave the trail here, and climb W up tundra and talus towards an obvious saddle (13,200') on Ellingwood's north ridge. Continue to the saddle, dealing with 4th and possibly easy 5th class rock as the terrain steepens below the saddle.

From the saddle follow the ridge to the summit, working the west side when the going gets tricky. A final dicy section blocks the way to the summit; take this with care. Descend your ascent route, having paid attention to variations on the way up!

Safety notes: This technical route requires experience with complex route finding and movement on rock where dangerous falls are possible. Beware of lightning hazard, and use standard sunrise for sunhit.

2.2.10	**Little Bear Peak—West Ridge & Southwest Face**	
	Ratings:	Ski Descent—Extreme Snow Climb—Intermediate Summer Climb—Advanced
	Season:	Spring snow or Summer
	RT Data:	Overnight, 13 miles, 6,177′↑
	Start:	Como Lake Trailhead, 8,020′
	1 Day from Rd:	High camp recommended; can be done in one day by mountain gods.
	Map:	Blanca Peak, pg. 86
	Photos:	pg. 98

Climbers headed for Little Bear will suffer from the access problems so common in the Sangre De Cristo. Private land surrounds the peak, and the Como Lake Road is the only access available without permission. Even though this is the most popular route from Como Lake, it is exceedingly dangerous because of rockfall, and the 4th class crux pitch is perhaps the hardest rock climbing (for any significant length) of any fourteener "standard" route.

Summer after snow melt-off: Park on the Como Lake Road (see section introduction), and hike the 4x4 trail to Como Lake (11,750′). All but the strongest climbers should overnight at a high camp above or slightly below the private land at Como Lake. Continue 1/4 mile upvalley past Como Lake to 11,960′. Swing S and leave the valley by climbing directly up an obvious couloir to a notch (12,990′) on the ridge crest (this is the west ridge of Little Bear). You may find snow in this couloir through mid-summer. When dry, it's a scree slog and scramble.

Take Little Bear's west ridge 1/4 mile to a rocky bump (12,990′), then drop about 80 vertical feet E to a saddle. Swing to the right on Little Bear's southwest face, then take a climbing traverse E to a major couloir that splits the face. Climb the couloir, which includes a 4th class rock section. After several hundred feet the couloir widens into a ledgy area with lots of loose rock. Take care not to knock rocks on climbers below you, and continue up and slightly left (N) to the summit. Descend your ascent route.

Spring snow season: Use the summer route above as a snow route—it's safer (less rockfall) and more fun. The first ski descent of Little Bear used the couloir on the southwest face described above, then continued directly down into Tobin Creek. This couloir has several steep sections that exceed 45°, and is often icy. Below timberline, Tobin Creek is choked with almost impassable deadfall and brush, and permission is required to drive across private land. Thus, a true ski descent of Little Bear is only for the hardy and resourceful.

Safety notes: The watchword on this route is *rockfall!* It's advisable to never be on this route with other climbers above you—that means only climbing on non-holiday week days. Wear a helmet. Sun hits Little Bear's southwest face couloir several hours after official sunrise.

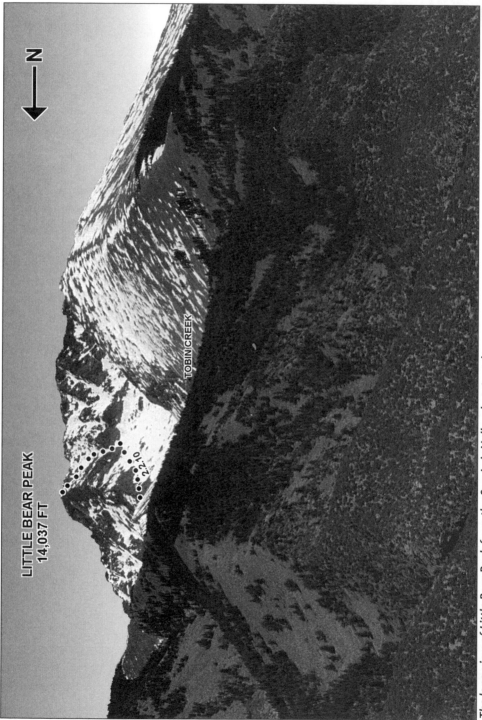

LITTLE BEAR PEAK
14,037 FT

TOBIN CREEK

The long view of Little Bear Peak from the San Luis Valley desert, spring.

2.2.11	**Little Bear Peak—Northwest Face Direct**	
Ratings:	Ski Descent—N.R. Snow Climb—Advanced Summer Climb—Advanced	
Season:	Spring Snow or Summer	
RT Data:	Overnight, 13 miles, 6,097'↑	
Start:	Como Lake Trailhead, 8,020'	
1 Day from Rd:	High camp recommended	
Map:	Blanca Peak, pg. 86	

Experts can use this classic fourteener climb to avoid the crowds and rockfall on the standard Little Bear route (2.2.10). Even so, you'll probably want to use the trade route for your descent, so to avoid crowds climb during non-holiday weekdays.

Summer after snow melt-off: Park at the Como Lake Trailhead. Approach using the Como Lake jeep trail. Hike past Como Lake to 12,080'. Take the time to check your map and identify Little Bear's summit. Your goal is the ridge crest several hundred yards left (N) of the summit. Once you know your goal, exit the valley by climbing S up Little Bear's slabby northwest face (3rd and 4th class). Bear left as you climb to avoid a steep face that drops directly from the summit. If you pick the correct line, your crux will be a steep section just below the ridge. Take the ridge (more 4th class terrain) several hundred yards to the summit. Descend route 2.2.10.

Safety notes: For this route you should be familiar with 5th class rock climbing. Carry a rope and know how to use it. Use standard sunrise time for sunhit.

2.2.12	**Mount Lindsey—Northwest Ridge**		
Ratings:	Summer Climb—Advanced Ski Descent—N.R. Snow Climb—Advanced		
Season:	Summer	Winter	Spring
RT Time:	10 hours, 8 miles 3,362'↑	Overnight, 20 miles 5,062'↑	Overnight, 20 miles 5,062'↑
Start:	Huerfano Valley (summer) 10,680'	Huerfano Valley 8,980'	Huerfano Valley 8,980'
1 Day from Rd:	Yes	High camp	High camp
Map:	Mount Lindsey, pg. 100		
Photo:	pg. 102		

An elegant scramble on a high ridge makes this the most aesthetic climb on Mount Lindsey. This is a good route for avoiding avalanche danger in winter, and it keeps summer climbers safely above the rubble-covered north face. Moreover, using this route causes less erosion.

Summer after snow melt-off: Follow route 2.2.13 to the saddle (13,100') between the Iron Nipple and Mount Lindsey. Continue up the obvious ridge to the summit. You'll encounter some hand-and-foot moves with a little exposure. Carry a rope for emergencies,

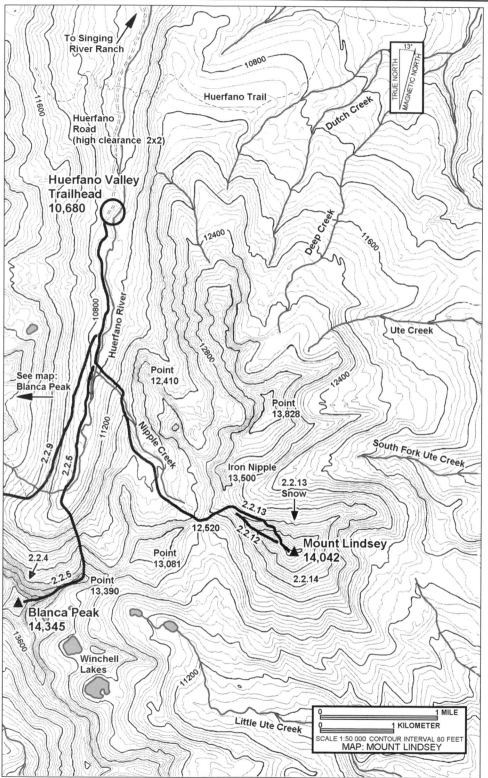

but you probably won't need it. Descend your ascent route if you found it easy enough. If not, you can use the standard north face couloirs route (2.2.13), or in an emergency, descend the southeast face (2.2.14).

Spring snow season: Use the summer route above and carry snow climbing gear for your descent.

Winter: Plan on an overnight and use the summer route above. While the scramble sections of the ridge are easy in the summer, winter conditions could increase the difficulty to 5th class. Bring a rope and a light selection of climbing hardware.

Safety notes: While this is not a technical climbing route, you must be comfortable with hand-and-foot climbing—with fall potential. Summer climbers should start early to avoid lightning.

2.2.13	Mount Lindsey—North Face Couloirs	
Ratings:	Ski Descent—Extreme Snow Climb—Advanced	
	Summer Climb—Advanced	
Season:	Spring Snow or Summer	
RT Data:	10 hours, 8 miles, 3,362'↑	
Start:	Huerfano Valley Trailhead, 10,680'	
1 Day from Rd:	Yes	
Map:	Mount Lindsey, pg. 100	
Photo:	pg. 102	

While this is the easiest route up Mount Lindsey, a more aesthetic line sticks with the Northwest Ridge (2.2.12) to the summit.

Summer after snow melt-off: From parking at the Huerfano Valley Trailhead (section introduction), follow an obvious closed roadcut on the west side of the valley. The route is fairly obvious to the Lily Lake Trail intersection at 10,740'. There is usually a sign here, and plenty of tree blazes. Don't take the Lily Lake Trail. Stay on the Huerfano Trail here as it drops down a short hill, swings close to the river, and takes you a flat 1/4 mile to 10,760'.

Using map, compass and altimeter, carefully identify the drainage (known as Nipple Creek) that climbs from 10,760' SE into the basin on the west side of the Iron Nipple. Hikers will want to follow the tree "cut-line" to the left of the creek, then where prudence dictates, work right into the narrow creek bed. There is a well-traveled trail in this area, but it's easy to miss. If you get on the trail, it climbs through steep forest, crosses the creek at 11,300', then climbs up out of the creek bed via the rib forming the right (SW) side of the creek bed. The trail (or the creek bed) both lead into a beautiful, low-angled alpine basin. Snow or no snow, stroll up the basin to the pass at the head of the basin (12,520'). This is the pass 3/4 mile southwest of the Iron Nipple. All the routes in this section diverge from here. To reduce trail braiding, try to stick with a beaten and cairned trail in this area.

From the 12,520' pass mentioned above, ascend the ridge NE to an obvious 13,100' saddle on the ridge connecting Lindsey with the Iron Nipple. From the saddle, expert rock climbers can enjoy a 4th class ascent of the Lindsey's Northwest Ridge (2.2.12). The easier way is to traverse E from the saddle across the N face. After about 1/4 mile of traversing, climb a series of couloirs that eventually intersect the summit ridge west of the summit, then hike the summit ridge.

Spring snow season: Use the summer route above. The flat area at 10,760' is a good place for a high camp, since the steeper climbing begins at this point. If you're looking for snow climbing, from the 13,100' saddle consider traversing farther E across the north face— the couloirs become wider and even easier to ascend. For a fine snow climb or ski descent, an

MOUNT LINDSEY
14,042 FT

NORTHWEST RIDGE 2.2.12

13,100 FT
SADDLE

2.2.13

2.2.13

2.2.13
SNOW

N

SOUTH FORK UTE CREEK

Mount Lindsey from the northwest, summer.

obvious couloir leads directly to the summit. This is shown on the map at the head of an intermittent stream in Lindsey's north face bowl. For the most aesthetic snow climb, take this couloir from the bottom by first descending into the bowl from the 13,100′ saddle.

Safety notes: Be careful of rockfall on the north face. These northerly couloirs get a late sunhit.

2.2.14	Mount Lindsey—Southeast Face	
Ratings:	Ski Descent—Intermediate Snow Climb—Intermediate	
	Summer Climb—Intermediate	
Season:	Spring Snow or Summer	
RT Data:	10 hours, 9 miles, 3,362′↑	
Start:	Huerfano Valley Trailhead, 10,680′	
1 Day from Rd:	High camp in early Spring	
Map:	Mount Lindsey, pg. 100	

This is a fine ski route and a nice summer hike, but much of the route is on private land. While this route might qualify for historic access, inquire locally for permission from the Forbes Ranch (see section introduction) to be sure of legality.

Summer after snow melt-off and spring snow season: Take route 2.2.13 to the 12,520′ pass southwest of the Iron Nipple. Continue on a long contour from the pass SE then E to Lindsey's beautiful southeast face. Climb the rocky face to the summit, then descend your ascent route. With spring snow cover, you can find continuous snow for your whole route.

Safety notes: Subtract at least an hour from standard sunrise for sunhit on this high southeast face.

SECTION 2.3
Culebra Peak (14,047′)

Culebra Peak is the southernmost fourteener in Colorado, and it lies completely on the private land of the Taylor Ranch—with limited access. This fourteener is another "giant gravel pile." As such, it has limited appeal to technical climbers. Snow climbers and hikers will find it to be worthwhile, but skiers should remember that the southern Sangre De Cristos offer limited skiing on all but the heaviest snow years. To top all that, Taylor Ranch charges a fee for bagging Culebra ($25 in 1989). Considering the fact that hunters pay thousands of dollars to hunt on the ranch, the peak fee is really a pittance. Yet if you're used to climbing in Colorado's vast public lands, paying to climb a peak may be less than attractive. At least it makes you appreciate our public lands.

Because of these access problems, many climbers never bother with Culebra Peak. Indeed, some climbers say they don't count Culebra as a fourteener—but most do. If you do go after Culebra, take time to enjoy the local culture. Spend some time in San Luis and drive some of the back roads around Chama. Southwestern Colorado is a melting pot of ranching and mining, multi-generational Hispanic and Anglo families, and Indians. For outsiders, traveling here is like journeying to another country. Founded in 1851, the town of San Luis is the oldest town in Colorado, and it has a rich Hispanic heritage. While in San Luis, be sure to enjoy a meal of Mexican food, and check out the San Luis Museum and Cultural Center.

You must make advance arrangements for climbing Culebra Peak. To do so, call or write the ranch manager at the Taylor Ranch (see directory). In the past, climbers have been allowed to camp at the ranch. Camping outside of the ranch is not recommended because of problems with crime. There are few accommodations in San Luis, but you'll find several inexpensive motels 15 miles north in Fort Garland.

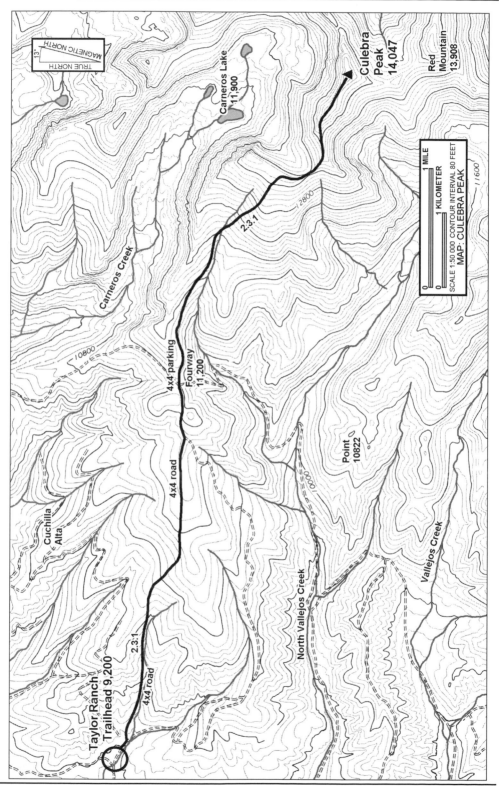

Culebra is best enjoyed as a simple ridge hike. Because this peak is located so far south, in a low precipitation area, and very windy, snow climbers and skiers will find little of their medium, even in deep winter. However, patient skiers can wait for the rare spring snowstorm such as the May 1990 blizzard that blanketed the Sierra Blanca with several feet of sticky spring snow. After a few days of consolidation, snow like that makes for incredible skiing.

ROADS AND TRAILHEAD

USGS Map: Taylor Ranch
USFS Forest Visitors Map: none

Taylor Ranch

Follow Highway 159 to San Luis. From Main Street in San Luis, turn E onto 4th Street (which becomes Highway 152, the road to Chama). Drive Highway 152 for 4 miles to a T intersection at Chama. Take a left (E) at the T, and drive Road L.7 for 3.6 miles to the second of two bridges that are a short distance apart. Just feet past the second bridge, turn right (S) onto Road 25.5, and drive .5 mile to another T intersection. Turn left here onto Road M.5, then drive .9 mile and take an obvious right, and continue 1.9 miles to the ranch (9,080'). Summer 2-wheel-drive parking is a short distance past the ranch at 9,200'. The jeep road past the ranch is obvious, and well-marked on the USGS Taylor Ranch and El Valle Creek maps. The jeep road is benign by Sangre standards, but it has a few steep hills and deep ruts. Ranch policy about allowing climbers to drive the road has varied, so bring your walking shoes. Remember to call the ranch in advance (see directory).

2.3.1	Culebra Peak—West Ridge From Taylor Ranch	
Ratings:	Summer Climb—Novice; Ski Descent—Intermediate/Advanced from summit Snow Climb—Intermediate	
Season:	Summer	Spring
RT Data:	10 hours, 12.5 miles, 4,847'↑	12 hours, 14 miles, 4,967'↑
Start:	Taylor Ranch Trailhead (Sum) 9,200'	Taylor Ranch 9,080'
1 Day from Rd:	Yes	Yes
Map:	Culebra, pg. 104	
Photo:	pg. 106	

Summer after snow melt-off: Though you could find other easy climbing routes for Culebra Peak, the west ridge is the most accessible from Taylor Ranch and is, consequently, the route recommended by the owners of the ranch. If you are interested in other routes, your best bet would be to do the standard route in order to get acquainted with the ranch manager, then discuss the options with him. The problem is that Taylor Ranch is a hunting ranch. An intricate network of roads and trails are used by guided hunting parties, and climbers on approaches to varied routes could interfere. The hunting clients pay thousands of dollars for elite hunting, and since a climb costs merely tens of dollars, climbers must play second fiddle.

This route is a long trek, but easy to navigate. Start at Taylor Ranch, and travel up the 4x4 road (section introduction) 3^1/4 miles to an open area and junction (called Fourway) at 11,200'. With permission, you can 4x4 to Fourway. From here, stay on the right (S) fork of the road as it makes a climbing traverse up an obvious cut to timberline (11,600'). You'll be at the base of an attractive alpine bowl. Climb 1 mile to gain the ridge at the head of the bowl, then follow the ridge (easy hike terrain) another mile to the summit. Return via your ascent route.

Spring snow season: Follow the summer route above, taking care at Fourway to follow the right-hand fork of the road on to the south face of the ridge. Ask about road access when you call the ranch. Snowmobile travel is possible in early spring after a normal winter. For a summit ski descent, avoid the cliffs on the north face and pick any other line with snow. Consult your map for the most efficient return (usually a climb back to the summit ridge, then descent of the summer route). If an exact summit ski descent is of little concern, stash your skis when you first gain the long summit ridge, then click in on your return.

Winter: The crux of this route as a winter climb lies in getting permission from the ranch. With careful planning, the whole climb can be done via avalanche-safe ridges.

Safety notes: Remember that help is far away from all but the Taylor Ranch side of the mountain. For sunhit use standard sunrise since exposures vary.

Climbing Culebra's long ridge for a spring ski descent.

Just a moment from the summit, Mount Sneffels.

3
NORTH
SAN JUAN
MOUNTAINS

USFS Forest Visitor Maps: San Juan National Forest, Uncompahgre National Forest, Gunnison National Forest

North San Juan summer climbs are usually straightforward, with good road access and well-defined trails. The afternoon thunderstorm cycle is predictable and must be avoided. Occasional cold fronts and low pressure systems bring bad weather. But you can climb through most summer storms with an early start to take advantage of the morning cloud lift. Lake City is a hopping place in the summer, with full amenities. Camping in the area is casual, with a choice of many sites.

Winter climbing in the North San Juans is a challenge. Long approaches and multi-day trips are the rule. The weather is often heinous and hard to predict. Using a snowmobile can help with winter access up long snow-closed roads. Call the Lake City Snowmobile Club (see directory) for information. In winter and early spring, Lake City is a ghost of its summer bustle. Few restaurants and lodges are open, so plan ahead.

During the spring snow season, the North San Juan Mountains have terrific access due to early snow removal from key roads. Sometime in May, the Willow Creek Road from Creede and the Cinnamon Pass and Engineer Pass roads from Lake City are driveable with a 4x4 to elevations that make spring skiing from your tailgate a commonplace occurrence.

Unfortunately, the times when these roads are open vary from year to year, depending on snow depth and the county road budget.

SECTION 3.1
San Luis Peak (14,014')

San Luis Peak sits alone to the east of all other San Juan fourteeners. Access is remarkably easy in the summer, with good roads to the north and south. During winter, however, road closures are likely to be farther than a day's travel from the mountain. Even in spring many of the logical approach roads remain gated by the Forest Service. One road, however, remains ungated and dries early: the Willow Creek Road to the Creede Pack Trail and Equity Mine Trailhead (see below). This is the best approach for winter and spring trips.

For skiers, the awesome drop of the Yawner Gullies (3.1.2) beckons on the west side of San Luis. In the summer a wilderness hike and climb up Stewart creek (3.1.3) is a sure cure for your civilized blahs. As icing, moose have been re-introduced to Stewart Creek—if you're lucky and look sharp you'll see these noble creatures.

ROADS AND TRAILHEADS

USGS Maps: San Luis Peak, Creede

Equity Mine Trailhead & Willow Creek Road

To reach the Equity Mine Trailhead, start from the town of Creede on Highway 149. Drive N on Creede's main street. Just outside of town this becomes the gravel and dirt Willow Creek Road. It is 7.5 miles to public parking just to the W of the Equity Mine gate (11,090'). Stay out of the Equity Mine compound; it is private property. Later in the spring, when the Willow Creek Road has been graded, it is passable for low-geared, high-clearance two-wheel drive. Early in the spring use a 4x4. Winter closure varies with mining activity. If unplowed, the road is frequently used by snowmobiles and maintenance snowcats, so you can count on at least a based trail, and possibly a packed highway. To check on the condition of the Willow Creek Road, call the Mineral County road department (see appendices).

Stewart Creek Trailhead

Start in the classic Colorado ranching town of Gunnison on Highway 50. Drive 7.6 miles E on Highway 50 and turn R on Highway 114. Drive S on Highway 114, and at 27 miles from Gunnison turn R on Road NN14, then drive south 6 miles on Road NN14 and pass Dome Lakes State Wildlife Area on your right. Just past Dome Lakes (at 34 miles from Gunnison), turn right on Road 15GG. Drive Road 15GG as it climbs above Dome Lakes, and enjoy tantalizing glimpses of San Luis and its satellite peaks.

At 37.4 miles from Gunnison (while still on Road 15GG), you'll come to a confusing intersection just past a cattle guard. Turn right here on Forest Service Road 794 (A.K.A. the Stewart Creek Road). Travel gets tougher here, and you should have at least a medium clearance 2x2 vehicle to continue. Follow the Stewart Creek Road 16 miles to the well-signed Stewart Creek Trailhead on the right side of the road (10,450', 53.5 miles from Gunnison). Parking is obvious. You'll find one campsite at the trailhead and a few more several hundred yards down the road in the Cochetopa Creek drain.

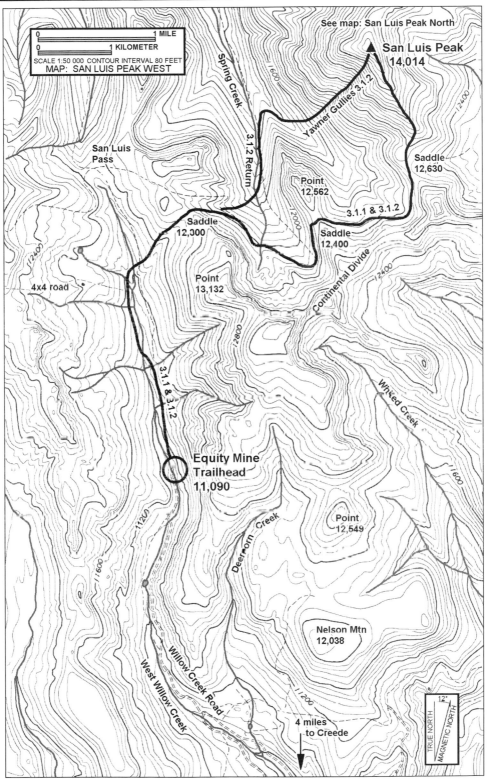

See map: San Luis Peak North

San Luis Peak
14,014

Yawner Gullies 3.1.2

Saddle
12,630

San Luis
Pass

3.1.2 Return

Spring Creek

Point
12,562

3.1.1 & 3.1.2

Saddle
12,300

Saddle
12,400

Continental Divide

4x4 road

Point
13,132

3.1.1 & 3.1.2

Wicked Creek

Equity Mine
Trailhead
11,090

Deermorn Creek

Point
12,549

Nelson Mtn
12,038

Willow Creek Road

West Willow Creek

4 miles
to Creede

1 MILE
1 KILOMETER
SCALE 1:50 000 CONTOUR INTERVAL 80 FEET
MAP: SAN LUIS PEAK WEST

12°
TRUE NORTH
MAGNETIC NORTH

3.1.1	**San Luis Peak—South Ridge from West Willow Creek**	
Ratings:	Summer Climb—Intermediate Ski Descent—Advanced Snow Climb—Intermediate	
Season:	Summer or Spring	Winter
RT Data:	10 hours, 13 miles, 3,424' ↑	16 hours, 214 miles, 3,824' ↑
Start:	Equity Mine Trailhead 11,090'	Equity Mine Trailhead 11,090'
1 Day from Rd:	Summer or Late Spring Yes, with open road	Winter Yes, with open road
Map:	San Luis Peak West, pg. 109	
Photo:	pg. 111	

Everyone enjoys this all-season route. In summer, it's a beautiful alpine hike. Spring skiers can enjoy a vast area of alpine terrain, and winter climbers will find that good road access makes this more of a climb and less of a slog.

Summer after snow melt-off: From the Equity Mine Trailhead (see section introduction), walk N up the 4x4 road that follows Willow Creek. At 11,520' the 4x4 trail swings left up a steep hill. Don't stay on the main road. Instead, follow an old road and foot trail that continues up Willow Creek several hundred yards, then swings NE and climbs 3/4 mile to a nondescript saddle (12,300') on the Continental Divide. From here you get your first view of San Luis Peak to the northeast.

From the saddle, contour into the basin to the east and follow the Colorado Trail as it traverses through the basin, climbs to another saddle (12,400'), then traverses another basin and makes a short climbing traverse to an obvious saddle at 12,630' on the south ridge of San Luis Peak. Follow tundra and scree up the south ridge to the summit, and descend your ascent route.

Spring snow season: For the most part, the snow route follows the summer route described above. From the Equity Mine Roadhead (see section introduction), ski or walk up the Creede Trail on the west side of the valley for 1/2 mile to the point where it crosses West Willow Creek. If you're on skis you have two choices here: with sparse snow stay in the stream bed, or with plentiful snow stay on the pack trail. If you're on foot because of a high snow line, use the pack trail route.

At 11,667' elevation, climb NE out of the West Willow Creek drainage, either by staying on the route of the pack trail or by following an obvious side drainage with good skiing, to a nondescript saddle (12,300') on the Continental Divide. From here you get your first view of San Luis Peak to the northeast.

From the saddle, contour into the next basin to the east. Use a high traverse if avalanche conditions are safe. If the snow is questionable, use a lower traverse through the trees at timberline. Contour through the basin and make a short climbing traverse up to the next major saddle to the east (12,400'). From the saddle, contour E through another bowl, then make another short climbing traverse up to an obvious saddle at 12,630' on the south ridge of San Luis Peak. Follow the south ridge to the summit. For descent, your ascent route yields plenty of skiing.

Winter: Use the ski route described above, with variations to avoid avalanche slopes.

Safety notes: Summer climbers will find no unusual hazards on this route. Start early to avoid lightning. During snow seasons, West Willow Creek is reasonably safe—it is exposed to large but infrequent slides from the east. Once you enter the two bowls you are in prime avalanche terrain, and you will be exposed to different slope aspects. Winter climbers should avoid avalanche slopes by using windblown ribs and dropping to timber when necessary. This

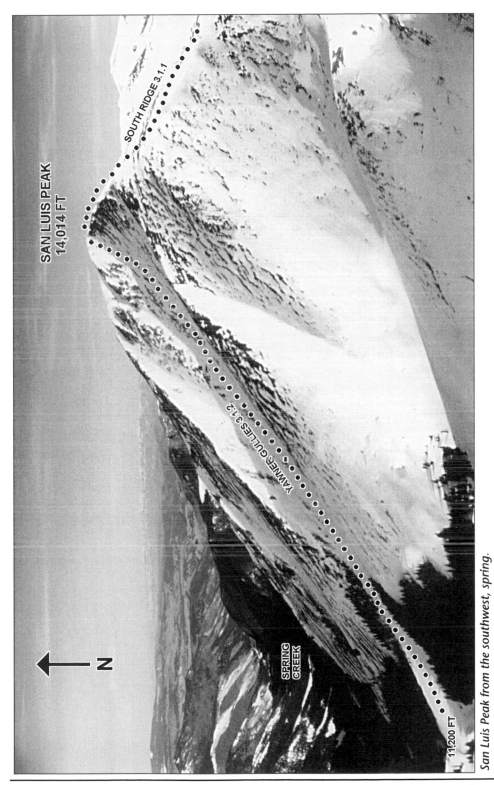

SOUTH RIDGE 3.1.1

SAN LUIS PEAK
14,014 FT

YAWNER GULLIES 3.1.2

SPRING
CREEK

N

11,200 FT

San Luis Peak from the southwest, spring.

is another route that is fantastic and safe when done on compacted spring snow. Add several hours to standard sunrise for sunhit.

3.1.2	San Luis Peak—Yawner Gullies	
Ratings:	Ski Descent—Advanced Snow Climb—Intermediate	
	Summer Climb—N.R.	
Season:	Spring Snow	
RT Data:	12 hours, 10 miles, 4,224'↑	
Start:	Equity Mine Trailhead, 11,090'	
1 Day from Rd:	Yes	
Map:	San Luis Peak West, pg. 109	
Photo:	pg. 111	

A beautiful tour, this is the best ski route off San Luis Peak.

Spring snow season: Park at the Equity Mine Trailhead (section introduction) and follow route 3.1.1 to the summit of San Luis Peak. From the first saddle on the route, note the good view of San Luis' southwest face, with the Yawner Gullies in plain view.

At the summit you can pick one of the three Yawner Gullies. The North Yawner tends to have the most snow on lean years, but the center and South Yawner have the best continuous fall line skiing. The South Yawner drops directly SW off the summit—you literally hang your ski

Classic style in the classic Yawner Gullies, San Luis Peak.

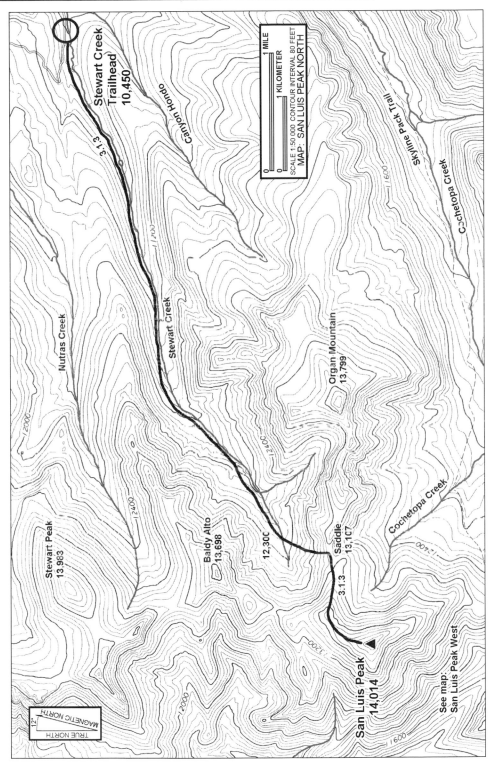

Stewart Creek Trailhead
10,450

Canyon Hondo

3.1.3

SCALE 1:50,000 CONTOUR INTERVAL 80 FEET
MAP: SAN LUIS PEAK NORTH

1 MILE

1 KILOMETER

Skyline Pack Trail

Cochetopa Creek

Nutras Creek

Stewart Creek

Organ Mountain
13,799

Cochetopa Creek

Stewart Peak
13,983

Baldy Alto
13,698

12,300

Saddle
13,107

3.1.3

San Luis Peak
14,014

See map:
San Luis Peak West

MAGNETIC NORTH

TRUE NORTH

12°

tips off the summit to start. The other two Yawner Gullies start a short distance down the west summit ridge. Ski your choice down to about 11,280', then put your skins back on, traverse W around Point 12,562, climb back to the saddle on the Continental Divide, and follow West Willow Creek back to the Equity Mine Trailhead.

Safety notes: West Willow Creek is exposed to large but infrequent slides falling from the east. Once you get into the two bowls you are in prime avalanche terrain, and will be exposed to many different slope aspects. This is another route that is fantastic and safe during stable snow periods of the spring season. Add several hours to standard sunrise for sunhit.

3.1.3	San Luis Peak—East Flanks from Stewart Creek	
Ratings:	Ski Descent—Intermediate Snow Climb—Intermediate	
	Summer Climb—Intermediate	
Season:	Spring Snow or Summer	
RT Data:	13 hours, 12.5 miles, 3,564'↑	
Start:	Stewart Creek Trailhead, 10,450'	
1 Day from Rd:	Yes, w/ melt-off to trailhead	
Map:	San Luis Peak North, pg. 113	

A fine wilderness hike, this route on San Luis Peak is less crowded than many other four-teener trails. Due to access problems this route is only recommended for summer climbs after roads are open. Nonetheless, it would make a decent winter climb for tough winter campers looking for a multi-day trip. Another plus for this route is that it requires less driving for people coming from the north.

Looking up Stewart Creek from the trailhead. Pristine wilderness awaits.

Summer after snow melt-off: Park at the Stewart Creek Trailhead (section introduction). Hike the well-traveled tread of the Stewart Creek Trail past innumerable beaver ponds, through aspens and stands of alpine conifer, to timberline in a huge alpine basin (12,040').

Continue on less-defined trails SW up the right (west) arm of Stewart Creek. At 12,300" swing S and climb 807 vertical feet to the saddle (13,107') between the west summit of Organ Mountain and San Luis Peak. Swing west at the saddle, climb a mellow ridge to a bump (13,700'), then walk the ridge 1/2 mile SW and S to the noble crest of San Luis Peak. Descend your ascent route.

Safety notes: While this is a supremely easy route, novice fourteener baggers should start early to avoid afternoon storms. Remember essential clothing and equipment, and use standard sunrise for sunhit.

SECTION 3.2
Wetterhorn Peak (14,015'), Uncompahgre Peak (14,309')

Wetterhorn and Uncompahgre peaks, though only 3 miles apart (and connected by a high plain), are two very different mountains. Wetterhorn is a beautiful rock arete, while Uncompahgre is a mound of broken volcanic rubble. Both peaks offer easy climbing routes. Uncompahgre is no more than a strenuous hike, while Wetterhorn finishes with an exposed but reasonable scramble up a rock face. Wetterhorn's ski and snow climbing route, the East Face (3.2.2), collects plenty of snow, thereby providing good mountaineering almost every spring. Indeed, skiing or snow climbing on Wetterhorn should be on everyone's list of essential ticks. Uncompahgre's west facing gullies, on the other hand, are often devoid of snow due to windscour. Nonetheless, if you catch Uncompahgre with snow cover, you will be justly rewarded.

Summer climbers can tick both summits in one day by crossing the divide between the peaks. If you do this, park cars at both trailheads to make the trip a pleasant loop rather than retracing your steps from Uncompahgre back to Matterhorn Creek. Plan on a hard day—more than 9 miles and 6,000' of climbing. For such an effort, climb Wetterhorn first via the Southeast Ridge (3.2.1), contour E through Matterhorn Basin and climb a few hundred vertical feet to the divide above the Cimarron drain. Cross the head of the Cimarron, suffer up an obvious gully on the west face of Uncompahgre (better with snow, see 3.2.3), then descend 3.2.5 to your stashed vehicle at the Nellie Creek Wilderness boundary. Be sure your cooler of cold drinks is left in the Nellie Creek vehicle—or in a snowbank nearby

ROADS AND TRAILHEADS

USGS Maps: Lake City, Uncompahgre Peak, Wetterhorn Peak

Nellie Creek Trailhead

From downtown Lake City, follow a well-signed turn W off the main street on to the Henson Creek/Engineer Pass Road. Drive the Henson Creek Road 5.2 miles to the well-signed turn off for the Nellie Creek Road. Park 2 wheel drives here (9,310'). With a 4x4, drive the Nellie Creek Road 4.1 miles to road closure at the wilderness boundary (11,390'). During your 4x4 crawl (or hike) up the Nellie Creek Road, be sure to take a left at a fork 2 miles from the Henson Creek Road. Nellie Creek Road melt-off is complete by late May or early June. This is not a popular ski route or snowmobile ride in winter, so expect to break trail.

Matterhorn Creek Trailhead

For Matterhorn Creek, follow the aforementioned Henson Creek—Engineer Pass Road 9.1 miles from Lake City to an obvious, well-signed intersection at the Capitol City town-

FITZ/PFEIFFER COLLECTION

At the keyhole on Wetterhorn Peak, spring.

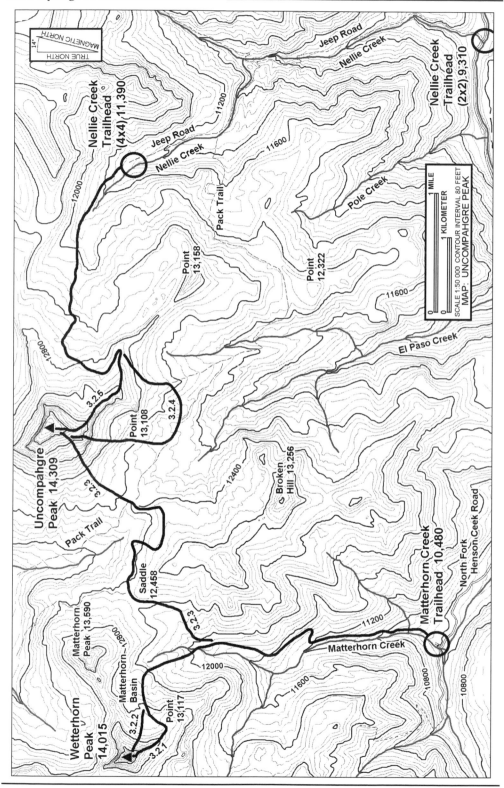

TRUE NORTH
MAGNETIC NORTH
14°

Nellie Creek
Trailhead
(4x4)11,390

Jeep Road

Nellie Creek

Nellie Creek

Jeep Road

Nellie Creek

Nellie Creek
Trailhead
(2x2),9,310

11200

11600

Pack Trail

Pole Creek

12000

Point
13,158

Point
12,322

11600

SCALE 1:50 000 CONTOUR INTERVAL 80 FEET
MAP: UNCOMPAHGRE PEAK
1 MILE
1 KILOMETER

El Paso Creek

12800

3.2.5

3.2.4

Point
13,108

Uncompahgre
Peak 14,309

12400

3.2.3

Broken
Hill 13,256

Pack Trail

Henson Creek Road

Saddle
12,458

Matterhorn
Peak 13,590

3.2.3

Matterhorn Creek
Trailhead 10,480

North Fork

11200

Matterhorn Creek

Matterhorn ~12800

12000

10800

11600

10800

Wetterhorn
Peak
14,015

Basin

3.2.2

Point
13,117

3.2.1

site. Take a right (NW) here on to the North Fork Henson Creek Road. Follow the North Fork Road for 2 miles to another turn to the right on to the Matterhorn Creek Road. Signage here is inconsistent, so use your car odometer (2 miles from Capitol City) and altimeter (10,370') to locate the point where the North Fork Road passes over Matterhorn Creek. From here, back-track downvalley a few hundred feet and turn onto the only, albeit unlikely looking, double-track on the north side of the road. This subsidiary road (high clearance 2-wheel-drive) leads 3/4 mile to wilderness road closure at 10,480' elevation.

Henson Creek Road Information

The Henson Creek—Engineer Pass Road to Capitol City is well-suited to regular automo-biles. The road gradually deteriorates after that, and becomes a jeep trail several miles below Engineer Pass. A vast array of high altitude hiking and terrific skiing is accessible from the upper reaches of this road, and with the county plowing it early in the season, it is a popular destination for Southern Colorado ski mountaineers. Cycling this road is popular, but it is heavily traveled and quite dusty, especially lower down on the Lake City side.

Henson Creek Road snow closure varies by season. During winters with below average snow, the road might be open more than 5 miles from Lake City. During average winters clo-sure is lower down, usually about 4 miles from Lake City—possibly at 9,340', just past the junction with the Nellie Creek Road. In late April the road is open 9.1 miles to Capitol City, several miles past there soon after, and all the way to Engineer Pass sometime in May.

The county does not plow the North Henson Creek Road to the Matterhorn Creek Trailhead, hence it may not be driveable until melt-out in late April or May. It is a snowmobile trail, so you may find it packed. The short section of Matterhorn Creek jeep trail is always closed by snow until mid or late May, or later if any large avalanches have covered it. During spring mud-season, both roads require 4-wheel-drive, but when dry, high clearance 2-wheel-drive is sufficient. For road information call the Lake County road department (see directory).

3.2.1	**Wetterhorn Peak—Southeast Ridge**	
Ratings:	Summer Climb—Intermediate Ski Descent—N.R.	
	Snow Climb—Intermediate	
Season:	Summer or Spring	Winter
RT Data:	8 hours, 6.5 miles, 3,535'↑	Expedition, 4,675'↑
Start:	Matterhorn Creek Trailhead	Henson Creek Road (closure)
	10,480'	9,340'
1 Day	Summer or Late Spring	Winter
from Rd:	Yes	Depends on closure
Map:	Uncompahgre Peak, pg. 116	
Photos:	pgs. 118, 120	

This is Wetterhorn's standard peak bagger's route, and a fine winter climb as well.

Summer after snow melt-off: Travel to the Matterhorn Creek Trailhead (section intro-duction). If your trip is early in the spring season, you may not be able to drive past the Capitol City fork. If this is the case, a high camp might be necessary. If you can drive to a point near the roadhead you can easily do the climb in one day.

From the trailhead, carefully follow the old jeep trail north (actually a pack trail since the Wilderness area was established). In the large open area, starting at 11,160', be sure to climb approximately 200 vertical feet NE up the mountainside, then follow a climbing traverse to enter Matterhorn Basin at 11,640'. Continue up the main trail about 1/2 mile to 11,980'. Leave the main trail here, and climb NW into the upper reaches of Matterhorn Basin until you reach the 12,800' level. Stay to the left (S) side of the basin. At around 12,800' climb south, gaining the southeast ridge of Wetterhorn on the northwest side of point 13,117.

For the most part, stick to the ridge (a bit of scrambling) until you reach a small notch known as the Keyhole at the base of the summit block. To your left will be the large rock known as the Ship's Prow. Scramble through the keyhole, and follow easy hand and foot climbing up a ledgy rock gully to the summit. A rope may be useful here for inexperienced

Matterhorn Creek and Wetterhorn Peak from the southeast, winter.

climbers, or when the rock is icy or snowcovered. Descend your ascent route, and stick to established trails to prevent undue erosion.

Spring snow season: Use the route described above. You should be expert with ice axe and crampons.

Winter: Use the route detailed above, perhaps gaining the ridge lower than that described to avoid avalanche slopes. During winter, miles of snowbound road distance the Henson Creek snow closure (usually near Lake City) and the spring and summer roadheads. However, the Henson Creek Road is usually packed by snowmobiles. Call the Lake City Snowmobile Club for road information (see directory).

Safety notes: Luckily, much of this route is "ridgy" enough to avoid the rock fall danger you encounter on many summer fourteener routes. However, the rock pitch on the summit block is exposed to projectiles if any bombardiers are climbing above you. Use standard sunrise for sunhit.

3.2.2 Wetterhorn Peak—East Face

Ratings:	Ski Descent- Extreme	Snow Climb—Advanced
Season:	Spring snow or Summer Snow	
RT Data:	8 hours, 6.5 miles, 3,615'↑	
Start:	Matterhorn Creek snow closure, 10,400'	
1 Day from Rd:	Yes	
Map:	Uncompahgre Peak, pg. 116	
Photos:	pgs. 118, 120, 122	

East Face of Wetterhorn Peak, spring.

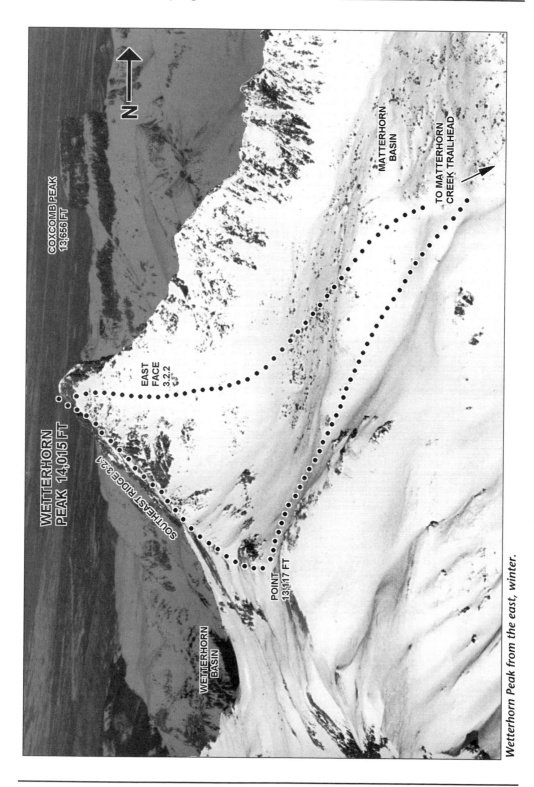

COXCOMB PEAK
13,656 FT

MATTERHORN
BASIN

TO MATTERHORN
CREEK TRAILHEAD

EAST
FACE
3.2.2

WETTERHORN
PEAK 14,015 FT

SOUTHEAST RIDGE 3.2.1

WETTERHORN
BASIN

POINT
13,117 FT

Wetterhorn Peak from the east, winter.

A ski or snow climb classic, this route takes one of the most beautiful snow faces in Colorado. It provides superb skiing and an aesthetic climb. For skiers, 2,000 vertical feet of bowls below the face put icing on your cake.

Snow season, spring or early summer: Drive the Henson Creek and North Henson Creek Roads to the Matterhorn Creek roadhead (section introduction). If your trip is early in the spring season, you may not be able to drive past the Capitol City fork. If this is the case, a high camp may be necessary. If you can drive to a point near the roadhead, the trip can easily be done in a day.

From the trailhead carefully follow the old "jeep trail" (actually a pack trail since the Wilderness was established). In the large open area, starting at 11,160', be sure to climb approximately 200 vertical feet NE up the mountainside, then follow a climbing traverse to entry into Matterhorn Basin 11,640' elevation. Leave the official trail here, and follow a climbing traverse NW into the upper reaches of Matterhorn Basin until you are below Wetterhorn's obvious E face. Snow climb the face (bearing a bit left) to the summit block. Maximum angle is 56°.

Once at the summit block, make a short traverse left (still on snow) to the obvious notch between the summit block and the large rock to the south known as the Ship's Prow. Scramble through the keyhole, and follow easy climbing up a ledgy rock gully to the summit. A rope may be useful here for inexperienced climbers or poor conditions such as icy rock.

Descent is via the same route. Most skiers start at the Keyhole, since the summit block is usually devoid of snow. The skiing is superb (maximum angle 48°). For snow climbers a descent via the Southeast Ridge "walk up route" (3.2.1) is a good alternative to downclimbing the face.

Safety notes: Though the first ski descent of this route was made in mid-winter, it is an avalanche path, and thus can only be safely climbed on consolidated spring snow. Of further note, it is also an east face, so spring skiers must make an early start to avoid avalanche danger and slushy snow due to sun warming. Figure standard sunrise for sunhit.

3.2.3	**Uncompahgre Peak—West Face Snow Route**		
	Ratings:	Ski Descent—Advanced	Snow Climb—Advanced
		Summer Climb-N.R.	
	Season:	Spring Snow	
	RT Data:	10 hours, 9.5 miles, 4,309'↑	
	Start:	Matterhorn Creek Trailhead; spring snow closure, 10,400'	
	1 Day from Rd:	Yes	
	Map:	Uncompahgre Peak, pg. 116	
	Photos:	pgs. 123, 124	

Spring snow season: Uncompahgre has several couloirs that snow climbers and ski mountaineers will find attractive. A steep slot cuts the south buttress of the peak (3.2.4), and several wider, less steep couloirs drop down the west face. None of these couloirs lead directly to the summit, so climbing them to check out the route is mandatory for a ski descent. Since these couloirs get a late western sunhit, it's possible to combine this route with Wetterhorn's East Face (3.2.2). Do Wetterhorn first, then enjoy Uncompahgre.

Uncompahgre's west face couloirs are probably best approached via Matterhorn Creek, though a heavy snow year and low road closure might make the Nellie Creek approach more attractive (see section introduction and route 3.2.4)

Drive to the Matterhorn Creek Trailhead (section introduction), and follow the Matterhorn Basin Trail up Matterhorn Creek 4 1/2 miles to the pass next to Matterhorn Peak (12,458'). From

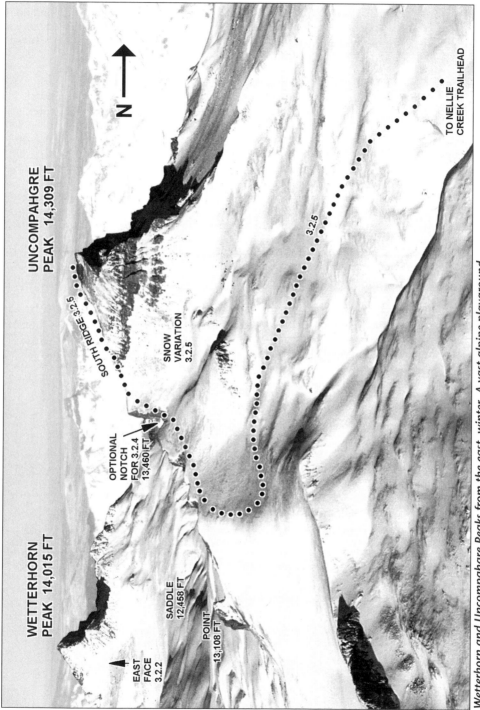

UNCOMPAHGRE PEAK 14,309 FT

WETTERHORN PEAK 14,015 FT

N

SOUTH RIDGE 3.2.5

SNOW VARIATION 3.2.5

3.2.5

TO NELLIE CREEK TRAILHEAD

OPTIONAL NOTCH FOR 3.2.4 13,460 FT

EAST FACE 3.2.2

SADDLE 12,458 FT

POINT 13,108 FT

Wetterhorn and Uncompahgre Peaks from the east, winter. A vast alpine playground.

here the couloirs are obvious, and you can pick the one with the most continuous snow. From the pass, contour and climb E to the base of your choice, then enjoy the climb.

Making a summit ski descent via any of these couloirs requires careful route finding. In general, try to find continuous snow off the south corner of the summit that leads to your couloir. You'll only get a summit ski descent off Uncompahgre when the snow is just right, probably after a winter and early spring with above-average snow accumulation and below-average wind.

Safety notes: At least one person has been caught in a major avalanche in these gullies. They should only be skied with very stable snow, probably in the spring, but possibly when they have been heavily scoured by west winds. For sunhit, add several hours to standard sunrise.

3.2.4	Uncompahgre Peak—South "Fin" Couloir	
Ratings:	Ski Descent—Extreme　　Snow Climb—Intermediate	
	Summer Climb—N.R.	
Season:	Spring Snow or Summer Snow	
RT Data:	10 hours, 14 miles, 4,999' ↑	
Start:	Nellie Creek Trailhead, 9,310'	
1 Day from Rd:	Yes	
Map:	Uncompahgre Peak, pg. 116	
Photos:	pgs. 122, 123, 124	

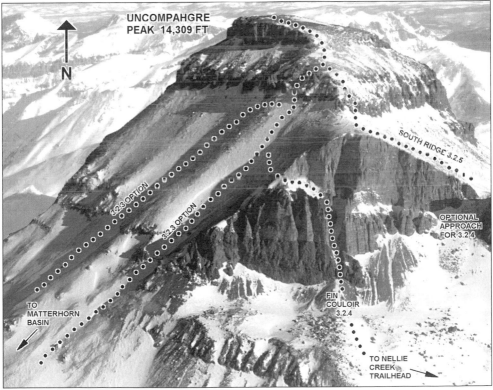

Uncompahgre Peak from the south, spring.

UNCOMPAHGRE PEAK 14,309 FT

N

OPTIONAL NOTCH
TO OR FROM SOUTH RIDGE
USE ONLY WITH SNOW COVER

POINT
13,108 FT

TO NELLIE CREEK
& SOUTH RIDGE 3.2.5

SADDLE
12,458 FT

3.2.3

3.2.4

3.2.3
OPTION

TO MATTERHORN
CREEK TRAILHEAD

Climbing Wetterhorn Peak, looking east at Uncompahgre Peak, spring.

This eccentric slot on Uncompahgre's convoluted south face is a fun snow climb. After a winter with heavy snow, it makes an interesting ski descent.

Spring snow season: Though you can approach the "Fin Couloir" from Matterhorn Creek, spring road closures may make Nellie Creek a better choice. Even so, starting from Nellie Creek with spring snow closure on the Henson Creek Road may make this an arduous one-day route. Consider using a high camp.

Park on the Henson Creek Road at the Nellie Creek intersection (section introduction). Follow the Nellie Creek Road and Trail to timberline in Uncompahgre's great east basin. From here, simply follow any logical route W up the basin then S over Uncompahgre's southeast shoulder at 12,880' elevation. With good snow cover, another option is to climb Uncompahgre's South Ridge (3.2.5) to 13,460', where an improbable notch gives you access to the south. You can descend from this notch, traverse NW, and be at the base of the Fin Couloir very quickly.

At any rate, assuming you take the low route rather than the notch, after you pass over the shoulder at 12,880', drop about 500 vertical feet and contour W below rocky Point 13,108. Approximately 1/4 mile past the base of Point 13,108 you will arrive below a convoluted portion of Uncompahgre's south face; climb the main slot, which leads up then left below unclimbable and unskiable cliffs, eventually ejecting you out into the southern-most couloir on the peak's west face (route 3.2.3). Climb this couloir to the South Ridge (3.2.5), then take the South Ridge to the summit. If you're snow climbing, descend Uncompahgre's south ridge and east bowl. Skiers can descend the couloir if it's in condition.

Safety notes: Though this couloir faces south, it's protected from the sun by its side walls. The slopes above and below the slot, however, get strong sunlight starting at mid-morning, and the summit snow gets sun at standard sunrise.

3.2.5 Uncompahgre Peak—South Ridge Hike Trail

Ratings:	Summer Climb—Novice Ski Descent—Intermediate		
	Snow Climb—Novice		
Season:	Summer	Winter	Spring
RT Time:	8 hours, 7 miles	Overnight, 15 miles	14 hours, 15 miles
	3,829' ↑	4,999' ↑	4,999' ↑
Start:	Nellie Creek	Henson Creek	Henson Creek
	10,480'	9,310'	9,310'
1 Day from Rd:	Yes	No	Yes
Map:	Uncompahgre Peak, pg. 116		
Photos:	pgs. 122, 123		

This is the standard hike route for Uncompahgre, and it makes an excellent "first four-teener." It's also a good snow climb, and gets you to good skiing in Uncompahgre's grand east bowls. It is popular to combine this route with a climb of Wetterhorn Peak. To do so, summer climbers can simply descend their ascent route back down to 12,880' on the southeast ridge, then follow a beaten trail that heads a relatively flat 2 miles W into Matterhorn Basin, where you then climb Wetterhorn via the Southeast Ridge (3.2.1). During spring snow season, a short cut takes a notch in Uncompahgre's south ridge at 13,460'. To prevent erosion only use this option with snow cover. If you do both peaks in a day consider stashing cars at both trailheads, or a car at one and bicycles at the other.

Summer after snow melt-off: Start at the Nellie Creek Trailhead, and hike up the Nellie Creek Trail 1 1/2 miles W to 12,640' in Uncompahgre's east basin. Stay on the trail as it turns south and makes a climbing traverse to intersect the crest of Uncompahgre's southeast ridge at 12,880′. Follow a well-beaten path on the ridge to a rocky area a few hundred vertical feet below the summit. The easiest route traverses slightly right (E) on to a rocky face, then swings back left (W) to the summit. Descend your ascent route.

Spring snow season: This is a terrific novice snow route. Use the summer route above to reach timberline, then take a more direct line up the peak's ridge. The skiing in the "bonus" bowls is superb, but doing a summit ski descent usually entails doing a bit of downclimbing through the rocky area.

Winter: Because of windscour and good ridge access, this is a very accessible winter route. Plan on an overnight.

Safety notes: In summer, though novice climbers will find a well-worn path to the summit of Uncompahgre, they should still realize that high altitude hiking is a serious endeavor. Proper equipment is a must, and awareness of such dangers as lightning a prerequisite. Use standard sunrise for sunhit.

SECTION 3.3
Redcloud Peak (14,034′), Sunshine Peak (14,001′), Handies Peak (14,048′)

As many mountaineers attest, Redcloud and Sunshine peaks are enticing from a distance; they lord over Lake San Cristobal with sublime majesty. Up close, while the view from their summits is good, these large piles of gravel offer little more than hikes to dry season mountaineers. Add snow, however, and these peaks offer ski mountaineers and snow climbers several aesthetic lines.

Redcloud and Sunshine are connected by a ridge about a mile long, and both peaks are usually climbed or skied during the same trip. During winter and early spring, when roads are still closed with snow, climbers occasionally use a rough route on the east ridge of Sunshine (3.3.5).

Four miles southwest of Sunshine and Redcloud, Handies Peak rises from Grizzly Gulch. While technical climbers should look elsewhere, Handies yields fine hikes, snow climbs, and ski descents. Access is good, and you can find everything from novice skiing in American Basin to extreme skiing and steep snow climbing on Handies' north face.

ROADS AND TRAILHEADS

USGS Maps: Handies Peak, Lake San Cristobal, Redcloud Peak.

Mill Creek Campground Trailhead

Winter or summer, the best road access to Redcloud, Sunshine and Handies peaks is via the Lake Fork/Cinnamon Pass Road. Finding this road is easy. Drive south on Lake City's main street—it becomes CO 149. A short distance out of town, take a right (W) on to the well-signed Lake Fork/Cinnamon Pass Road, and drive this road (it soon becomes dirt) for 11 miles to Mill Creek Campground Trailhead (park at the campground, 9,440′). For the trailheads described below, continue on the main road.

Grizzly & Silver Creek Trailhead

Continue on the main Lake Fork/Cinnamon Pass Road as described above. At 13 miles from Lake City, you'll hit a fork where a left takes you to the Sherman Townsite and a right takes you onto Shelf Road (which is also part of the Cinnamon Pass Road). Stay to the right, and drive the hairy Shelf Road 3.5 miles to the well-signed GRIZZLY & SILVER CREEK TRAILHEAD (10,400′). For Redcloud and Sunshine, a "double track" trail (now closed to motor vehicles) heads up the Silver Creek drainage. It leaves the Cinnamon Pass Road about 200 feet downvalley from the trailhead sign, on the downvalley side of the old broken down cabin, and about

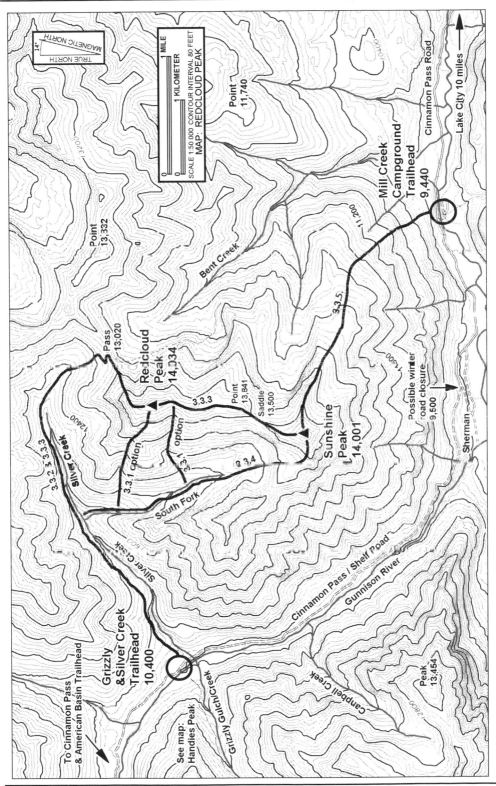

MAGNETIC NORTH

TRUE NORTH

14°

SCALE 1:50,000 CONTOUR INTERVAL 80 FEET
MAP: REDCLOUD PEAK

1 MILE

1 KILOMETER

Point
11,740

Cinnamon Pass Road

Lake City 10 miles

Mill Creek
Campground
Trailhead
9,440

11,200

3.3.5

14,500

9,500

Possible winter
road closure

Sherman

Point
13,332

Bent Creek

13,200

Pass
13,020

Redcloud
Peak
14,034

3.3.3

Point
13,841

Saddle
13,500

Sunshine
Peak
14,001

3.3.2, 3.3, 3.3.3

Silver Creek

12,400

3.3.1 option

3.3.1 option

3.3

3.3.4

South Fork

Silver Creek

12,600

Cinnamon Pass / Shelf Road

Gunnison River

Peak
13,454

12,800

Grizzly
& Silver Creek
Trailhead
10,400

To Cinnamon Pass
& American Basin Trailhead

See map:
Handies Peak

Grizzly Gulch Creek

Campbell Creek

600 feet up the Cinnamon Pass Road from the culvert where Silver Creek passes beneath the road. This double track soon becomes a well-worn single track foot trail that follows the north side of the Silver Creek drainage all the way into the bowl at the head of Silver Creek.

American Basin Trailhead

For the American Basin Trailhead, continue from the Grizzly Creek Trailhead up the Cinnamon Pass road 2 miles to obvious parking (11,320') at the start of the American Basin jeep trail. During some years, plows open the road to here in early spring. Because of mud and deep puddles, use a 4x4 for spring access. Depending on the winter's snowfall the closure may be lower in the valley. As is usually the case with fourteener road approaches, a reconnaissance the day before your trip would be smart.

Cinnamon Pass Road Information

In summer you can reach these trailheads with average clearance 2-wheel-drive. You'll find good car camping in the upper valley past Shelf Road.

In winter and early spring, the Lake Fork/Cinnamon Pass Road is usually open to the Sherman Junction (9,500'). Hinsdale County makes a great effort to open this road early, often using a bulldozer as a snow plow. Several parties have reported the road being open in early May—with unbelievable skiing from their tailgate. During winters with average snowfall, snowmobilers use the road on occasion, but dry sections and avalanche terrain discourage heavy snowmobile use. Call the Lake City Snowmobile Club for information (see directory)—at the very least you can find out if the road is packed. On dry years a bicycle can be useful. During morning thaws the road may be bombarded by dangerous rockfall.

Grouse Gulch Trailhead

From the famous southern Colorado cowboy town of Durango, drive north to Silverton on Highway 550. Drive through Silverton, then drive Road 110 for 11.5 miles to the Grouse Gulch.

3.3.1	**Redcloud Peak—West Face from South Fork Silver Creek**	
	Ratings:	Ski Descent—Advanced Snow Climb—Intermediate
		Summer Climb—Intermediate
	Season:	Snow Route, Spring
	RT Data:	7 hours, mileage varies, 3,634'↑
	Start:	Grizzly and Silver Creek Trailhead, 10,400'
	1 Day from Rd:	Yes
	Map:	Redcloud Peak, pg. 127

With a coating of consolidated spring snow, the west side of Redcloud Peak is loaded with snow climbs and ski routes. While climbers use this side of the peak for dry-season routes, doing so may cause erosion and is not recommended.

Spring snow season: From the Silver Creek Trailhead (see introduction), hike or ski the trail up Silver Creek. Because of its south aspect, this trail is often dry to about 11,000' in late April or early May. At 11,280' elevation, at the confluence of Silver Creek and the South Fork of Silver Creek, leave the Silver Creek drainage and travel S up the South Fork drainage.

You have two choices for west face routes from the South Fork drainage; choose according to snow cover. For the first option, travel a short distance up the South Fork to 11,600' elevation, and follow a gully system with an intermittent stream to the summit. For another option, climb the South Fork to 12,080' and then follow a gully system to the ridge just south of the summit. Descend your ascent route, or run the ridge to Sunshine Peak and ski back into the South Fork of Silver Creek from there (3.3.4).

Safety notes: These gullies should only be climbed or skied with a stable compacted spring snow pack, or extremely wind-hammered winter snow. Add several hours to standard sunrise for sunhit.

Happy skiers atop Redcloud Peak. Wetterhorn Peak on left horizon.

3.3.2	**Redcloud Peak—Silver Creek and East Ridge**	
Ratings:	Summer Climb—Novice Ski Descent—Intermediate Snow Climb—Novice	
Season:	Summer or Spring	Winter
RT Data:	7 hours, 8.5 miles, 3,634'↑	Multi-day, 16 miles, 4,534'↑
Start:	Grizzly and Silver Creek 10,400'	Cinnamon Pass Road 9,500'
1 Day *from Rd:*	Summer or Late Spring Yes, with open road	Winter No, with closed road
Map:	Redcloud Peak, pg. 127	
Photo:	pg. 131	

Summer peak baggers use this route for Redcloud, then go on to Sunshine Peak via the connecting ridge (3.3.3). This route also includes terrific ski terrain.

Summer after snow melt-off: Park at the Silver Creek Trailhead (section introduction) and hike the Silver Creek Trail 4 miles to a pass on Redcloud's East Ridge (13,020'). Leave the main trail at the pass and climb W then S up the ridge up easy ground to the summit. Descend your ascent route, or continue to Sunshine Peak, then reverse your route.

Spring snow season: Use the summer route described above. Skiers and snow climbers will find plenty of moderate terrain.

Winter: Getting up Shelf Road might be considered the crux of this route if you tackle it during the winter. In doing so, you'll encounter everything from avalanche slopes to rockfall. Nonetheless, during an early-winter dry spell or after a late-winter thaw, this certainly is a viable approach.

Safety notes: Don't let the moderate nature of this route make you lazy. Start early, read your map, and carry proper equipment. Use standard sunrise for sunhit.

3.3.3	**Sunshine Peak from Redcloud Peak via Connecting Ridge**	
Ratings:	Summer Climb—Intermediate Ski Descent—Intermediate Snow Climb—Intermediate	
Season:	Summer or Spring	Winter
RT Data:	Round trip varies, 4,669'↑	Multi-day, 5,569'↑
Start:	Grizzly and Silver Creek 10,400'	Cinnamon Pass Road 9,500'
1 Day *from Rd:*	Summer or Late Spring Yes	Winter No
Map:	Redcloud Peak, pg. 127	
Photos:	pgs. 131, 133	

You can bag two teeners in a day using this ridge run, but don't beat your chest; getting your second peak only costs you 534 vertical feet—well under the 3,000 vertical that pundits claim qualifies a "real" climb. Skiers should note that this is one of the classic "raid blanc" ski tours in the San Juans. Moreover, given a coating of firm snow, this is also a good beginner snow climb.

Because of the vast scree fields on Sunshine and Redcloud, this route may be less than fun without snow to hold everything together. Nevertheless, many peak baggers do a double

Spring climbing on Redcloud Peak's northeast ridge (routes 3.3.2 and 3.3.3.)

day by traversing these two peaks. Well-used trails on all portions of this route help with such an endeavor. To reduce erosion, avoid scree-running and try to stick with lower-angled and marked trails.

Summer after snow melt-off: From the Silver Creek Trailhead (section introduction), climb the East Ridge route (3.3.2) to the summit of Redcloud Peak. From Redcloud, traverse the ridge (easy ground) S to Sunshine. It has a drop of 534 feet, with terrific views to occupy your mind while you hike the mellow terrain. From the summit of Sunshine reverse the ridge.

Spring snow season: Use the summer route described above, with variations using any of the snow climbs and ski descents described in this section. With good snow cover, you'll find a good ski pitch when you drop off Redcloud towards Sunshine.

Winter: After climbing Sunshine via the long East Ridge (3.3.5), you can bag Redcloud via this ridge.

Safety notes: See other routes in this section. Remember you'll be spending time high on an exposed ridge. Use standard sunrise for sunhit.

3.3.4	**Sunshine Peak—Northwest Face Snow Route**	
Ratings:	Ski Descent—Intermediate	Snow Climb—Novice
Season:	Snow Route, Spring	
RT Data:	9 hours, 6 miles, 3,601'↑	
Start:	Grizzly and Silver Creek 10,400'	
1 Day from Rd:	Yes	
Map:	Redcloud Peak, pg. 127	
Photo:	pg. 133	

Use this for a pleasant and relatively direct snow route to the summit of Sunshine.

Spring snow season: From the Grizzly & Silver Creek Trailhead (see section introduction), hike or ski the trail up Silver Creek. At 11,280' elevation you will arrive at the confluence of Silver Creek and the South Fork of Silver Creek. Leave the Silver Creek drainage and travel up the South Fork drainage.

Follow the drainage (routes are obvious) to the band of cliffs blocking the head of the drainage at 13,000'. Turn these to the right (W), or climb a short but steep slot to the left. Once above the cliffs cross a low-angled shelf and climb Sunshine's west ridge or northwest face, depending on snow conditions. Descend your ascent route. The slot is skiable (maximum angle 40°).

Safety notes: This whole valley is exposed to avalanches, so only travel at times of little or no risk. The northwest face of Sunshine Peak is often wind scoured. Be careful of cornices on the west ridge. Add several hours to standard sunrise for sunhit.

SUNSHINE PEAK
14,001 FT

3.3.3

REDCLOUD PEAK
TO/FROM

3.3.4

N

TO
GRIZZLY & SILVER CREEK
TRAILHEAD

Sunshine Peak from the north, spring

3.3.5	**Sunshine Peak—Long East Ridge**	
Ratings:	Ski Descent—N.R.	Snow Climb—Advanced
	Summer Climb—N.R.	
Season:	Winter or Spring Snow	
RT Data:	8 hours, 6.5 miles, 4,561′↑	
Start:	Mill Creek Campground 9,440′	
1 Day from Rd:	Yes	
Map:	Redcloud Peak, pg. 127	

The only time to use this rough and exceedingly tedious route is when the road to the Silver Creek Trailhead is closed by snow.

Winter or spring snow: Park at Mill Creek Campground (see section introduction). Cross the road and hike up steep brushy terrain. Climbing the fall line will lead you to timberline on Sunshine's east ridge, and you'll breathe a sigh of relief now that all the slogging is below you. Stick with the ridge to the summit, and descend your ascent route.

Safety notes: Beware of cliff areas on either side of the true east ridge. Use standard sunrise for sunhit.

3.3.6	**Handies Peak—North Ridge from Grizzly Gulch**	
Ratings:	Ski Descent—Intermediate	Snow Climb—Intermediate
	Summer Climb—Intermediate	
Season:	Summer or Spring Snow	
RT Data:	6 hours, 7.5 miles, 3,648′↑	
Start:	Grizzly and Silver Creek 10,400′	
1 Day from Rd:	Yes	
Map:	Handies Peak, pg. 137	
Photo:	pg. 135	

During snow seasons, while this route up Handies can get you into severe timber bashing, it could be the only practical choice for a day trip if the road is not open to the American Basin route (3.3.8). It is a fine route in summer, with a reasonably defined trail to timberline.

Summer after snow melt-off: Begin at the Grizzly Gulch Trailhead on the Cinnamon Pass Road (section introduction). Head W and cross a bridge over the Lake Fork of the Gunnison River, then stick with the pack trail that follows the valley on the north side of Grizzly Gulch Creek. Use the trail to reach timberline at 11,800′.

From timberline you have several options. A simple choice is to climb NW to the 13,000 foot saddle between Whitecross Mountain and Handies, then follow Handies' north ridge to the summit. This involves a bit of scrambling along the ridgecrest. For more excitement, pick one of the ribs to the left (W) of the saddle, follow it to the crest of the ridge, then follow the ridge to the summit. Descend your ascent route, or for a long tour, descend the South Ridge to American Basin (3.3.8), and follow the Cinnamon Pass Road back to the Grizzly Gulch Trailhead.

Spring snow season: Use the summer route described above. Extreme skiers and snow climbers can consider several couloirs on the north face.

Handies Peak from the northeast, spring.

N

HANDIES PEAK
14,048 FT

WHITECROSS
MOUNTAIN
13,542 FT

CINNAMON
PASS

SADDLE
13,000 FT

3.3.6

3.3.7

3.3.6

P.INT
12,792 FT

GRIZZLY
GULCH

TO
GRIZZLY & SILVER CREEK TRAILHEAD
10,400 FT

Safety notes: Less experienced climbers should be ready for a bit of slow movement on the north ridge. Snow climbers should note that this side of Handies gets an early sunhit. Other than the crest of the north ridge, every part of this route is exposed to avalanche danger.

3.3.7	Handies Peak—East Face Snow from Grizzly Gulch	
Ratings:	Ski Descent—Advanced Snow Climb—Advanced Summer Climb—N.R.	
Season:	Snow Route, Spring	
RT Data:	8 hours, 7 miles, 3,648′↑	
Start:	Grizzly and Silver Creek 10,400′	
1 Day from Rd:	Yes	
Map:	Handies Peak, pg. 137	
Photo:	pg. 135	

Snow climbers and skiers enjoy this route, but the approach may dim your initial enthusiasm if you're used to access such as that provided by the American Basin Trailhead (section introduction).

Spring or early summer snow: Begin at the Grizzly Gulch Trailhead on the Cinnamon Pass Road (section introduction). Head W and cross a bridge over the Lake Fork of the Gunnison River, then stick with the pack trail that follows the valley on the north side of Grizzly Gulch Creek. Use the trail to reach timberline at 11,800′.

From timberline, climb SW into the upper right (N) arm of the basin, below the Handies/Whitecross ridge. Continue up to the East Face. While you'll see several choices for routes, perhaps the best snow line is on the far right (N) side of the face. Descend your ascent route, or descend Handies' North Ridge (3.3.6).

Safety notes: Use standard sunrise for sunhit on this eastern aspect.

3.3.8	Handies Peak from American Basin		
Ratings:	Summer Climb—Novice Ski Descent—Intermediate Snow Climb—Novice		
Season:	Summer	Winter	Spring
RT Time:	6 hours, 5 miles 2,728′↑	10 hours, 11 miles 4,548′↑	Multi-day 3,648′↑
Start:	American Basin 11,320′	Cinnamon Pass Rd 9,500′	Grizzly and Silver Creek 10,400′
1 Day from Rd:	Yes	No	Yes
Map	Handies Peak, pg. 137		

This is the quickest and easiest way up Handies Peak. It is an excellent hike for a first fourteener, and it's a classic ski descent.

Summer after snow melt-off: Your route is simple. Follow the Cinnamon Pass Road to the American Basin Trailhead (section introduction). From parking, follow the drainage S to 12,400′ in American Basin. Head E from here and climb the south side of Handies' prominent west shoulder. Obvious grassy slopes and gullies lead to the south summit ridge saddle (13,460′). Take the ridge to the summit. Descend your ascent route.

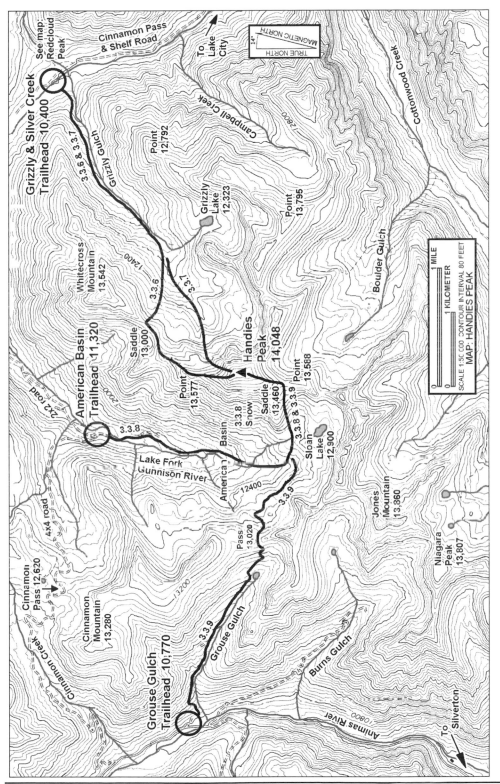

Spring powder in American Basin.

Spring snow season: Use the summer route described above, but start at snow closure on the Cinnamon Pass Road, possibly at the Grizzly & Silver Creek Trailhead (section introduction). For skiing and snow climbing, you can find steeper terrain by taking a direct line to the summit by climbing E from 12,200' in American Basin.

Winter: Start at winter road closure and use the the summer route described above. To avoid avalanche terrain, make variations using windscoured ribs and shoulders.

Safety notes: This route is a good choice for beginners. But even though it is an easy hike, novices should remember they are still at high altitude, and exposed to lightning danger in the event of a storm. Summer hikers should be fit and get an early start. Snow season climbers s136hould note that this route, including the approach, is exposed to many avalanche paths and should only be climbed during very stable periods. For sunhit, add several hours to standard sunrise.

3.3.9	Handies Peak—South Ridge from Grouse Gulch		
Ratings:	Ski Descent—Advanced		Snow Climb—Intermediate
		Summer Climb—Intermediate	
Season:	Spring Snow or Summer		
RT Data:	9 hours, 7 miles, 4,478' ↑		
Start:	Grouse Gulch Trailhead 10,770'		
1 Day from Rd:	Yes		
Map:	Handies Peak, pg. 137		

While this route is not as direct as those from the north, it involves much less driving for climbers coming from southern Colorado. Summer climbers will enjoy this high tour, as will spring skiers.

Summer, or spring snow season: Park at the Grouse Gulch Trailhead (see section introduction) and follow the 4x4 road/trail to the pass at the head of Grouse Gulch (13,020'). Continue E on the trail as it drops into American Basin, then circles to the center of the basin (12,400'). Remember that this section of the route, when also used for your return, adds about 1,200 feet to your total vertical gain. Leave the main trail here, and climb E through the upper basin to the south (R) side of Handies' west shoulder. Take the right (S) side of the west shoulder up easy ground to a saddle on the south ridge (13,460') then follow the ridge to the summit. Descend your ascent route.

Safety notes: You won't find any unusual hazards on this route. Allow extra time for the climb back out of American Basin. Use standard sunrise for sunhit.

SECTION 3.4
Mount Sneffels (14,150')

Undeniably the most spectacular peak in the San Juans, Mount Sneffels rises 6,000 vertical feet from its northern foothills. Any mountaineer driving from the north is sure to get an itch when he or she sees this spectacular arete in a stupendous view unrivaled anywhere else in Colorado.

No discussion of Mount Sneffels would be complete without pondering its unusual name. The most likely origin is as a homonym to Mount Snaefell from Jules Verne's book, *Journey to the Center of the Earth.* It also bears a resemblance to a Nordic word meaning "snowfield." Whatever the case, at least the peak is named for something other than a politician. My favorite explanation is that miners working high on Sneffels' slopes always had colds, so the name derives from "sniffles." However, if you look up similar words in Webster's, you will find "snaffle," which means a horse's muzzle or birds beak—another likely derivative.

Mount Sneffels has fine climbing on numerous ridges. Due to the riven nature of this volcanic peak, skiable couloirs are prevalent as well. Winter climbs of the peak involve quite a bit of avalanche exposure. If you don't care for the extreme, but still like to get out in winter, forego a summit bid and try a ski trip into Yankee Boy Basin. Here, acres of slopes entice every level of skier, with many slopes gentle enough to make avalanches less likely. Aside from terrific terrain and snow, another incentive for mountaineering in Yankee Boy Basin is all-season access via the Camp Bird Mine Road.

ROADS AND TRAILHEADS

USGS Maps: Mount Sneffels, Ridgway, Telluride

Yankee Boy Basin Trailhead

Drive U.S. 550 (the Red Mountain Pass Road) S from Ouray for slightly less than 1/2 mile. Just past the first switchback, turn off to the SW on the well-signed Imogene Pass/Camp Bird Mine Road (Road #361). After snow melt-off, two-wheel-drive will take you 7 miles to parking at a spur road that heads left (10,720'). With four-wheel-drive you can continue 2 miles up into Yankee Boy Basin to 11,400' (if you come to any unsigned intersections, bear right.) The 4x4 section is of average difficulty.

Great effort is made to keep the Camp Bird Mine open during snow seasons. During winters with light snow, it's often plowed to 10,720'. In the spring it's often punched higher. You must use a 4x4 vehicle (with chains or studded tires) to navigate the road during snow seasons.

Blaine Basin Trailhead

This trailhead is only useful after the spring snow melt-off. Drive Colorado Highway 62 for 5 miles W from Ridgway, or 19 miles E from its intersection with Highway 145. Turn S off the highway on to Ouray County Road 7 (average clearance 2-wheel-drive), which is indicated by an obvious sign. Continue up the road (known as the East Dallas Creek Road). At 9 miles you'll hit several intersections. Take the central (main road) options and continue a short distance to obvious parking (9,330'). To reach Blaine Basin, locate the road-closure gate at the trailhead, and continue on foot up the closed road. Don't take the trail to Blue Lakes. Instead, stick with the old road as it crosses the creek and heads northeast about 1 mile to Wilson Creek. The trail then follows the Wilson Creek drainage up into Blaine Basin.

While the complete East Dallas Creek Road doesn't melt out until sometime in May, during some years you can drive quite a distance up the road earlier in the spring, possibly to 8,500' or above.

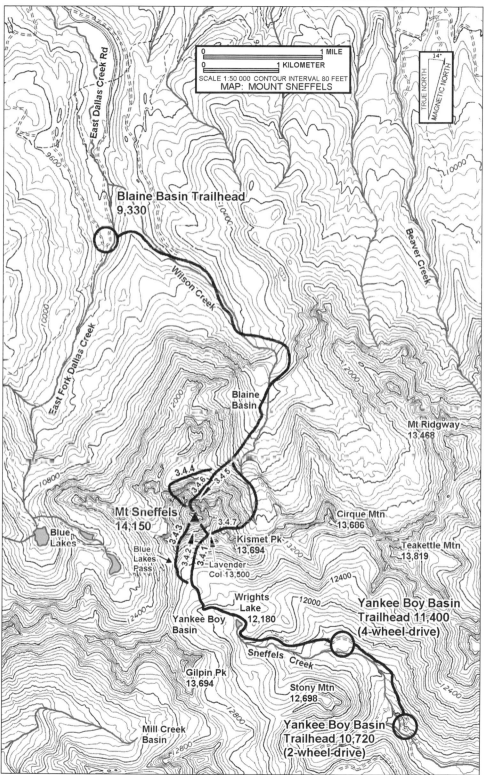

3.4.1	**Mount Sneffels via Lavender Col from Yankee Boy Basin**	
Ratings:	Summer Climb—Intermediate Ski Descent—Extreme	
	Snow Climb—Advanced	
Season:	Summer/Spring	Winter
RT Data:	6 hours, 4 miles, 3,430′↑	7 hours, 4 miles, 3,430′↑
Start:	Yankee Boy Basin Trailhead	Yankee Boy Basin Trailhead
	10,720′	10,720′
1 Day from Rd:	Yes	Road may be closed midwinter
Map:	Mount Sneffels, pg. 141	
Photos:	pgs. 143, 145	

This is the all-season standard route for Mount Sneffels. It includes a terrific little couloir that's a perfect entry-level snow climb during spring snow season.

Summer after snow melt-off: Follow the Camp Bird Mine Road to Yankee Boy Basin (section introduction). Hike the old road and trail up the basin to the higher basin above Wrights Lake (12,180′), then climb NW for about 3/4 of a mile to 13,000′ elevation in the small amphitheater below Sneffels' south face.

For the standard route, climb NE out of the amphitheater up steep scree to Lavender Col, the obvious 13,500′ saddle on Sneffels' southeast ridge. From Lavender Col, climb an obvious, steep couloir to the summit ridge. If conditions in the couloir are unpleasant, you can scramble up the rocks on the left side. If you do climb out of the couloir, this will be the real crux of the route, but the steep scree below Lavender Col could be considered a crux as well! Descend your ascent route.

Spring snow season: Your route from the higher Yankee Boy Basin to Lavender Col will vary with snow conditions. With complete spring snow coverage, try staying on the north side of Yankee Boy Basin as you enter the area below Sneffels' south face. Skiing this route is serious because of the fall potential encountered while descending the terrain above Lavender Col.

Winter: Because of good road access (section introduction), Mount Sneffels is climbed quite often in the winter. The standard route via Lavender Col is the best, but it has a great deal of avalanche danger; some can be avoided by using rock ribs and windscoured areas, but snow stability evaluation is a must, since some potentially dangerous slopes can not be avoided. Make sure at least one person in your group is skilled in avalanche hazard evaluation and avoidance, or hire a guide.

Safety notes: Summer climbers should take precautions for rockfall in the summit gully. In winter, all routes on Sneffels have a great deal of avalanche potential. Thus, if you're after snow, hit this route when it's covered with compacted spring snow. The sun hits this side of Sneffels early; use standard sunrise for sunhit.

MOUNT SNEFFELS
14,150 FT

DYKE COL
13,041 FT

KISMET PEAK
13,694 FT

LAVENDER
COL 13,500 FT

YANKEE BOY
BASIN

YANKEE BOY
BASIN

WRIGHTS
LAKE 12,180 FT

TO YANKEE BOY
BASIN TRAILHEAD

GILPIM PEAK
13,694 FT

BLUE LAKES
PASS 13,000 FT

3.4.2

3.4.1

N

Mount Sneffels from the south, winter.

3.4.2	Mount Sneffels—South Face "Birthday Chutes"	
Ratings:	Ski Descent—Extreme Snow Climb—Advanced	
	Summer Climb—N.R.	
Season:	Snow route, Spring	
RT Data:	7 hours, 6 miles, 3,430'↑	
Start:	Yankee Boy Basin Trailhead 10,720'	
1 Day from Rd:	Yes	
Map:	Mount Sneffels, pg. 141	
Photos:	pgs. 143, 145	

A number of classic couloirs split the south face of Mount Sneffels. The ones to the left side of the face are shorter and steeper, while those to the right (closer to Lavender Col) are longer and slightly lower-angled (though still at least 45°).

Spring snow season: Park at the Yankee Boy Basin Trailhead. Follow route 3.4.1 to 13,200' at the base of Sneffels' south face. A jagged mountain known as Kismet Peak (13,694) rises southeast of Mount Sneffels, and newcomers looking for couloirs have mistaken this for Sneffels. Read your map.

Once below Sneffels' south face, pick one of the obvious couloirs. A popular line takes the couloir leading most directly to the summit. It starts out as an obvious rift, then branches into several shallow gullies leading to a steep 50° flank just below the summit. Descend the Lavender Col route (3.4.1), or ski the couloir.

Safety notes: A fall in the upper part of this route could eject you over cliffs and rock-studded snow. Use standard sunrise for sunhit.

3.4.3	Mount Sneffels—Southwest Ridge	
Ratings:	Summer Climb—Advanced	Ski Descent—N.R.
	Snow Climb—Advanced	
Season:	Summer/Spring	Winter
RT Data:	8 hours, 7.5 miles, 3,430'↑	12 hours, 7.5 miles, 3,430'↑
Start:	Yankee Boy Basin 10,720'	Yankee Boy Basin 10,720'
1 Day from Rd:	Yes	Yes, unless road closed lower
Map:	Mount Sneffels, pg. 141	
Photo:	pgs. 143	

You'll see fewer people on this airy ridge, and it's slightly more challenging than the Sneffels standard route (3.4.1). This is not a 5th class climb, but you may face sections of 4th class hand-and-foot scrambling.

Summer after melt off: Park at the 2-wheel or 4-wheel-drive Yankee Boy Basin Trailhead (section introduction). Continue on foot up the jeep trail into Yankee Boy Basin. Stick with the road as it becomes a trail and leads to Blue Lakes Pass (13,000', the Gilpin/Sneffels saddle). Leave the trail at the saddle and head N up the ridge. Now the climbing begins.

Your first obstacle is a group of stately gendarmes. Turn these on the left (W), and continue to a major notch at 13,500'. Continue up the ridge from the notch. The remainder of the route sticks with the ridgetop, with a few minor deviations to the right (E). Descend the

N

KISMET PK
13,694 FT

3.4.1

LAVENDER COL
13,500 FT

DYKE COL
13,040 FT

3.4.2

TEAKETTLE MTN
13,819 FT

CIRQUE MTN
13,686 FT

Skiing Mount Sneffels, South Face (spring). Looking east.

Lavender Col route (3.4.1).

Spring snow season: Use the summer route above. Be prepared for snow climbing on both the approach and descent.

Safety notes: Until mid-summer, you'll need both crampons and ice axe for the approach and descent. While this route does not require roped climbing, you will be in situations where a fatal fall is possible. Use standard sunrise for sunhit.

3.4.4	Mount Sneffels—West Couloir	
Ratings:	Ski Descent—Extreme Snow Climb—Advanced	
	Summer Climb—N.R.	
Season:	Snow Route or Spring	
RT Data:	Overnight, 16 miles, 5,650'↑	
Start:	Dallas Creek Road 8,500'	
1 Day from Rd:	No, via Dallas Creek; yes from Yankee Boy	
Map:	Mount Sneffels, pg. 141	
Photo:	pg. 147	

Easily viewed from Highway 62, this magnificent couloir is often mistaken for the Snake Couloir (3.4.6). Actually, both lines share the same upper section, but they are two very different routes. The Snake is north facing and is a good ice or snow climb during most seasons, while the West Couloir gets harsh sun and melts out by late spring.

Spring snow season: You can choose among several strategies for approaching this route. For climbers, perhaps the most elegant option is a drop off at snow closure on the Dallas Creek Road. You then do the Blaine Basin approach (section introduction), climb the West Couloir, then descend the Lavender Col route (3.4.1) to a stashed car or pick-up at the Yankee Boy Basin Trailhead. Another option for climbers is to leave from the Yankee Boy Basin Trailhead and climb to Lavender Col (3.4.1), descend the East Couloir (3.4.7), circle up through Blaine Basin and climb the West Couloir, then descend the Lavender Col route back to Yankee Boy Basin. The only drawback of this option is an early morning descent of the icy East Couloir, which may have the added horror of frozen scree near the top. Still another option is to climb the West Couloir from Blaine Basin, then go over the summit and back down the East Couloir to Blaine Basin. This latter option is the most circuitous, and involves a late descent of the East Couloir, exposing you to the danger of wet snow avalanches.

Skiers who feel certain of snow conditions could do opposite routines, but icy patches can develop in these couloirs, so it's better to climb before you ski. Thus, a high camp in Blaine Basin might be the best choice for skiers.

At any rate, the route is quite simple. Indeed, the crux is probably locating the start of the couloir (you can't see it till you're there.) To begin, be aware that Blaine Basin splits into two arms at the 12,000' level, with a central slope leading up to Sneffels' gothic north face. East Blaine Basin leads to the base of Sneffels' East Couloir route, while West Blaine Basin takes you to the West Couloir. Climb low angled snow into West Blaine Basin, which narrows into a classic cirque. Continue to 12,600' at the head of the cirque, where the start of the West Couloir is obvious. Climbing in the couloir is straightforward (maximum angle 48°), and it leads you to a saddle at 13,600' where the route joins up with the Snake Couloir (3.4.6). Continue up the Snake Couloir, and climb an easy rock pitch (4th Class) to the summit.

Skiers will find the West Couloir to be a fine extreme route, but hit it early in the spring season since sections of snow quickly melt out.

Safety notes: Skiers should beware of skiing this couloir without climbing it first. Climbers should take precautions for rockfall. Know the pros and cons of your access and descent strategy. This west facing couloir gets a late sunhit, but the top of the Snake Couloir gets sun at sunrise.

Mount Sneffels from the north, winter.

3.4.5	**Mount Sneffels—North Buttress**	
Ratings:	Ski Descent—N.R. Snow Climb—N.R.	
	Summer Climb—Advanced	
Season:	Summer	
RT Data:	9 hours, 7 miles, 4,820'↑	
Start:	Blaine Basin Trailhead 9,330'	
1 Day from Rd:	Yes	
Map	Mount Sneffels, pg. 141	
Photo:	pg. 147	

Dedicated mountaineers should place this "directisima" classic on their must-do list. The route follows an airy buttress up Mount Sneffels' majestic north face.

Summer after snow melt-off (technical 5.6 rock climbing): Drive to the Blaine Basin Trailhead and take the trail into Blaine Basin (section introduction). As soon as you have a good view of Sneffels' north face, identify the Snake Couloir (3.4.6)—the deeply notched cleft that splits the right side of the north face. The North Buttress forms the left (E) side of the Snake Couloir, and separates the Snake from another couloir farther to the left.

Hike to the base of the Snake Couloir, work a bit left, and climb an obvious rock pitch onto the buttress. Continue up the buttress, working the left side when necessary. From 13,600', near the dogleg in the Snake Couloir, take a direct line up the buttress to the summit. Descend to Lavender Col (3.4.1), then down the East Couloir (3.4.7).

Safety notes: Bring a good selection of rock hardware, and know how to use it. Time your ascent with afternoon lightning in mind. Use sunrise time for sun-hit.

3.4.6	**Mount Sneffels—Snake (Dogleg) Couloir**	
Ratings:	Ski Descent—Extreme Snow Climb—Advanced	
	Summer Climb—N.R.	
Season:	Snow Route, Spring or Summer	
RT Data:	8 hours, 7 miles, 4,930'↑	
Start:	Yankee Boy Basin Trailhead 10,720'	
1 Day from Rd:	Yes, from Yankee Boy, no from Blaine Basin	
Map:	Mount Sneffels, pg. 141	
Photo:	pg. 147	

This cleft on the north face of Mount Sneffels is one of the best ski descents and snow climbs in Colorado. Also known as the Dogleg Couloir, or simply the Sneffels Couloir, it's been a popular test piece among Southern Colorado mountaineers since 1933 when it was first climbed by Dwight Lavender and friends. While spring snow season is the best time for climbing or skiing in the Snake Couloir, ice climbers can ply their trade into early summer, and late fall can fill the Snake with alpine ice from top to bottom.

The problem with snow climbing and skiing the Snake Couloir is that the north side of Sneffels is relatively inaccessible during spring snow season. Road access does not open completely until early summer. It is possible to backpack up the East Fork of Dallas Creek to a high camp in Blaine Basin, especially when the Dallas Creek Road opens in late spring; but most

Camp Bird Mine Road, spring.

people choose to approach from Yankee Boy Basin. See the description of Sneffels' West Couloir (3.4.4) for more ideas on access strategy.

Summer or spring snow season. To climb the Snake Couloir from Yankee Boy Basin, take the Camp Bird Mine Road to parking for Yankee Boy Basin (section introduction). Climb into Yankee Boy Basin, then continue NW to 13,000' in the small amphitheater below Sneffels' south face (3.4.2). Your route to this point will vary with snow conditions. With complete spring snow coverage, staying up on the north side of Yankee Boy Basin is probably a good choice, but with more avalanche danger you will want to vary your route to avoid traveling below suspect slopes.

From the amphitheater, climb NE to Lavender Col—the obvious 13,500' saddle on Sneffels' southeast ridge. From Lavender Col, drop E down the wide East Couloir (3.4.7) to about 12,000' elevation. Traverse W for about 1/4 mile through easily negotiated rock outcrops into the small basin below Sneffels' spectacular jagged north face. Three couloirs run up the face. Take the right-hand couloir, which is deeply cleft and leads to the bend in the dog's leg, where the angle steepens to about 50° and the couloir takes a marked turn to the left (E). You'll see a small rock pillar in the middle of the couloir where it turns. Continue up the gully to its end. You may need a rope for the climb to the summit pyramid, as a slip could be fatal.

For skiing, most parties forgo the "climb it first principle." Instead, they take the Lavender Col Route (3.4.1) to the summit from Yankee Boy Basin, then rappel to the head of the couloir. I and several companions paid a price for that tactic one July. After skiing past the dogleg we discovered that a rock slide had made the gully entirely unskiable—and dangerous in the event of a fall because the runout was a pile of rocks.

A high camp in Blaine Basin, with an initial reconnaissance climb up the couloir, is a good tactic. But with high parking near Yankee Boy Basin, who can blame those who do not climb before they ski?

Safety notes: This route and its approaches have a great deal of avalanche potential. Thus, it's best to visit this area during the spring snow season when avalanche danger is predictable and avoidable. Most of the Snake (Dogleg) Couloir is very shaded and has a very late sunhit—if it even gets sun at all. The sun hits the summit pyramid above the couloir at just after sunrise in the spring, so figure an early sunhit for that reason.

3.4.7	Mount Sneffels—East Couloir to Lavender Col	
Ratings:	Summer Climb—Advanced	Ski Descent—Advanced
	Snow Climb—Advanced	
Season:	Spring Snow	Summer Snow
RT Data:	Overnight, 15 miles, 5,650'↑	8 Hours, 8 miles, 4,820'↑
Start:	Dallas Creek Road	Blaine Basin Trailhead
	8,500'	9,330'
1 Day	Spring	Summer
from Rd:	Yes	No
Map:	Mount Sneffels, pg. 141	
Photo:	pg. 147 and cover	

This is a fine climb in its own right, but is most often used as a connection between Yankee Boy Basin and Blaine Basin.

Summer after snow melt-off: Park at the Blaine Basin Trailhead (see section introduction), and hike to timberline in Blaine Basin. Observe that Blaine Basin splits into two arms at the 12,000' level, with a central slope leading up to Sneffels' gothic north face. East Blaine Basin leads to the base the East Couloir route, while West Blaine Basin takes you to the West Couloir (3.4.4). Also observe that another arm heads from timberline up a drainage on the northwest side of Cirque Mountain.

Read your map and compass at timberline and identify the jagged north ridge of Mount Sneffels. Climb Blaine Basin towards Sneffels to 11,800'. Work left, then head up an obvious, wide gully leading up and left of Sneffels' north ridge. This gully widens and leads to a lower-angled area at about 12,500'. Swing right (W) here, and climb an obvious dished couloir W to Lavender Col. Follow the remainder of the Lavender Col route (3.4.1) to the summit. Descend your ascent route.

Summer or spring snow season: Use the route above. It's better with snow.

Safety notes: Once this couloir is devoid of snow, it's still climbable, but may have more rockfall. Snow in the upper part of the couloir gets a sunrise sunhit.

4
SOUTH
SAN JUAN
MOUNTAINS

Near the summit of Wilson Peak, looking south at Mount Wilson, spring.

USFS Forest Visitor Maps: San Juan National Forest, Gunnison National Forest, Uncompahgre National Forest

The South San Juan Mountains, vaguely divided from their northern siblings by road access, are perhaps slightly more precipitous and somewhat harder to access. The Chicago Basin peaks (Windom, Sunlight, Eolus) require a backpack trip and railroad ride. The Wilsons and El Diente can be done as long day trips, but many people backpack for these as well. In the summer after most snow is melted, all these peaks have intermediate level climbing routes, albeit with tasty bits of hand-and-foot scrambling. The easiest are Wilson Peak (N), Sunlight Peak, Windom Peak, and North Eolus Peak. El Diente Peak, Mount Wilson (S) and South Eolus are slightly harder, but still "hikeable." If you're after more challenge, try the ridge connecting El Diente with Mount Wilson (4.1.10), or Sunlight Peak's west ridge (4.2.4).

Snowfall in the South San Juans is usually copious, making spring snow climbing and skiing consistently enjoyable. But dry winters hit as well, when a thin snowpack can spell disaster for mountaineers because these steep rocky peaks need plenty of snow to cover the stones and widen the couloirs. Call the Forest Service in Durango and Telluride to check on snow conditions (see directory).

SECTION 4.1
The San Miguel Mountains
Wilson Peak (N) (14,017'), Mount Wilson (S) (14,246'),
El Diente Peak (14,159')

The San Miguel Mountains (called "The Wilsons" by locals), are a cluster of high peaks to the southwest of Telluride. This is a beautiful massif with good road access, especially in late spring and summer. Two of the peaks have practically the same name: Wilson Peak and Mount Wilson. This situation has led to some confused conversations, and no small amount of guidebook writer's angst. For the sake of clarity all references to Mount Wilson in this book will be accompanied by the following parenthetic: (S). For a good view of The Wilsons drive the road to the Telluride airport.

The Wilsons provide good hiking, skiing, snow climbing and rock scrambling. The steeper rock faces are too loose for safe technical climbing. Speaking of rocks and stones, it should be noted that several routes, when devoid of snow from mid-summer to late fall, are covered with unpleasant scree. These routes may be climbed dry, but are more fun with snow cover. Moreover, such scree areas are easily eroded by too much climber traffic. Such scree problems are noted in the route descriptions.

ROADS AND TRAILHEADS

USGS Maps: Mount Wilson, Dolores Peak

Silver Pick Trailhead

The Silver Pick Road provides access to El Diente Peak and both Wilsons. Drive Highway 145 for 2.6 miles E from Sawpit, or 8.5 miles W from Telluride to the well-signed turn south on to the Silver Pick Road (2-wheel-drive). Drive the Silver Pick Road 6.9 miles to the well-signed Silver Pick Basin parking area. This is the start of the Silver Pick Basin Road, which is navigable by high clearance vehicles for three miles to the Silver Pick Trailhead at road closure (10,700') just below the Silver Pick Mill (an abandoned mining complex). Winter snow closure is near the lower parking area. In mid-May snow closure is usually on shaded hillsides (9,700') about 1 mile up from the parking area. After a light-snow winter, the road will open to the intersection of the Wilson Mesa Trail by May. Snowmobile travel is not practical on the Silver Pick Road.

Lizard Head Creek Trailhead

This trailhead provides access to the Slate Creek route on the E side of Mount Wilson (South Wilson). From Telluride, drive Highway 45 3 miles W and turn left on Highway 145. Drive Hwy. 145 for 12 miles to the summit of Lizard Head Pass, then continue down the west side of Lizard Head Pass 2 miles to a turnout at 10,050'. Park here. Up the hill to the north you will find signs for the trails. Highway 145 is an all-season paved highway, though it may be closed during extreme winter weather.

Kilpacker Creek Trailhead & Navajo Lake Trailhead

These trailheads are all located on the Dunton Road. Sadly, there is no snow removal done on the Dunton Road until May 15. Before that date you can travel by snowmobile if snow cover is good. In the spring the road may melt off earlier than that date, but do not count on it.

Two routes lead to the Dunton Road. From aforementioned Lizard Head Pass, drive Highway 145 for 5.4 miles W to a well-signed right turn onto the Dunton Road. Snow closure

---

in early May is at the first switchback just a mile or so from the highway. In the summer, if you come from the east, this is the shortest way to the Navajo Lake and Kilpacker Creek Trailheads, but the road is narrow and requires a high clearance vehicle. From the aforementioned highway turnoff, drive the Dunton road 5.1 miles to Dunton Meadows and a small spur road that turns off to the right (N); this spur leads a few hundred yards to the Kilpacker Creek Trailhead (10,060'). For the Navajo Lake Trailhead, continue 2 miles on the Dunton Road. The Navajo Lake Trailhead (9,350') is 1/4 mile up a well-signed spur off the Dunton Road.

The other route for the Dunton Road trailheads, (better in spring mud season or with a low clearance vehicle), is to drive Highway 154 for 38.6 miles W from Lizard Head Pass (or E from Cortez or Dolores) to the well-signed West Dolores Road. Follow this road 13 miles to a T intersection. Take a right at the T, and drive 8.9 miles to Dunton. Drive past Dunton for .6 miles to another T intersection. Turn right and continue 2.7 miles to a left turn off the Dunton Road on to a spur that leads 1/4 mile to the Navajo Lake Trailhead (9,350'). For the Kilpacker Creek Trailhead, continue 2 miles up the Dunton Road to a spur road that turns off to the left (marked as Road 207). Take this spur several hundred yards to the trailhead (10,060').

Bilk Basin Trailhead

Drive Highway 145 for 6 miles west from Telluride to the intersection with South Fork Road. Take a left (S) turn onto South Fork Road, and drive 2 miles to the Illium townsite. Leave the South Fork Road and take a right (W) on Road 623. After a bridge and short hillclimb, take a left and drive S on an old railroad grade for 3 miles, then turn right and drive up another steep hill .6 mile to a fork (9,050'). Park 2-wheel-drive here. With 4-wheel-drive, take the left fork and continue 31/2 miles on Road 623 to the Bilk Basin Trailhead (10,070') at the Morningstar Mine ruins.

4.1.1	Wilson Peak—Northeast Face	
Ratings:	Ski Descent—Extreme Snow Cllmb—Advanced	
	Summer Climb—N.R.	
Season:	Snow Route, Spring	
RT Data:	6 hours, 7 miles, 4,317'↑	
Start:	Silver Pick Trailhead (snow) 9,700' '	
1 Day from Rd:	Yes	
Map:	El Diente Peak, pg. 154; Mount Wilson, pg. 155	
Photos:	pgs. 156, 157	

Early summer or spring snow season: A ski descent of this route is a popular testpiece among mountaineers from Telluride. It is also a fine snow climb, but like any easterly face, snow conditions are likely to be poor. Thus, unless an "exact" summit ski is your priority, you'll find better snow on the Silverpick side of Wilson Peak.

Follow the Silver Pick Road (section introduction) to 10,500' elevation, about 1/4 mile before the Silver Pick Mill. Leave the road here and travel in as easterly direction, following timberline for about 11/2 miles to 11,500' in the basin below Wilson's North Face. Two obvious couloirs lead up the left (southeast) side of the face. The left couloir hits the summit ridge just to the north of the summit, and is the best route for both skiing and climbing.

Climbers can get an easier descent via the northwest face route (4.1.2). Skiers will find it hard to get into the couloir directly from the summit, but it has been done. A few turns down the north ridge allows easier access. The 50° crux is a short way down from the ridge. A fall in the crux section of the gully would have serious consequences since the gully is studded with

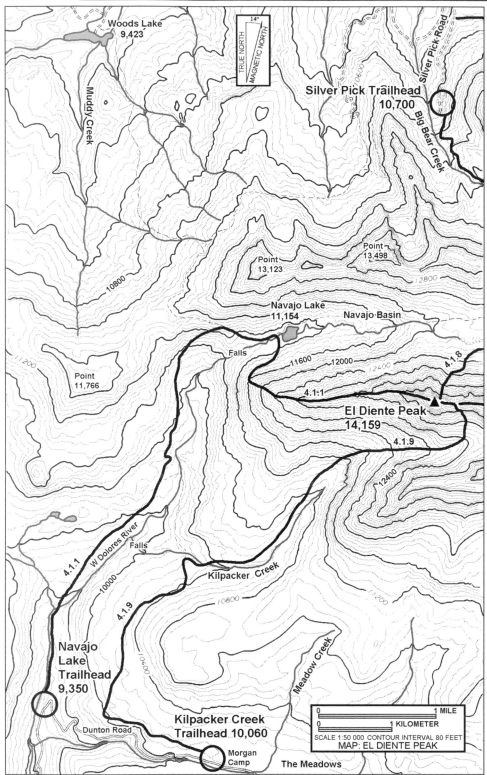

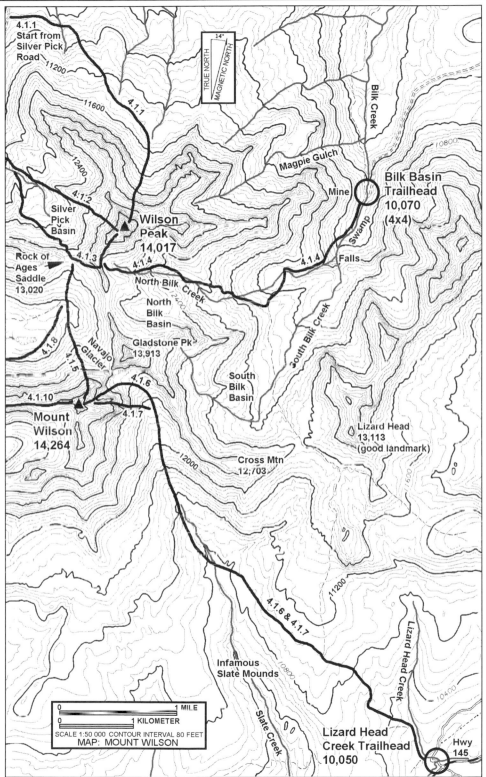

4.1.1
Start from
Silver Pick
Road

11200

11600

4.1.1

14°

TRUE NORTH

MAGNETIC NORTH

Bilk Creek

10800

12400

Magpie Gulch

4.1.2

Silver
Pick
Basin

Mine

Bilk Basin
Trailhead
10,070
(4x4)

Wilson
Peak
14,017

Rock of
Ages
Saddle
13,020

4.1.3

4.1.4

North Bilk Creek

Swamp

Falls

4.1.4

North
Bilk
Basin

2400

South Bilk Creek

4.1.8

Navajo
Glacier

Gladstone Pk
13,913

4.1.5

4.1.10

4.1.6

South
Bilk
Basin

Lizard Head
13,113
(good landmark)

Mount
Wilson
14,264

4.1.7

11600

Cross Mtn
12,703

12000

11200

4.1.6 & 4.1.7

Lizard Head Creek

Infamous
Slate Mounds

10800

Slate Creek

10400

0   1 MILE

0   1 KILOMETER

SCALE 1:50 000 CONTOUR INTERVAL 80 FEET
MAP: MOUNT WILSON

Lizard Head
Creek Trailhead
10,050

Hwy
145

Wilson Peak from the northeast, spring.

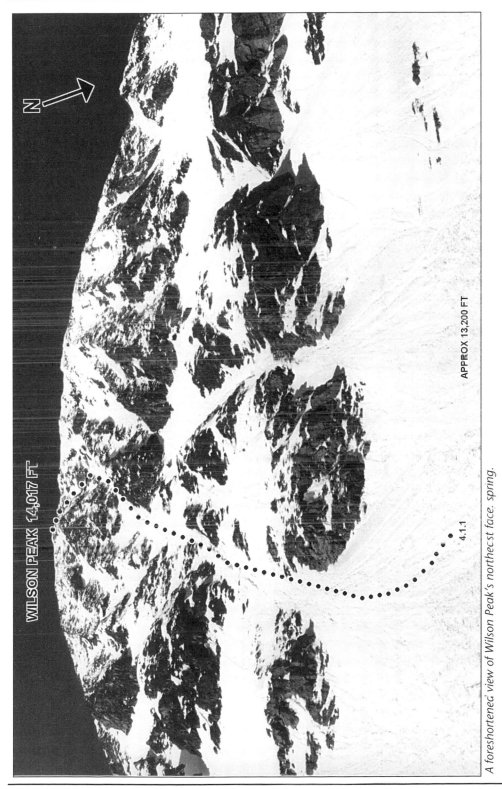

WILSON PEAK 14,017 FT

APPROX 13,200 FT

4.1.1

N

A foreshortened view of Wilson Peak's northeast face, spring.

rock outcrops. Both skiers and climbers should consider belaying.

Winter: This route is not recommended for winter climbing. See Appendix 1.

Safety notes: This route should only be attempted with compacted spring snow. As mentioned above, it has the usual problem of an easterly exposure, in that the snow receives a great deal of heat during the day. This may prevent proper freezing at night, and also creates deep melt channels early in the spring season. After a winter of heavy snow, this route can provide good snow climbing early in the summer. It should not be climbed without snow cover because of rockfall danger. Use standard sunrise for sunhit.

4.1.2	Wilson Peak—Northwest Face		
Ratings:	Summer Climb—Intermediate Ski Descent—Advanced		
	Snow Climb—Intermediate		
Season:	Summer	Winter	Spring
RT Time:	5 hours, 4.5 miles	multi-day,	7 hours, 7 miles
	3,317'↑	4,317'↑	4,317'↑
Start:	Silver Pick Trailhead	Silver Pick Trailhead	Silver Pick Trailhead
	(summer) 10,700'	(snow) 9,700'	(snow) 9,700'
1 Day from Rd:	No		
Map:	El Diente, pg. 154; Mount Wilson, pg. 155		

This route is a fine late season snow climb, and the whole Silver Pick Basin area provides fantastic skiing. If you're after a summer climb of Wilson Peak, this route is a good choice provided the scree is still covered by early summer snow. If the scree is exposed, avoid frustration and erosion by climbing the Southwest Ridge (4.1.3 or 4.1.4).

Spring or summer snow season: Follow the Silver Pick Road (section introduction), park at the highest snow closure or at the summer trailhead, and hike up into Silver Pick Basin. At 11,800' swing left (E) and follow the left side of Big Bear Creek to 12,200'. Bear left here, and instead of continuing with the creek, climb directly towards Wilson's summit into a small bowl.

Climb the bowl towards the summit. At the top of the bowl work left and you will find a nice gully that leads to the summit ridge several hundred feet southwest of the summit. Walk the ridge from here to the summit, then descend your ascent route. With good snow cover it's possible to ski (rated Extreme) from the summit back down the final couloir, but most skiers leave their planks at the top of the bowl.

Safety notes: During snow seasons all of this route (including portions of the Silver Pick Road) is exposed to avalanches. It is best done on stable snow during the spring season. Though experts would call this a "snow hike," bring your axe and crampons anyway. For sunhit, add several hours to standard sunrise.

4.1.3	Wilson Peak—Southwest Ridge from Rock of Ages Saddle		
Ratings:	Summer Climb—Advanced Ski Descent—N.R.		
	Snow Climb—Advanced		
Season:	Summer	Winter	Spring
RT Time:	7 hours, 6 miles	Overnight, 12 miles	10 hours, 9 miles
	3,317' ↑	5,017' ↑	4,317' ↑
Start:	Silver Pick Trailhead (summer) 10,700'	Silver Pick Trailhead (snow closure) 9,000'	Silver Pick Trailhead (snow) 9,700'
1 Day from Rd:	No		
Map:	El Diente, pg. 154; Mount Wilson, pg. 155		
Photo:	pg. 160		

If you're keen on preserving our fourteeners, use this relatively erosion-free route. It includes a little scrambling and route finding, but that's mountaineering!

Summer after melt off, or spring snow season: Park at the Silver Pick Trailhead (see section introduction), and hike (or ski) Silver Pick Basin 1½ miles to the main saddle at the head of the basin. This is known as Rock of Ages Saddle (13,020'). Summer climbers should note that a major track takes you to the ruins of a building at 12,140', and a less worn trail continues up to the Rock of Ages Saddle. Try to stick to the trail since it avoids difficult scree you'd encounter on a direct line up to the saddle.

Once at Rock of Ages Saddle, take a climbing traverse from the south side of the saddle for about ¼ mile to a minor saddle (13,280') on Wilson's south ridge. The remainder of the route involves much scrambling, but most parties do without a rope. Swing left (N) from the minor saddle, but instead of climbing the ridge crest, stay to the right (E) side of the ridge and contour through a cliffy area, then take a climbing traverse to reach the ridgetop at about 13,540'. Continue the ridge, with a deviation to the left if it looks appropriate, and perhaps a jog to the right just before the summit.

Winter: This is probably the most avalanche-safe route for Wilson Peak, but it's a major effort to do a winter ascent; the Silver Pick Road is closed in winter, and the scramble terrain on the ridge could be sinister with snow cover.

Safety notes: This is a scramble route with fall potential. Parties of varied ability should carry a rope for emergencies. Use standard sunrise for sunhit.

4.1.4	Wilson Peak—Southwest Ridge from Bilk Basin	
Ratings:	Ski Descent—N.R. Snow Climb—N.R.	
	Summer Climb—Advanced	
Season:	Summer or late Spring (no snow)	
RT Data:	9 hours, 8 miles, 3,947' ↑	
Start:	Bilk Basin Trailhead 10,070'	
1 Day from Rd:	Yes	
Map:	Mount Wilson, pg. 155	
Photo:	pg. 160	

This route takes the same upper section as 4.1.3, but involves a bit more distance from a lower trailhead. The advantages? More solitude and wilderness lend an aesthetic feel to this fine alpine hike and climb.

Summer after snow melt-off: Drive your 4x4 to the Bilk Basin Trailhead. With 2-wheel-drive, park lower (see section introduction) and add 1,200' gain and 7 miles to your trip data.

From parking at the 4x4 Bilk Basin Trailhead (10,070'), cross Bilk Creek, step over the Wilderness boundary, and hike the Bilk Basin Trail 1^1/2 miles to 11,400', where it splits. Climb the trail's north fork (which heads towards Wilson Peak) 1^3/4 miles to the 13,380' minor saddle on Wilson's south southwest ridge. Join route 4.1.3 here and follow it to the summit. Descend your ascent route.

Safety notes: See route 4.1.3; use standard sunrise for sunhit.

Looking northeast at Wilson Peak from El Diente Peak, late spring.

4.1.5	**Mount Wilson (S)—North Face**	
Ratings:	Summer Climb—Advanced	Ski Descent—Advanced
	Snow Climb—Advanced	
Season:	Summer	Spring snow
RT Data:	10 hours, 7 miles, 4,346'↑	12 Hours, 10 miles, 5,346'↑
Start:	SIlver Pick Trailhead	Silver Pick Trailhead
	10,700'	(snow) 9,700'
1 Day from Rd:	Summer	Spring
	Yes	Yes
Map:	Mount Wilson, pg. 155	
Photos:	pgs. 160, 161, 163, 170	

MOUNT WILSON
14,264 FT

← N

4.1.5
FROM
NAVAJO
BASIN

RIDGE
4.1.10

4.1.9
FROM
KILPACKER
CREEK

ORGAN
PIPES

Near the summit of El Diente, looking east at the rugged connecting ridge with Mount Wilson.

You'll find good snow climbing on this route until later in the summer. Once the snow melts you can scramble the same route, though you'll encounter patches of year-round snow. A popular "double bagger" day includes a traverse of the ridge to El Diente (4.1.10). If you like a casual schedule, consider a high camp in Navajo Basin.

Spring or early summer snow season: Park at the Silver Pick Trailhead, and climb Silver Pick Basin to the Rock of Ages Saddle (13,020', see route 4.1.2 for details). Use the excellent south view from the saddle to identify Mount Wilson and the Navajo Glacie,; a permanent snowfield that fills the cirque below the Wilson/Gladstone saddle. Continue S from the Rock of Ages Saddle and descend to 12,500', then contour the head of the basin to the north face of Mount Wilson. In late spring or early summer, when there's less snow, a good line takes a series of ribs to the right (W) of Navajo Glacier. Climb to just below the summit ridge, then parallel the summit ridge towards the summit, eventually reaching a break in the summit ridge. Gain the ridge here and scramble to the summit. Descend your ascent route, or make a few traverses to look for the best ski lines.

Given firm, avalanche-safe spring snow, you can climb any one of several couloirs that lead up this face. The ones that lead you to points closer to the summit are usually the best choice.

Summer: Climbers will find patches of snow in this area for most of the summer. With sparse cover, use one of the broken ribs leading to the summit ridge, then parallel the ridge as described above.

Safety notes: To avoid avalanches, this route should only be climbed and skied on stable spring and summer snow. Summer climbers should have crampons and ice axe, and know how to use them. For sunhit, add several hours to standard sunrise.

4.1.6	Mount Wilson (S)—East Cirque from Slate Creek		
Ratings:	Ski Descent—Advanced		Snow Climb—Advanced
	Summer Climb—Intermediate		
Season:	Spring snow or Summer		
RT Data:	overnight, 12 miles, 4,596↑		
Start:	Lizard Head Creek Trailhead 10,050'		
1 Day from Rd:	Yes		
Map:	Mount Wilson, pg. 155		
Photo:	pg. 163		

Though unpopular because of a lack of improved trails, this route is certainly the best way to ski Mount Wilson (S). What's more, this is is also an excellent snow climb. The East Cirque works as a summer route (it's more direct than any other), but it does involve bushwhacking and scree. If summer climbing is your game, still try to hit this route with at least a modicum of spring snow. You'll have a much better day as a result. The view from the Mount Wilson summit is exceptional; you get an unequaled panorama of the San Juans, as well as an impressive vista to the south.

Summer after snow melt-off: Drive the Lizard Head Pass Road (state 145) to the Lizard Head Creek Trailhead (section introduction). Park here and follow the Lizard Head Creek Trail about 1/4 mile uphill, then continue NW through conifer forest on a well-defined (closed) roadcut to 11,000'. The bushwhack starts here.

Leave the roadcut/trail and take a slightly dropping contour NW at 11,000' for just over a mile, then drop into Slate Creek at around 10,800'. All this monkey business is necessary to avoid the infamous "Slate Mounds" farther down the Slate Creek drainage. The crux is the bushwhack from 11,000'. Because of the bushwhack, most parties should do this trip as an

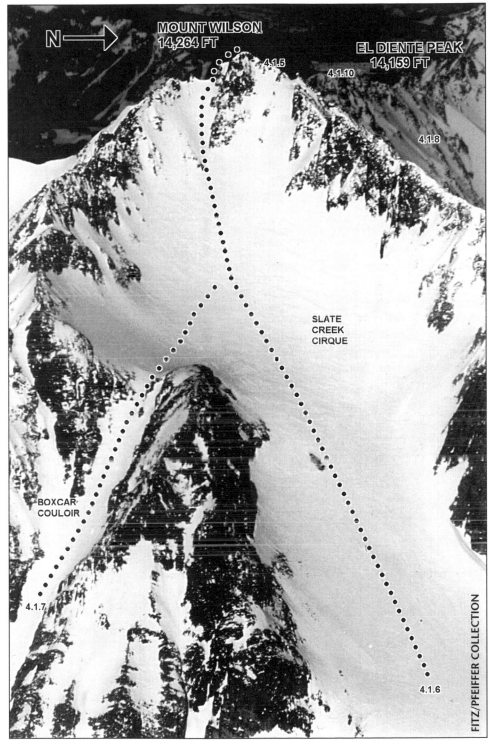

Mount Wilson's magnificent eastern routes, spring.

overnight with a camp in Slate Creek. Take a light pack—you'll find plenty of logs to climb over.

Follow the Slate Creek drainage up to timberline, then climb the narrow amphitheater at the head of the drainage (12,400'). Continue up the amphitheater as it takes a turn to the left and leads to a small saddle to the south of the summit rockpile. Scramble the last hundred feet to the summit. Descend your ascent route.

Spring snow season: Use the summer route described above. The cirque itself is magnificent, but the rough approach may detract from your enjoyment. Solitude, however, is a given.

Safety notes: This route should be climbed or skied only on stable spring season snow. Each party should have at least one member with exceptional orienteering skill. Use standard sunrise for sunhit.

FITZ/PFEIFFER COLLECTION   12,700 FT

Spring snow fills the Boxcar Couloir (4.1.7), Mount Wilson. Can you spot the skier?

4.1.7	**Mount Wilson (S)—Boxcar Couloir**	
Ratings:	Ski Descent—Advanced Snow Climb—Advanced	
	Summer Climb—N.R.	
Season:	Spring snow	
RT Data:	11 hours, 12 miles, 4,214'↑	
Start:	Lizard Head Creek Trailhead 10,050'	
1 Day from Rd:	No	
Map:	Mount Wilson, pg. 155	
Photos:	pgs. 163, 164	

Remote and hidden, this is a terrific snow climb or ski descent.

Spring snow season: Follow the East Cirque route (4.1.6) to 12,400' in the Slate Creek Cirque. From here the Boxcar Couloir cleaves Mount Wilson's east buttress. Once you're in the cirque below the couloir, the route follows an obvious narrow slot that splits the east face of the ridge, forming the left (W) wall of the cirque. The Boxcar leads to 13,600', where you rejoin the East Cirque route. Descend the couloir or the East Cirque (4.1.6). Skiers should be sure to climb the couloir first, since the entry point may be hard to find.

Safety notes: This route should be climbed or skied only on stable spring snow. Use standard sunrise for sunhit.

4.1.8	**El Diente Peak—North Couloir**	
Ratings:	Summer Climb—Novice	Ski Descent—Advanced
	Snow Climb—Intermediate	
Season:	Summer snow	Spring snow
RT Data:	10 hours, 8 miles, 5,259'↑	12 hours, 11 miles, 6,259'↑
Start:	Silver Pick Trailhead 10,700'	Silver Pick Trailhead 9,700'
1 Day from Rd:	Summer Yes	Spring Yes
Map:	El Diente Peak, p. 154; Mount Wilson, pg. 155	
Photos:	pgs.160, 163, 166, 167, 170	

This classic snow climb is also a beautiful ski descent. As a dry climb this route has a great deal of unpleasant loose rock, but it is popular as a descent route after doing the ridge from Mount Wilson (South Wilson). A better summer route for El Diente is the West Ridge (4.1.11).

Summer or spring snow season: Park at the Silver Pick Trailhead (section introduction) and follow route 4.1.2 to the Rock of Ages Saddle (13,020'). As an alternative, you can leave from the Navajo Lake Trailhead and backpack to a high camp in Navajo Basin.

Study your map at the Rock of Ages Saddle and identify El Diente's beautiful north face. Choose the most continuous snow line and commit it to memory. The photograph herein may be helpful, but the snow cover on this face varies greatly. The best route follows several wide, shallow couloirs to the east summit ridge, just to the west of the "Organ Pipe" gendarmes, then continues along the east ridge to the summit.

On El Diente's North Couloir, spring, route 4.1.8.

From Rock of Ages Saddle, descend and contour Navajo Basin to a depression in the basin at 12,120', located at the base of the face. Climb directly S to about 12,800'. Here you will be looking up into a well-defined, deep cleft couloir. Do not climb this couloir. Instead, climb and traverse right (W) into another, shallower and wider couloir, and follow it to the cliffs on the summit ridge. Traverse right (W) under the cliffs, and gain the ridge at the first reasonable opportunity. If you're carrying skis, leave them here. Follow the ridge to the summit. Descend your ascent route. The summit ridge is a short but unskiable rock-studded arete. Maximum angle in the couloir is 46° near the crest of the ridge, but the upper portion of the route is consistently steep and exposed to some even steeper, cliff-studded terrain. Thus, the skiing is rated as extreme. If you're not that hardcore, skiing from halfway up the route would still be fabulous, and is rated as expert.

Safety notes: These couloirs should only be climbed on stable spring or early summer snow. The upper part of the route gets sun at sunrise.

On El Diente Peak's north face, spring (route 4.1.8). Gladstone Peak on horizon.

4.1.9	**El Diente Peak—Kilpacker Creek**	
Ratings:	Ski Descent—Intermediate Snow Climb—Intermediate	
	Summer Climb—Intermediate	
Season:	All	
RT Data:	11 hours, 10 miles, 4,479'↑	
Start:	Kilpacker Creek Trailhead 10,060'	
1 Day from Rd:	Yes	
Map:	El Diente Peak, pg. 154	
Photo:	pg. 161	

If you want to race up El Diente in a day, this route could be your best bet. It is fairly simple, but involves a bit of orienteering because the trails are not frequently traveled. Interestingly, El Diente is officially a subpeak of Mount Wilson, but the peak is so beautiful and challenging that few people would argue its inclusion as a real "fourteener." Indeed, for grand slam bragging rights, this peak is a must do and this is possibly the best "bagger" route. If you climb this route after the spring snow melts, you'll encounter heinous scree above timberline. Thus, if you're planning a summer climb, consider doing the West Ridge (4.1.11) instead.

Summer after snow melt-off, or spring snow season: From the Kilpacker Creek Trailhead on the Dunton Road (section introduction), follow the trail (starts as a closed jeep trail) NW then W to its intersection with Kilpacker Creek (10,160'). Leave the main trail here and follow a fainter trail up the south side of Kilpacker Creek. After about a mile, switch to the north side of the creek and continue climbing into the basin.

You'll encounter cliff bands at 11,200'. Turn these to the left (N). Above here, follow the left side of the basin to 13,000'. Again, work your way to the left of obvious cliff bands, climbing a scree slope just below the Organ Pipe gendarmes. With the Organ Pipes above you, make a short traverse W below the ridge crest, then follow a gully to the ridge (13,900'). Follow the ridge W several hundred yards to the summit. If more obstacles block your way, try dropping a bit to the right (N) side of the ridge. Descend your ascent route.

Winter: This is a passable winter route, but involves a great deal of slide terrain. Use the spring/summer route described above, with variations to avoid avalanche slopes. Perhaps the crux of a winter climb is the approach, since the Dunton Road is closed during the winter months (see section introduction).

Safety notes: Summer climbers should be comfortable with steep scree and scrambling above cliffs. Because this route is exposed to many avalanche paths, skiers and snow climbers should tackle it after the spring consolidation. If you use it as a winter route, be sure you are climbing it during a period of very low hazard—on every exposure. For sunhit, add several hours to standard sunrise.

4.1.10	**El Diente Peak from Mount Wilson via Ridge Traverse**	
Ratings:	Ski Descent—N.R. Snow Climb—N.R.	
	Summer Climb—Advanced	
Season:	Summer	
RT Data:	16 hours, 8.5 miles, 4,959′↑	
Start:	Silver Pick Trailhead 10,700′	
1 Day from Rd:	Yes, for fit experts	
Map:	El Diente Peak, pg. 154; Mount Wilson, pg. 155	
Photos:	pgs. 161, 170	

While most climbers checking peaks off their list might be better off climbing Mount Wilson and El Diente via separate routes, experts will enjoy this classic connector ridge. The correct route has no 5th class climbing, but you'll find lots of exposed scrambling, and a rappel may be expedient in one place.

For access and egress, you can choose from several strategies. Perhaps the most classic routine is to get dropped off at Silver Pick Trailhead, and then picked up at the Kilpacker Creek Trailhead after descending El Diente's Kilpacker Creek route (4.1.9). This has the advantage of covering all new terrain, and is slightly easier because you don't have the 600 vertical foot climb back over Rock of Ages Saddle during your return.

The other strategy is the more popular, presumably because it involves less automobile logistics. You leave the Silver Pick Trailhead, do the ridge run, descend El Diente via the North Couloir (4.1.8), then return to Silver Pick Trailhead via Rock of Ages Saddle. The route described below assumes such a routine.

Summer after melt off: Park at the Silver Pick Basin Trailhead and climb Mount Wilson via the North Face (4.1.5). Steel yourself for the trials ahead. To avoid a direct attack on the ridge, descend Mount Wilson's north ridge for about 100′ into a small saddle, descend from the saddle a bit farther west, then cut west to a saddle on the El Diente Ridge (14,070″). Continue W on the ridge (it gets narrow and exposed) to an obvious cleft. Your best bet here is to make a 70′ rappel down into the cleft. This places you on a comfortable saddle (13,990′).

Stick to the ridge after the saddle. Nip a false summit that marks the approximate halfway point, then traverse around the south side of a group of gendarmes and regain the ridge. Take the ridge to your next obstacle, the famous Organ Pipe gendarmes, which you avoid by another traverse on the south side of the ridge. Climb back to the ridge after the Organ Pipes and follow the ridge to the summit with a few small deviations to the right (N). Descend El Diente's North Couloir (4.1.8) and return to Silver Pick via Rock of Ages Saddle.

Safety notes: The big problem with this route is that the ridge scrambling eats up time. Start early and try to be off the route before afternoon thunder booms. Bring a standard climbing rope, a small selection of hardware, and you favorite rappel device. Use standard sunrise for sunhit.

At Wilson Peak's summit, spring.

4.1.11 El Diente Peak—West Ridge		
Ratings:	Summer Climb—Advanced	Ski Descent—N.R.
	Snow Climb—Advanced	
Season:	Summer/Spring	WInter
RT Data:	12 hours, 14 miles, 4,809'↑	Multi-day
Start:	Navaho Lake Trailhead	Dunton Road
	9,350'	depends on snow closure
1 Day	Summer or Late Spring	Winter
from Rd:	Yes	No
Map:	El Diente Peak, pg. 154	
Photo:	pg. 170	

This route on El Diente Peak has a few exposed sections and lots of scenic high-altitude scrambling. If you want solitude, this is your line. While El Diente's West Ridge could be a challenging winter climb, and it might actually be the best winter route on the peak, access is problematic because of winter closures on the access roads.

Summer after snow melt-off, or spring snow season: Park at the Navajo Lake Trailhead and march the pack trail to Navajo Lake. While most fit and experienced climbers could do this whole route in a day, a high camp at Navajo Lake would certainly be appropriate. From Navajo Lake, do a climbing traverse SW to about 11,600' on the ridge crest, then stick to the ridge all the way to the summit, making small deviations for gendarmes and drop-offs. Return via the same route, or descend the Kilpacker Creek Route (4.1.9).

Winter: Use the route described above, with deviations to avoid avalanche danger. One such deviation might start lower down on the ridge.

Safety notes: The West Ridge route is simple on a grand scale, but care must be taken with micro-decisions while on the ridge crest: which side you pass a gendarme can mean the difference between dangerous exposure and safe passage. At least one person has made a fatal mistake here. Consequently, parties with varied ability levels should not hesitate to sit novice members down while the experts explore alternative routes. Also, bring your lightweight rope. Use standard sunrise for sunhit.

SECTION 4.2
Windom Peak (14,082'), Sunlight Peak (14,059'), South Mount Eolus (14,083), North Mount Eolus (14,039')

Windom Peak, Sunlight Peak, and the two summits of Mount Eolus form the boundaries of high, spectacular, and hard to reach Chicago Basin. These peaks offer fine summer climbing, snow climbing and skiing. Due to difficult access, winter climbs are unpopular. The Chicago Peaks are usually climbed from a high camp in Chicago Basin, reached via a rugged pack-in. On top of that, the only way you can get within a day's hike of Chicago Basin is via a train ride!

For climbers willing to plan and execute a major expedition, winter climbing in Chicago Basin is feasible, though it is hard to avoid avalanche hazard. Traveling safely through the narrow parts of the Needle Creek Valley is definitely a crux. In addition, following the trail in winter without getting caught in dense timber requires a major orienteering effort. Anyone who climbs the Chicago Basin fourteeners in winter deserves accolades for courage and skill.

ROADS AND TRAILHEADS

USGS Maps: Snowdon Peak, Mountain View Crest, Storm King Peak, Columbine Pass.

Animas River Railroad and Needleton Trailhead, Chicago Basin

Built in 1882, the Animas River Railroad serves 45 miles of the Animas River Valley between Durango and Silverton. The railroad is run mostly as a tourist attraction. Climbers heading to and from Chicago Basin have always enjoyed the fun of being transported to the trailhead by a coal-fired steam locomotive. Nowadays the railroad has a diesel-powered railbus which they use to transport hikers and climbers up and down the Animas. This is more convenient, but lacks the ambiance of the passenger train.

For transport to Needleton—the Chicago Basin trailhead—you catch the railbus at Rockwood, a whistle stop just off Highway 550, 17 miles north of Durango. The turnoff from Highway 550 to Rockwood has a small sign for ROCKWOOD and also one for LA PLATA COUNTY 200. The scenic railbus ride from Rockwood to Needleton takes about 2 hours. Reservations are required; call the Animas River Railroad (see appendices). There is no camping at Rockwood, but the Purgatory and Haviland Lake campgrounds are close by on Highway 550. As of 1988, parking at Rockwood requires a daily fee, so you may want to arrange a dropoff and pickup from Durango.

Whistle stop at Needleton Trailhead.

From Needleton (8,200'), cross the Animas River over an obvious suspension bridge, then follow signs and a well-defined trail S through about a mile of private property to the Needles Pack Trail. At this point you have two trail alternatives. The first, and better for the uphill, is to follow a steep, less-defined trail that switchbacks up the mountainside to the north of Needle Creek. Your other alternative is to follow a more-defined trail that parallels Needle Creek on the north side of the valley, gradually climbing higher and higher above the creek. The former trail is better for the hike up, while the latter may make a better descent route for fit backpackers, though it is more of a knee killer. Either way, the hike up the Needle Creek drainage to high camp at around 10,900' covers about 6 miles and 2,688 vertical feet. With a heavy pack, all but the most feral mountaineers will find this hike to be a true grunt.

Camp spots abound in the Chicago Basin area. Early in the spring, you'll find the highest dry ground on the north side of the valley around 10,900'. Groves of mature trees provide sheltered camping in this area. If you have the energy, consider bucking the crowds and camping higher in the basin.

4.2.1	Windom Peak—West Ridge	
Ratings:	Summer Climb—Novice	Ski Descent—Advanced
	Snow Climb—Novice	
Season:	Summer or Spring	Winter
RT Data:	6 hours, 7 miles, 3,182'↑	8 Hours, 7 miles, 3,182'↑
Start:	Chicago Basin high camp	Chicago Basin high camp
	10,900'	10,900'
1 Day	Summer or Late Spring	Winter
from Rd:	No	No
Map:	Chicago Basin, pg. 174	
Photos:	pgs. 175, 178	

Easy and enjoyable, this is the standard route for Windom Peak.

Summer after melt-off: From your high camp at 10,900' in lower Chicago Basin (see section introduction), follow the north side of the Needle Creek drainage to the first headwall in the basin. Turn this headwall on the left or right, depending on snow cover (the summer trail goes left, but there may be more snow to the right), and gain the shelf at 11,600', above the headwall.

Climb N to the 12,200' level, then follow a climbing traverse to Twin Lakes (12,500'). This is the summer trail route, and it is usually marked with cairns. Once at Twin Lakes climb into another basin to the S, below the NW face of Windom. At the 13,100' level follow a climbing traverse to the 13,240' saddle just to the E of Point 13,472. From here, climb the obvious route up Windom's West Ridge to the summit. Descend your ascent route.

Spring snow season: Use the route above, or with good snow cover use the gulch that forms the eastern of two drainages from Twin Lakes (steep, maximum angle approximately 40°). Intermediate skiers should leave their skis at the 13,240' saddle. Skilled mountain skiers should consider skiing from the summit via the other routes described here.

Winter: With minor variations, the route above is your best choice for a winter climb (using the summer trail route to climb to Twin Lakes). Even so, this whole route, including the approach from Needleton, is exposed to innumerable avalanche paths. Consequently, it must be done only at the most stable times. And since you will be traveling on all different exposures, be aware of hazard that varies by exposure. For example: the south facing slopes up to Twin Lakes my be very stable in the early spring, but the northwest slopes above the lakes may still have an unpredictable winter snowpack.

Safety notes: For sunhit on the west facing terrain, add several hours to standard sunrise.

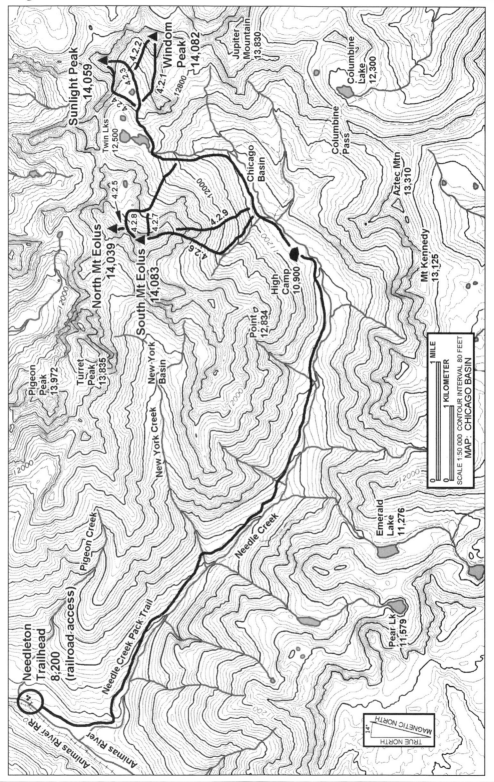

Sunlight Peak
14,059

Windom Peak
14,082

4.2.2

4.2.1

4.2.3

Jupiter
Mountain
13,830

Columbine
Lake
12,300

12,800

Twin Lks
12,500

Chicago
Basin

Columbine
Pass

4.2.5

North Mt Eolus
14,039

4.2.8

4.2.7

4.2.9

Aztec Mtn
13,310

12,000

South Mt Eolus
14,083

4.2.6

Mt Kennedy
13,125

High
Camp
10,900

Point
12,834

Pigeon
Peak
13,972

Turret
Peak
13,835

New York
Basin

New York Creek

Emerald
Lake
11,276

12,000

Pigeon Creek

Needle Creek

Pear Lk
11,579

Needleton
Trailhead
8,200
(railroad access)

Needle Creek Pack Trail

Animas River RR

Animas River

SCALE 1:50 000 CONTOUR INTERVAL 80 FEET
MAP: CHICAGO BASIN

1 MILE

1 KILOMETER

TRUE NORTH

MAGNETIC NORTH

14°

On Sunlight Peak, looking southwest at Windom Peak, spring.

4.2.2	**Windom Peak—Northwest Face**	
Ratings:	Ski Descent—Advanced	Snow Climb—Advanced
	Summer Climb—N.R.	
Season:	Spring Snow Route	
RT Data:	6 hours, 7 miles, 3,182'↑	
Start:	Chicago Basin high camp 10,900'	
1 Day from Rd:	High camp recommended	
Map:	Chicago Basin, pg. 174	
Photos:	pgs. 175, 180	

Though small by fourteener "nordwand" standards, this face is aesthetic and has several routes of varied difficulty.

Spring snow season: From your high camp at 10,900' in lower Chicago Basin (see section introduction), follow route 4.2.1 to the shelf at 11,600', above the headwall. From the 11,600' shelf you have two choices. The normal route climbs N to 12,200', then follows a climbing traverse to Twin Lakes (this is the summer trail route). Your other choice, if there is plenty of snow and you want more snow climbing, is to climb the gully that forms the eastern of two drainages from Twin Lakes (maximum angle approximately 40°). Either way, once at Twin Lakes climb into another basin to the south, below the Northwest Face of Windom. From here you have three obvious choices. The wide couloir on the right (W) side of the face is fairly easy, with a maximum angle of about 38°. The central part of the face is slightly more difficult, and to the left is the "hourglass" slot of the Windom Widowmaker Couloir, with a maximum angle of 45°

Descend the West Ridge (4.2.1), or downclimb the west couloir, or ski any one of these routes. For skiing, the Windom Widowmaker (see photo) offers a technically difficult "narrows" section, which is rated Extreme; the wider couloirs and broken terrain to the west is suitable for advanced level ski mountaineers.

Safety notes: These routes should only be done on stable spring snow. Be aware that the approach and descent have many different sun exposures, so use standard sunrise for sun-hit.

4.2.3	**Sunlight Peak—The Red Couloir**	
Ratings:	Ski Descent—Advanced	Snow Climb—Intermediate
	Summer Climb—Novice	
Season:	All	
RT Data:	8 hours, 7 miles, 3,159' ↑	
Start:	Chicago Basin high camp 10,900'	
1 Day from Rd:	High camp recommended	
Map:	Chicago Basin, pg. 174	
Photos:	pgs. 177, 178, 182	

The Red Couloir is the only non-technical route up Sunlight Peak. It's a summer scree hike, an excellent snow climb, and a good entry-level advanced ski descent. Because it faces southwest, it has mature snow earlier in the spring.

Summer after melt-off: From your high camp at the 10,900' level in lower Chicago Basin (see section introduction), follow route 4.2.1 to Twin Lakes. From Twin Lakes, climb E into another basin to about 13,000'. This puts you in position to follow the Red Couloir to the summit ridge, southeast of the summit. You then scramble the ridge to the summit, making obvious small detours, usually to the left (SW). The true summit is a large boulder, the top of which is quite airy and gained by a "boulder" style rock climbing move. For bragging rights do a handstand on the summit. Yes, this is the place for hero photographs. Descend your ascent route.

Spring snow season: Use the route above, perhaps with the Twin Lakes drainage variation mentioned in route 4.2.2. With good snow cover you can contrive a ski descent from the base of the summit block, but most skiers start slightly lower. Plan your descent while you climb.

Winter: While this is an avalanche path, it's the only route on Sunlight Peak that allows winter climbing without technical rock work. Winter strategy would involve expert hazard evaluation.

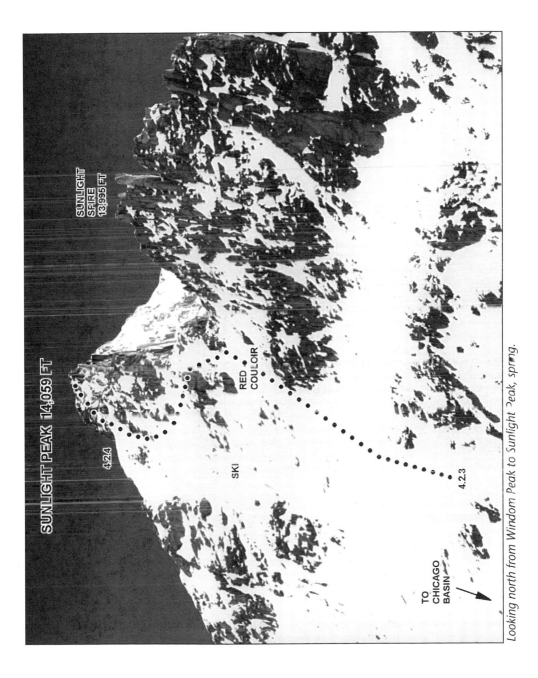

SUNLIGHT PEAK 14,059 FT

SUNLIGHT SPIRE 13,995 FT

4.2.4

RED COULOIR

SKI

4.2.3

TO CHICAGO BASIN

Looking north from Windom Peak to Sunlight Peak, spring.

SUNLIGHT PEAK 14,059 FT

SUNLIGHT SPIRE 13,995 FT

WINDOM PEAK 14,082 FT

N

4.21

4.22

4.23

4.24

Sunlight and Windom Peaks from the west, spring.

Safety notes: In the summer, this is another route exposed to "bowling balls" dislodged from climbers above. Since Sunlight's summit ridges are studded with gendarmes, this is the only practical snow route to the summit—it is also an avalanche path. Thus, it should only be climbed during the most stable times: either on frozen spring snow or in the winter when it's windscoured and compacted. Be aware that the approach and descent are exposed to many different aspects. Perhaps use a belay while you play on the summit boulder. For sunhit, add several hours to standard sunrise.

4.2.4	**Sunlight Peak—West Ridge**	
Ratings:	Summer Climb—Advanced	Ski Descent—N.R.
	Snow Climb—Advanced	
Season:	Summer or Spring	Winter
RT Data:	9 hours, 6.5 miles, 3,159'↑	Multi-day, Expedition
Start:	Chicago Basin high camp	Chicago Basin high camp
	10,900'	10,900'
1 Day	Summer or Late Spring	Winter
from Rd:	High camp recommended	High camp
Map:	Chicago Basin, pg. 174	
Photos:	pgs. 177, 178, 180	

If you're after a summer climb of Sunlight Peak, but the scree in the Red Couloir (4.2.3) discourages you, consider this route. The West Ridge involves a bit of talus slogging, but also includes an elegant arete that leads you to the summit. The complete West Ridge involves 5th class climbing on a jagged section known as Needle Ridge. The route below avoids Needle Ridge by starting higher.

Summer after snow melt-off, or spring snow season: Start from your high camp in Chicago Basin (see section introduction), and hike up to Twin Lakes (4.2.1). Continue E into the bowl above Twin Lakes. At 13,000', swing left (N) and take a talus-filled couloir up to the Needle Ridge/Sunlight saddle (13,300'). During spring snow season this couloir will be a

On the top, Sunlight Peak.

JUPITER MTN
13,830 FT

WINDOM PEAK
14,082 FT

4.2.4

NEEDLE
CREEK

PEAK 18
13,472 FT

APPROX 11,000 FT

SUNLIGHT PEAK
14,059 FT

4.2.4

UPPER
CHICAGO
BASIN

NEEDLE RIDGE

N

In Chicago Basin, spring.

pleasant snow climb. Stick with the ridge and tackle a series of 4th class headwalls, interspersed with mellow sections. When you're close to the summit, weave slightly right (south) and take easy ground back to the summit boulder.

Safety notes: Carry a rope and small selection of rock climbing hardware. Remember the time consuming nature of 4th class ridge climbing, so get an early start. Add 1 hour to standard sunrise for approximate sunhit.

4.2.5	North Mount Eolus—East Face		
Ratings:	Ski Descent—Advanced		Snow Climb—Intermediate
	Summer Climb—Intermediate		
Season:	Spring snow or Summer		
RT Data:	5.5 hours, 6 miles, 3,139' ↑		
Start:	Chicago Basin high camp 10,900'		
1 Day from Rd:	High camp recommended		
Map:	Chicago Basin, pg. 174		
Photos:	pgs. 182, 185, 188		

North Mount Eolus is not an "official" member of the 54 highest, but it qualifies for many people as a distinct fourteener. It's a wonderful mountain offering good skiing, an easy summer climbing route, and a nice view into an abyss to the north.

Summer after melt off: From your high camp at the 10,900' level in lower Chicago Basin (see section introduction), follow the north side of the Needle Creek drainage to the first headwall in the basin. Turn this headwall on the left or right, depending on snow cover (the summer trail goes left, more snow to the right), and gain the shelf at the 11,600' level above the headwall.

From the shelf, climb NW up the elongated bowl leading to the base of South Mount Eolus' east face (13,400'). At this point you will be under East Couloir of South Mount Eolus—a beautiful hidden slot you can climb to the summit of South Mount Eolus (4.2.7). From the base of the East Couloir, do a climbing traverse for about 2,000' NE into the bowl beneath the east face of North Eolus. From the bowl, you can climb either of the easterly faces on the north or south summit ridges, then follow either of these to the summit. The north ridge has more ups and downs, but can be skied from higher up. The south ridge is better if you're not concerned about skiing. For your descent, either ridge is fine for foot travel.

Spring snow season: Use the same route. It would be hard to ski directly from the summit, as it's very rocky. Instead, you can launch from a short distance down either ridge. To make a truly superb ski, head directly E out of the summit basin, past the small unnamed hanging lake, then E from the lake down a beautiful gully to Twin Lakes (maximum angle 40°). From Twin Lakes ski the east-most intermittent stream down into the Needle Creek drainage (maximum angle 40°).

This route uses a great deal of avalanche terrain. Consequently, it should only be snow climbed or skied when the snow is very stable, i.e., on consolidated spring snow. You will be traveling on all different exposures, so be aware of hazard that varies by exposure. For example, the south facing slopes up to Twin Lakes my be quite stable in the early spring, but the northwest facing slopes above the lakes may still have an unpredictable winter snowpack.

Winter: Take the south ridge to the summit. See section introduction for information on winter climbing in Chicago Basin.

Safety notes: During spring snow season, beware of an early sunhit on these east facing slopes.

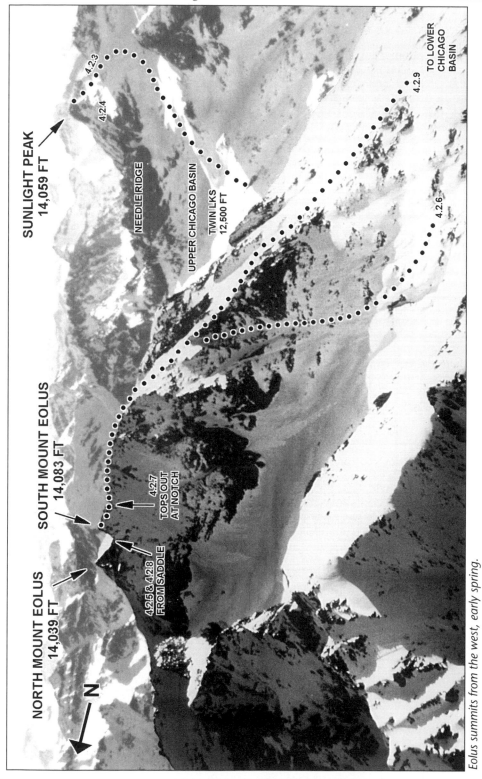

Eolus summits from the west, early spring.

4.2.6	**South Mount Eolus—Pfeifferfitz Couloir**	
Ratings:	Ski Descent—Advanced Snow Climb—Advanced Summer Climb—N.R.	
Season:	Spring snow or summer snow	
RT Data:	5.5 hours, 4.5 miles, 3,183'↑	
Start:	Chicago Basin high camp 10,900'	
1 Day from Rd:	High camp recommended	
Map:	Chicago Basin, pg. 174	
Photos:	pgs. 182, 183	

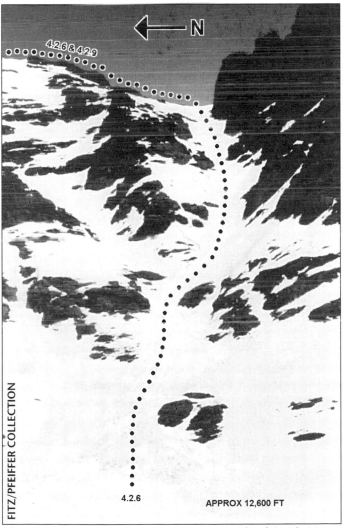

The ski and snow climb route on the west side of South Mount Eolus, spring.

For snow climbers and skiers, this route on the southwest face of Mount Eolus provides the sought after late morning sunhit. Yet the slopes you use to approach the couloir are south facing, as are certain slopes above the couloir, so you still need an early start. Also, these south slopes melt off early in the season, so you may have to hike much of the approach.

Spring snow season: The route is obvious. From your high camp at 10,900' in lower Chicago Basin, follow the pack trail route upvalley for about 1/2 mile to the first permanent stream dropping down the north side of the valley (11,000'). Leave the main valley here, and follow this stream as it leads into the basin under the west face of Mount Eolus. At 11,840', the main stream splits into two intermittent streams. Follow the route of the right hand (E) stream; it will lead you to the base of the couloir. Climbing the couloir will take you to the south ridge of the peak. Follow this ridge to the summit.

Descend your ascent route. As an alternative, descend the North Ridge (4.2.8)—a manageable rock scramble to the saddle between Mount Eolus and North Eolus. From here, continue down to the 13,600' level in the basin on the east side of North Eolus. A southerly traverse will bring you into the basin below the east face of Mount Eolus. Follow this basin down into Chicago Basin.

Safety notes: This route should only be climbed or skied on stable spring snow. For sunhit, add several hours to standard sunrise.

4.2.7	South Mount Eolus—East Couloir		
Ratings:	Ski Descent—Advanced	Snow Climb—Intermediate	
	Summer Climb—N.R.		
Season:	Spring snow		
RT Data:	7 hours, 6 miles, 3,183'↑		
Start:	Chicago Basin high camp 10,900'		
1 Day from Rd:	High camp recommended		
Map:	Chicago Basin, pg. 174		
Photos:	pgs. 182, 185, 186		

Provided this route's couloir has snow, this excellent snow climb or ski descent is the most direct route to Mount Eolus' summit. Do not climb this route without snow, as there is a great deal of rockfall potential without snow cover.

From your high camp at the 10,900' level in lower Chicago Basin (see section introduction), follow the N side of the Needle Creek drainage to the first headwall in the basin. Turn this headwall on the left or right, depending on snow cover (the summer trail goes left), and gain the shelf above.

From the shelf, climb NW for about 2,000' to 13,600' in the basin below the east face of Mount Eolus. Here you will be under the East Couloir, a beautiful hidden slot (maximum angle 44°). Climb the couloir, then at the top of the couloir traverse the east face for a few hundred feet till you are below the summit, then climb directly up to the summit.

Descend the couloir or the summer route described below. The couloir makes a good ski descent; a summit ski descent can be done by skiing a short way down on the west face of the summit, then traversing to the notch at the top of the couloir.

Safety notes: Use standard sunrise for sunhit, but beware of icy snow on the shaded west face below the summit.

East Couloir, South Mount Eolus. Spot the climber?

In the East Couloir (route 4.2.7.), South Mount Eolus, spring.

4.2.8	**South Mount Eolus—North Ridge**	
Ratings:	Summer Climb—Intermediate	Ski Descent—N.R.
	Snow Climb—Intermediate	
Season:	Summer or Spring	Winter
RT Data:	7 hours, 6 miles, 3,183'↑	10 Hours, 6 miles, 3,183'↑
Start:	Chicago Basin high camp	Chicago Basin high camp
	10,900'	10,900'
1 Day	Summer or Late Spring	Winter
from Rd:	No	No
Map:	Chicago Basin, pg. 174	
Photos:	pgs. 182, 188	

Summer, or spring snow season: From your high camp at about 10,900' in lower Chicago Basin (see section introduction), follow the north side of the Needle Creek drainage to the first headwall in the basin. Turn this headwall on the left or right, depending on snow cover (the summer trail goes left), and gain the shelf (11,500' elevation) above the headwall.

From the shelf, climb NW for about 2,000 vertical feet to 13,600' in the basin below the east face of Mount Eolus (you will be under the East Couloir (4.2.7). From here, do a climbing traverse NE into the basin below North Eolus' east face. From the basin, hike and scramble to the saddle between South Mount Eolus and North Eolus. Leave the saddle and scramble your way S up an obvious but exposed ridge to the summit. Descend your ascent route. If you don't like the look of the ridge, try wandering up the slopes and ledges on the east face (to climber's left). This route can be a bit confusing, but it will get you to the top.

Winter: Use summer route, with variations on rock ribs to avoid avalanche slopes.

Safety notes: This ridge has a few steep rock steps. Though most parties do not use a rope, a tumble could send you flying, so only attempt this route if you are comfortable with exposed scrambling. Carry a rope and know how to use it. Use standard sunrise for sunhit.

4.2.9	**South Mount Eolus—South Ridge**	
Ratings:	Summer Climb—Intermediate	Snow Climb—Intermediate
Season:	Spring Snow or Summer	
RT Data:	8 hours, 5 miles, 3,183'↑	
Start:	Chicago Basin high camp, 10,900'	
1 Day		
from Rd:	High camp recommended	
Map:	Chicago Basin, pg. 174	
Photos:	pgs. 182, 188	

This long 4th Class route is seldom climbed. Nonetheless, it's a good way to find solitude and more challenge.

Summer after snow melt-off: Backpack into Chicago Basin. Start from the pack trail at 10,880', directly below the South Eolus' monolithic south ridge. Wander N and slightly left (W) up the lower-angled area, always heading for the true crest. Above 12,200' the terrain steepens and sections may require use of a rope. Stick with the ridge to the summit, with slight variations to avoid steeper headwalls. Descend the North Ridge route (4.2.8), or the East Couloir (4.2.7) if the snow hasn't thawed too much by the time you're there.

Safety notes: Only experienced technical climbers should attempt this route. Carry a rope and a selection of rock hardware. Use standard sunrise for sunhit, and start early.

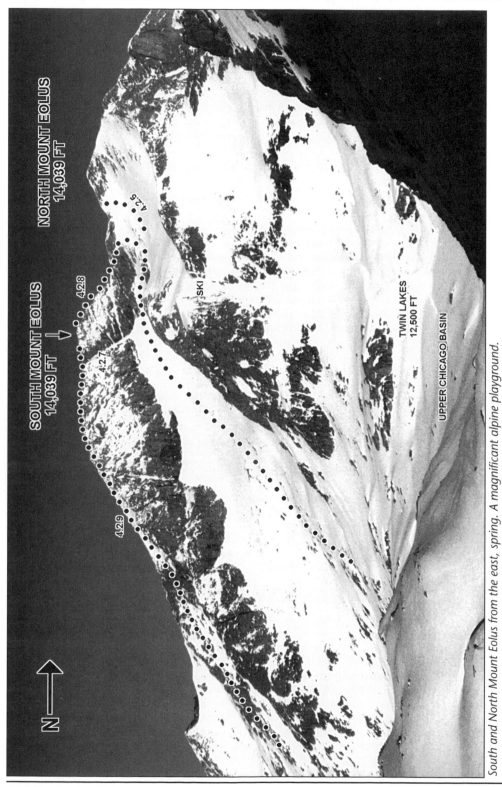

NORTH MOUNT EOLUS
14,039 FT

SOUTH MOUNT EOLUS
14,039 FT

4.2.5

4.2.8

4.2.7

4.2.9

SKI

TWIN LAKES
12,500 FT

UPPER CHICAGO BASIN

N

South and North Mount Eolus from the east, spring. A magnificent alpine playground.

Approaching South Mount Eolus from the southeast, spring.

Skiing in upper Chicago Basin, looking west at Peak 18.

Appendix 1
ROUTE RATINGS AND RECOMMENDATIONS

Asterisks indicate recommended routes. Not every peak has a recommended route. If your goal is to climb every peak, look ahead at the Grand Slam route lists.

1.1	**Summer Climbs—Novice**
1.1.1	Pikes Peak via Barr Trail
*1.1.6	Pikes Peak—Road Access Hiking and Skiing
*1.1.7	Pikes Peak from the Crags Campground
*2.1.1	Humboldt Peak—West Ridge
2.2.1	Blanca Peak—Northwest Face & North Ridge
2.3.1	Culebra Peak—West Ridge from Taylor Ranch
3.2.5	Uncompahgre Peak—South Ridge Hike Trail
3.3.2	Redcloud Peak—Silver Creek & East Ridge
*3.3.8	Handies Peak from American Basin
*4.2.1	Windom Peak—West Ridge
4.2.3	Sunlight Peak—The Red Couloir

1.2	**Summer Climbs—Intermediate**
2.1.6	Crestone Peak—North Couloir
*2.1.10	Kit Carson Mountain—East Ridge from S. Colony Lakes
2.1.15	Kit Carson Mountain from Challenger Peak
2.1.16	Challenger Peak—East Ridge from Kit Carson Mountain
2.1.17	Challenger Peak—North Face
2.2.6	Ellingwood Peak—South Face
*2.2.7	Ellingwood Peak—Southwest Ridge
2.2.8	Ellingwood Peak from Blanca Peak
*3.1.1	San Luis Peak—South Ridge from West Willow Creek
*3.2.1	Wetterhorn Peak—Southeast Ridge
3.3.3	Sunshine Peak from Redcloud Peak via Connecting Ridge
*3.3.6	Handies Peak—North Ridge from Grizzly Gulch
3.3.9	Handies Peak —South Ridge from Grouse Gulch
*3.4.1	Mount Sneffels via Lavender Col from Yankee Boy Basin
4.1.2	Wilson Peak—Northwest Face
4.1.6	Mount Wilson (S)—East Cirque from Slate Creek
4.1.9	El Diente Peak—Kilpacker Creek
4.2.5	North Mount Eolus—East Face
*4.2.8	South Mount Eolus—North Ridge

1.3	**Summer Climbs—Advanced**
2.1.3	Crestone Needle—South Ridge & South Couloir
*2.1.4	Crestone Needle—Ellingwood Arete
2.1.5	Crestone Needle to Crestone peak via Connecting Ridge
2.1.7	Crestone Peak—North Buttress
2.1.9	Crestone Peak to Crestone Needle via Connecting Ridge
2.1.11	Kit Carson Mountain—North Ridge
*2.1.13	Kit Carson Mountain—The South Prow
2.2.2	Blanca Peak from Little Bear via Connecting Ridge
2.2.3	Blanca Peak from Ellingwood Peak
2.2.4	Blanca Peak—North Face
2.2.5	Blanca Peak—Gash Ridge
*2.2.9	Ellingwood Peak—North Ridge from Huerfano Valley
2.2.11	Little Bear Peak—Northwest Face Direct
*2.2.12	Mount Lindsey—Northwest Ridge
2.2.13	Mount Lindsey—North Face Couloirs
*3.4.3	Mount Sneffels—Southwest Ridge
3.4.5	Mount Sneffels—North Buttress
*4.1.3	Wilson Peak—Southwest Ridge from Rock of Ages Saddle
4.1.4	Wilson Peak—Southwest Ridge from Bilk Basin
4.1.5	Mount Wilson (S)—North Face
4.1.10	El Diente Peak from Mount Wilson via Ridge Traverse
*4.1.11	El Diente Peak—West Ridge
*4.2.4	Sunlight Peak—West Ridge

1.4	**Ski Descents—Novice**

There are no novice ski descents in this guide

1.5	**Ski Descents—Intermediate**

(NFS=not from summit; all routes depend on snow conditions)

*1.1.6	Pikes Peak—Road Access Hiking and Skiing
2.1.1	Humboldt Peak—West Ridge (NFS)
2.3.1	Culebra Peak—West Ridge from Taylor Ranch (NFS)
*3.2.5	Uncompahgre Peak—South Ridge Hike Trail (NFS)
*3.3.2	Redcloud Peak—Silver Creek and East Ridge
3.3.3	Sunshine Peak from Redcloud Peak via Connecting Ridge
3.3.4	Sunshine Peak—Northwest Face Snow Route
3.3.6	Handies Peak—North Ridge from Grizzly Gulch (NFS)

*3.3.8	Handies Peak from American Basin	*4.1.1	Wilson Peak—Northeast Face
4.1.9	El Diente Peak—Kilpacker Creek (NFS)	*4.1.7	Mount Wilson (S.)—Boxcar Couloir
		*4.1.8	El Diente Peak—North Couloir

1.6   Ski Descents—Advanced
*1.1.2	Pikes Peak—East Face Snow Route
*1.1.4	Pikes Peak—Railroad Couloir
*2.1.2	Humboldt Peak—Southeast Flank Snow Route
*2.1.17	Challenger Peak—North Face
*2.1.18	Challenger Peak—Kirk Couloir
*2.2.1	Blanca Peak—Northwest Face
*2.2.6	Ellingwood Peak—South Face
3.1.1	San Luis Peak—South Ridge from West Willow Creek (NFS)
*3.1.2	San Luis Peak—Yawner Gullies
3.2.3	Uncompahgre Peak—West Face Snow Route
3.3.1	Redcloud Peak—West Face from South Fork Silver Creek
3.3.7	Handies Peak—East Face Snow from Grizzly Gulch
3.3.9	Handies Peak—South Ridge from Grouse Gulch (NFS)
*3.4.7	Mount Sneffels—East Couloir to Lavender Col
*4.1.2	Wilson Peak—Northwest Face
4.1.5	Mount Wilson (S)—North Face
*4.1.6	Mount Wilson (S)—East Cirque from Slate Creek
4.2.1	Windom Peak—West Ridge (NFS)
4.2.2	Windom Peak—Northwest Face
4.2.3	Sunlight Peak—The Red Couloir
4.2.5	North Mount Eolus—East Face
4.2.6	South Mount Eolus—Pfeifferfitz Couloir (NFS)
*4.2.7	South Mount Eolus—East Couloir

1.7   Ski Descents—Extreme
*1.1.3	Pikes Peak—Y Couloir
2.1.3	Crestone Needle—South Couloir
*2.1.8	Crestone Peak—South Couloir
2.1.12	Kit Carson Mountain—O.B. (North) Couloir
2.1.14	Kit Carson Mountain—South Couloir
2.2.10	Little Bear Peak—Southwest Face
2.2.13	Mount Lindsey—North Face Couloirs
*3.2.2	Wetterhorn Peak—East Face
3.2.4	Uncompahgre Peak—South "Fin" Couloir
*3.4.1	Mount Sneffels via Lavender Col from Yankee Boy Basin
*3.4.2	Mount Sneffels—South Face "Birthday Chutes"
3.4.4	Mount Sneffels—West Couloir
*3.4.6	Mount Sneffels—Snake Couloir

1.8   Snow Climbs—Novice
(all snow climbs are seasonal and vary with snow cover)
*1.1.1	Pikes Peak via Barr Trail
*1.1.6	Pikes Peak—Road Access Hiking and Skiing
1.1.7	Pikes Peak from the Crags Campground
*2.1.1	Humboldt Peak—West Ridge
*3.2.5	Uncompahgre Peak—South Ridge Hike Trail
3.3.2	Redcloud Peak—Silver Creek and East Ridge
*3.3.4	Sunshine Peak—Northwest Face Snow Route
*3.3.8	Handies Peak from American Basin
4.2.1	Windom Peak—West Ridge

1.9   Snow Climbs—Intermediate
*2.1.2.	Humboldt Peak—Southeast Flank Snow Route
2.1.10	Kit Carson Mountain—East Ridge from S. Colony Lakes
*2.2.1	Blanca Peak—Northwest Face & North Ridge
*2.2.6	Ellingwood Peak—South Face
2.3.1	Culebra Peak—West Ridge from Taylor Ranch
3.1.1	San Luis Peak—South Ridge from West Willow Creek
*3.1.2	San Luis Peak—Yawner Gullies
*3.2.1	Wetterhorn Peak—Southeast Ridge
*3.2.4	Uncompahgre Peak—South "Fin" Couloir
3.3.1	Redcloud Peak—West Face from South Fork Silver Creek
3.3.3	Sunshine Peak from Redcloud Peak via Connecting Ridge
3.3.6	Handies Peak—North Ridge from Grizzly Gulch
*3.3.9	Handies Peak—South Ridge from Grouse Gulch
*4.1.2	Wilson Peak—Northwest Face
*4.1.9	El Diente Peak—Kilpacker Creek
*4.2.3	Sunlight Peak—The Red Couloir
*4.2.5	North Mount Eolus—East Face
*4.2.7	South Mount Eolus—East Couloir
4.2.8	South Mount Eolus—North Ridge

1.10   Snow Climbs—Advanced
*1.1.2	Pikes Peak—East Face Snow Route
*1.1.3	Pikes Peak—Y Couloir
*1.1.4	Pikes Peak—Railroad Couloir
*2.1.3	Crestone Needle—South Ridge & South Couloir

1.11 Snow Climbs —Extreme

1.12 Technical Climbs

Appendix 2
2.1 SUMMER CLIMBER'S GRAND SLAM ROUTES

In the interest of preservation, more than one route per peak is sometimes listed. If your goal is simply to have climbed all the 54 "official" four-teeners, pick your route of this list for the peaks covered in this guide.

2.2.13   Mount Lindsey—North Face
          Couloirs
2.3.1   Culebra Peak—West Ridge from
          Taylor Ranch
3.1.1   San Luis Peak—South Ridge from
          West Willow Creek
3.1.3   San Luis Peak—East Flanks from
          Stewart Creek
3.2.1   Wetterhorn Peak—Southeast Ridge
3.2.5   Uncompahgre Peak—South Ridge
          Hike Trail
3.3.2   Redcloud Peak—Silver Creek and
          East Ridge
3.3.3   Sunshine Peak from Redcloud Peak
          via Connecting Ridge
3.3.6   Handies Peak—North Ridge from
          Grizzly Gulch
3.3.7   Handies Peak—East Face Snow from
          Grizzly Gulch
3.3.8   Handies Peak from American Basin
3.3.9   Handies Peak—South Ridge from
          Grouse Gulch
3.4.1   Mount Sneffels via Lavender Col
          from Yankee Boy Basin
4.1.2   Wilson Peak—Northwest Face
4.1.4   Wilson Peak—Southwest Ridge
          from Bilk Basin
4.1.5   Mount Wilson (S)—North Face
4.1.8   El Diente Peak—North Couloir
4.1.10   El Diente Peak from Mount Wilson
          via Ridge Traverse
4.1.11   El Diente Peak—West Ridge
4.2.1   Windom Peak—West Ridge
4.2.3   Sunlight Peak—The Red Couloir
4.2.8   South Mount Eolus—North Ridge

2.2. SKIER'S GRAND SLAM ROUTES

If your goal is to ski all 54 fourteeners, here are
the routes you need for the peaks covered in this
volume. These routes are not always the most
aesthetic, but they're the ones that most often
start at the summit and have the best access.
1.1.2   Pikes Peak—East Face Snow Route
1.1.4   Pikes Peak—Railroad Couloir
2.1.2   Humboldt Peak—Southeast Flank
          Snow Route
2.1.3   Crestone Needle —South Ridge &
          South Couloir
2.1.8   Crestone Peak—South Couloir
2.1.14   Kit Carson Mountain—South
          Couloir
2.1.17   Challenger Peak—North Face
2.1.18   Challenger Peak—Kirk Couloir
2.2.1   Blanca Peak—Northwest Face &
          North Ridge
2.2.6   Ellingwood Peak—South Face

2.2.10   Little Bear Peak—West Ridge &
          Southwest Face
2.2.14   Mount Lindsey —Southeast Face
2.3.1   Culebra Peak from Taylor Ranch
3.1.1   San Luis Peak—South Ridge from
          West Willow Creek
3.1.2   San Luis Peak—Yawner Gullies
3.2.2   Wetterhorn Peak—East Face
3.2.3   Uncompahgre Peak—West Face
          Snow Route
3.2.5   Uncompahgre Peak—South Ridge
          Hike Trail
3.3.1   Redcloud Peak—West Face from
          South Fork Silver Creek
3.3.4   Sunshine Peak—Northwest Face
          Snow Route
3.3.8   Handies Peak from American Basin
3.4.1   Mount Sneffels via Lavender Col
          from Yankee Boy Basin
3.4.2   Mount Sneffels—South Face
          "Birthday Chutes"
4.1.1   Wilson Peak—Northeast Face
4.1.5   Mount Wilson (S)—North Face
4.1.6   Mount Wilson (S)—East Cirque
          from Slate Creek
4.1.7   Mount Wilson (S)—Boxcar Couloir
4.1.8   El Diente Peak—North Couloir
4.2.2   Windom Peak—Northwest Face
4.2.3   Sunlight Peak—The Red Couloir
4.2.7   South Mount Eolus—East Couloir

2.3. WINTER CLIMBER'S GRAND SLAM ROUTES

To date only one man, Tom Mereness of
Boulder, Colorado, has climbed all 54 official
fourteeners in winter. If you'd like to be next,
here are perhaps the best winter routes for the
peaks in this book. "Winter" means any day
between the winter solstice and the vernal
equinox.
1.1.1   Pikes Peak via Barr Trail
2.1.1   Humboldt Peak—West Ridge
2.1.3   Crestone Needle—South Ridge &
          South Couloir
2.1.6   Crestone Peak—North Couloir
2.1.10   Kit Carson Mountain—East Ridge
          from S. Colony Lakes
2.1.16   Challenger Peak—East Ridge from
          Kit Carson Mountain
2.1.17   Challenger Peak—North Face
2.2.1   Blanca Peak—Northwest Face &
          North Ridge
2.2.6   Ellingwood Peak—South Face
2.2.10   Little Bear Peak—West Ridge &
          Southwest Face
2.3.1   Culebra Peak—West Ridge from
          Taylor Ranch

3.1.1	San Luis Peak—South Ridge from West Willow Creek
3.2.1	Wetterhorn Peak—Southeast Ridge
3.2.5	Uncompahgre Peak—South Ridge Hike Trail
3.3.2	Redcloud Peak—Silver Creek and East Ridge
3.3.3	Sunshine Peak from Redcloud Peak via Connecting Ridge
3.3.5	Sunshine Peak—Long East Ridge
3.3.8	Handies Peak from American Basin
3.4.1	Mount Sneffels via Lavender Col from Yankee Boy Basin
4.1.2	Wilson Peak—Northwest Face
4.1.3	Wilson Peak—Southwest Ridge from Rock of Ages Saddle
4.1.5	Mount Wilson (S.)—North Face
4.1.11	El Diente Peak—West Ridge
4.2.1	Windom Pea—West Ridge
4.2.3	Sunlight Peak—The Red Couloir
4.2.8	South Mount Eolus—North Ridge

2.4. RECOMMENDED WINTER CLIMBS
HARD

1.1.1	Pikes Peak via Barr Trail
1.1.7	Pikes Peak from the Crags Campground
2.1.1	Humboldt Peak—West Ridge
3.2.5	Uncompahgre Peak—South Ridge Hike Trail

HARDER

2.2.1	Blanca Peak—Northwest Face & North Ridge
2.2.6	Ellingwood Peak—South Face
2.3.1	Culebra Peak—West Ridge from Taylor Ranch
3.1.1	San Luis Peak—South Ridge from West Willow Creek
3.4.1	Mount Sneffels via Lavender Col from Yankee Boy Basin

DESPERATE

2.2.12	Mount Lindsey—Northwest Ridge
3.2.1	Wetterhorn Peak—Southeast Ridge
3.3.5	Sunshine Peak—Long East Ridge
4.1.11	El Diente Peak—West Ridge

Appendix 3
RESOURCE DIRECTORY

3.1. COUNTY PHONE NUMBERS FOR ROAD INFORMATION AND EMERGENCIES

In Colorado the County Sheriff handles emergency calls; try 911 first—if there is no response call the sheriff directly.

Boulder County (county seat: Boulder)
County office	(303)441-3131
Sheriff	(303)441-4609

Chaffee County (county seat: Salida)
County office	(719)539-4004
Sheriff	(719)539-2814

Clear Creek County (county seat: Georgetown)
County office	(303)534-5777
Sheriff	same

Costilla County (county seat: San Luis)
County office	(719)672-3962
Sheriff	(719)672-3302

Custer County (county seat: Westcliffe)
County office	(719)783-2441
Sheriff	(719)783-2270

Dolores (county seat: Dove Creek)
County office	(719)677-2383
Sheriff	(719)677-2257

Eagle County (county seat: Eagle)
County office	(970)328-7311
Sheriff	(970)328-6611

El Paso County (county seat: Colorado Springs)
County office	(719)630-2800
Sheriff	(719)520-7100

Fremont County (county seat: Cañon City)
County office	(719)275-7521
Sheriff	(719)275-2000

Gunnison County (county seat: Gunnison)
County office	(970)641-0248
Sheriff	(970)641-1113

Hinsdale County (county seat: Lake City)
County office	(970)944-2225
Sheriff	(970)944-2291

Huerfano County (county seat: Walsenberg)
County office	(719)738-2370
Sheriff	(719)738-1600

Lake County (county seat: Leadville)
County office	(719)486-1410
Sheriff	(719)486-1249

La Plata County (county seat: Durango)
County office	(970)259-4000
Sheriff	(970)247-1157

Larimer County (county seat: Fort Collins)
County office	(970)221-7000
Sheriff	(970)498-5101

Las Animas County (county seat: Trinidad)
County office	(719)846-3481
Sheriff	(719)846-2211

Mineral County (county seat: Creede)
County office	(719)658-2440
Sheriff	(719)658-2600

Montezuma County (county seat: Cortez)
County office	(970)565-8317
Sheriff	(970)565-8441

Park County (county seat: Fairplay)
County office	(719)838-7509
Sheriff	(719)836-2494

Pitkin County (county seat: Aspen)
County office	(970)920-5180
Sheriff	(970)920-5300

Saguache County (county seat: Saguache)
County office	(719)655-2231
Sheriff	(719)655-2544

San Juan County (county seat: Silverton)
    County office   (970)387-5671
    Sheriff   (970)387-5531
San Miguel County (county seat: Telluride)
    County office   (970)728-3954
    Sheriff   (970)728-4442
Summit County (county seat: Breckenridge)
    County office   (970)453-2561
    Sheriff   (970)453-2232

3.2 MECHANIZED ACCESS
Aspen
    T Lazy Seven Ranch, Snowmobile Rentals
    (970)925-7254
Buena Vista
    Buena Vista Snowdrifters (snowmobile club)
    Bx. 3133, Buena Vista, CO, 81211
Lake City
    Continental Divide Snowmobile Club
    Bx. 797, Lake City CO, 81235
    Lake City Nordic Association 944-2625
Leadville
    High Riders Snowmobile Club
    400 E. 6th St., Leadville, CO 80461
Westcliff
    Sangre Snow Runners
    Bx 145, Silvercliff, CO 81249
Minturn
    Nova Guides (970)949-4232
Durango—Silverton Railroad
    Animas River Railway (970)247-2733

3.3. CHAMBERS OF COMMERCE PHONE NUMBERS
Lake City   (970)944-2527
Aspen   1-800-26-ASPEN
Durango   1-800-525-8855
Leadville   1-800-933-3901
Estes Park   1-800-44-ESTES

3.4. FOREST SERVICE and PARK SERVICE
The supervisor's office can give you the numbers of appropriate district offices for your trip.
Arapaho/Roosevelt National Forests
    (970)498-1100 Ft. Collins
Gunnison/Uncompahgre National Forests
    (970)874-7691 Delta
Pike/San Isabel National Forests
    (719)545-8737 Pueblo
Rio Grande National Forest
    (719)852-5941 Monte Vista
Rocky Mountain National Park
    (970)586-2371 Estes Park
San Juan National Forest
    (970)247-4874 Durango
White River National Forest
    (970)945-2521 Glenwood Springs

3.5. COLORADO STATE PATROL
Road conditions   (719)630-1111 Ext. 7623

3.6. GUIDE SERVICES
Adventures to the Edge
Crested Butte, CO (800)349-5219

Aspen Alpine Guides
Aspen, CO (970)625-6618

Elk Mountain Guides
Aspen, CO (970)925-5601

Fantasy Ridge
Telluride, CO (970)728-3546

Pikes Peak Alpine School
Colorado Springs, CO (800)358-6867

Pikes Peak Mtn. Sports Climbing School & Guide Service
Colorado Springs, CO (719)634-3575

3.7. AVALANCHE INFORMATION FOR COLORADO
Aspen   (970)920-1664
Boulder/Denver   (303)275-5360
Colorado Springs   (719)520-0020
Durango   (970)247-8187
Frisco   (970)668-0600
Ft. Colllns   (970)482-0457
Minturn (Vail)   (970)827-5687
On-Line: Travel Bank   (303)671-7669

3.8. WEATHER
The avalanche information numbers provide good weather information.
Denver area weather   (303)398-3964
Weather radio VHF band 162.55 MHZ
(this is the best source of current information)

3.9 LODGING/CLUBS/ROADS

HUTS
Fred Braun Huts and Friends Hut
c/o Tenth Mountain Trail Association
(hut reservations)
1280 Ute Avenue
Aspen, CO 81612 (970)925-5775

San Juan Hut Systems
(970)728-6935

Ouray Victorian Inn
800-443-7391

Taylor Ranch
Box 96
San Luis, CO 81152
(719)672-3580

Pikes Peak Highway
(719)684-9383

Colorado Mountain Club
3375 W. 31st Ave.
Denver CO 80211 (303)477-6343

Appendix 4
BIBLIOGRAPHY

Bein, Vic. _Mountain Skiing_. Seattle: The Mountaineers, 1982.

Borneman and Lampert. _A Climbing Guide to Colorado's Fourteeners, 3rd. ed._ Boulder: Pruett Publishing, 1988.

Bueler, William. _Roof of the Rockies._ Boulder, Colorado: Pruett, 1974.

Colorado Mountain Club & Robert Ormes. _Guide to the Colorado Mountains, 9th ed._ Boulder: Colorado Mountain Club, 1992.

Dawson, Louis. _Colorado 10th Mountain Trails._ Aspen: WHO Press, 1991.

Dawson, Louis. _Colorado High Routes._ Seattle: The Mountaineers, 1987.

Dawson, Louis. _Dawson's Guide to Colorado's Fourteeners, Volume 1, The Northern Peaks._ Monument, CO: Blue Clover Press, 1994.

Hart, John L. Jerome. _Fourteen Thousand Feet._ Denver, Colorado: Colorado Mountain Club, 1971. (out of print)

Kelner, Alexis and Hanscom, David. _Wasatch Tours._ Salt Lake City: Wasatch Publishers, Inc., 1995.

LaChapelle, Edward R. _The ABC of Avalanche Safety, 2nd ed._ Seattle: The Mountaineers, 1985.

Litz, Brian and Lankford, Kurt. _Skiing Colorado's Backcountry._ Golden: Fulcrum, 1989

Perla, Ronald and Martinelli, M. _Avalanche Handbook._ Washington, D.C.: U.S. Department of Agriculture #489, 1976.

Peters, Ed, ed. _Mountaineering: The Freedom of the Hills._ Seattle: The Mountaineers, 1991

Roach, Gerry. _Colorado's Fourteeners._ Golden: Fulcrum Press, 1992.

Schniebs, Otto Eugene. _American Skiing._ N.Y.: E.P. Dutton, 1939. (out of print)

Tejada-Flores, Lito. _Backcountry Skiing._ San Francisco: Sierra Club Books, 1981.

Watters, Ron. _Ski Camping._ San Francisco: Solstice Press/Chronicle Books, 1979.

Williams, Knox and Armstrong, Betsy. _The Avalanche Book._ Golden, Colorado: Fulcrum, 1986.

Williams, Knox and Armstrong, Betsy. _The Snowy Torrents—Avalanche Accidents in the United States 1972-1979._ Jackson, Wyoming: Teton Bookshop Publishing Company.

Appendix 5
TIMING YOUR ASCENT

The following suggestions, combined with the sun chart, will help you time your route for the most enjoyment and safety.

During the spring compacted snow season, when the snowpack is undergoing the daily melt-freeze cycle, use the following rules of thumb:
- be off E by 9:00 MST
- be off S by 11:00 MST
- be off W by 12:30 MST
- be off N by 2:00 MST

You must be certain that north facing snow is in the spring melt-freeze. Otherwise, you're dealing with a winter snowpack, and possible soft slab avalanches. If the north facing snow is in the spring cycle, your safety depends on the air temperature during the day and how well it froze the night before. That's because, even in the spring, north facing snow doesn't get much sun. Beware, however, of how much sun the east and west sides of a north facing gully are getting. If the temperature at timberline, before sunrise, is warmer than 32°F, abort your trip with no question. During years with a deep snowpack, the snow may mature to a point where it can be skied safely without being frozen. Such snow is very dense, and rare before June.

Roughly speaking, the sun will hit the east side of a fourteener at sunrise time. An intervening peak that is high and close will delay east sunhit. But few east facing routes are blocked significantly in this fashion. Of more concern is that a peak facing out over the eastern plains will have an earlier sunhit—sometimes 45 minutes earlier than standard sunrise.

South facing mountain sides will receive sunhit several hours after sunrise time. The exact delay depends on the date. During the shortest winter days the delay is shorter; towards the longer days of spring, the delay increases. Intervening mountains are not a factor, since by the time the sun moves around to the south it is high enough in the sky to be above any mountains.

West facing routes get the latest sunhit, and often provide the best skiing and snow climbing—often into mid-day.

In the winter, most north faces get little or no sun. In the spring, north faces get hit early in the morning or in the late afternoon, depending on exact aspect and horizon angle, how deeply the face is cupped, and how deep the gullies are. A deep gully on any face will receive a later sunhit than an equivalent smooth slope. But remember that couloirs usually open out onto less riven areas near the summit, and the snow here will still receive sun, even while the more deeply cleft portions of the gully are shaded. For example, the North Face of North Maroon Peak gets its spring sunhit at sunrise.

SUNRISE AND SUNSET TIMES

These times are figured for an average latitude and longitude of Colorado's fourteeners. The differences possible because of variation from this average amount only to minutes. Of more concern are variations due to your horizon. In other words, the horizon when you're in a valley is the ridge above you, and the sun will hit the vally later than standard sunrise. Conversely, if you're on the side of a mountain above the horizon, the sun will hit earlier.

SUNRISE TIMES FOR CENTRAL COLORADO TIMES: MOUNTAIN STANDARD AND MOUNTAIN DAYLIGHT AS NOTED

TIMES BELOW:
MOUNTAIN STANDARD

DATE	SUNRISE	SUNSET
1 JAN	7:27	16:54
5 JAN	7:27	16:57
10 JAN	7:27	17:02
15 JAN	7:25	17:07
20 JAN	7:23	17:13
25 JAN	7:20	17:19
30 JAN	7:16	17:25
5 FEB	7:10	17:32
10 FEB	7:04	17:38
15 FEB	6:58	17:43
20 FEB	6:52	17:49
25 FEB	6:45	17:55
1 MAR	6:39	17:59
5 MAR	6:33	18:03
10 MAR	6:25	18:09
15 MAR	6:18	18:14
20 MAR	6:10	18:19
25 MAR	6:02	18:24
30 MAR	5:54	18:29
5 APR	5:44	18:35

TIMES BELOW:
DAYLIGHT SAVINGS

10 APR	6:36	19:40
15 APR	6:29	19:45
20 APR	6:22	19:50
25 APR	6:15	19:55
30 APR	6:08	19:59
5 MAY	6:03	20:04
10 MAY	5:57	20:09
15 MAY	5:52	20:14
20 MAY	5:48	20:18
25 MAY	5:45	20:23
1 JUN	5:41	20:28
5 JUN	5:40	20:30
10 JUN	5:39	20:33
15 JUN	5:39	20:35
20 JUN	5:39	20:37
25 JUN	5:41	20:38
1 JUL	5:43	20:38
5 JUL	5:45	20:37
10 JUL	5:48	20:35
15 JUL	5:52	20:33

20 JUL	5:56	20:29
25 JUL	6:00	20:25
1 AUG	6:06	20:19
5 AUG	6:10	20:14
10 AUG	6:14	20:08
15 AUG	6:19	20:02
20 AUG	6:24	19:55
25 AUG	6:28	19:48
5 SEP	6:39	19:31
10 SEP	6:43	19:23
15 SEP	6:48	19:15
20 SEP	6:52	19:07
25 SEP	6:57	18:58
1 OCT	7:03	18:49
2 OCT	7:04	18:47
3 OCT	7:05	18:46
4 OCT	7:06	18:44
5 OCT	7:07	18:42
6 OCT	7:08	18:41
7 OCT	7:09	18:39
8 OCT	7:10	18:38
9 OCT	7:11	18:36
10 OCT	7:12	18:35
11 OCT	7:13	18:33
12 OCT	7:14	18:32
13 OCT	7:15	18:30
14 OCT	7:16	18:29
15 OCT	7:17	18:27
16 OCT	7:18	18:26
17 OCT	7:19	18:24
18 OCT	7:20	18:23
19 OCT	7:21	18:21
20 OCT	7:22	18:20
21 OCT	7:23	18:19
22 OCT	7:24	18:17
23 OCT	7:25	18:16
24 OCT	7:26	18:15
25 OCT	7:27	18:13

TIMES BELOW:
MOUNTAIN STANDARD

26 OCT	6:28	17:12
27 OCT	6:29	17:11
28 OCT	6:31	17:09
29 OCT	6:32	17:08
30 OCT	6:33	17:07
31 OCT	6:34	17:06
1 NOV	6:35	17:05
2 NOV	6:36	17:04
3 NOV	6:37	17:02
4 NOV	6:38	17:01
5 NOV	6:39	17:00
6 NOV	6:41	16:59
7 NOV	6:42	16:58
8 NOV	6:43	16:57
9 NOV	6:44	16:56
10 NOV	6:45	16:55
11 NOV	6:46	16:54
12 NOV	6:47	16:54
13 NOV	6:49	16:53
14 NOV	6:50	16:52

15 NOV	6:51	16:51
16 NOV	6:52	16:50
17 NOV	6:53	16:50
18 NOV	6:54	16:49
19 NOV	6:55	16:48
20 NOV	6:56	16:48
21 NOV	6:58	16:47
22 NOV	6:59	16:47
23 NOV	7:00	16:46
24 NOV	7:01	16:46
25 NOV	7:02	16:45
26 NOV	7:03	16:45
27 NOV	7:04	16:44
28 NOV	7:05	16:44
29 NOV	7:06	16:44
30 NOV	7:07	16:43
1 DEC	7:08	16:43
2 DEC	7:09	16:43
3 DEC	7:10	16:43
4 DEC	7:11	16:43
5 DEC	7:12	16:43
6 DEC	7:13	16:42
7 DEC	7:14	16:42
8 DEC	7:15	16:42
9 DEC	7:15	16:43
10 DEC	7:16	16:43
11 DEC	7:17	16:43
12 DEC	7:18	16:43
13 DEC	7:19	16:43
14 DEC	7:19	16:43
15 DEC	7:20	16:44
16 DEC	7:21	16:44
17 DEC	7:21	16:44
18 DEC	7:22	16:45
19 DEC	7:22	16:45
20 DEC	7:23	16:46
21 DEC	7:24	16:46
22 DEC	7:24	16:47
23 DEC	7:24	16:47
24 DEC	7:25	16:48
25 DEC	7:25	16:48
26 DEC	7:26	16:49
27 DEC	7:26	16:50
28 DEC	7:26	16:50
29 DEC	7:26	16:51
30 DEC	7:27	16:52
31 DEC	7:27	16:53

Appendix 6
FOURTEENER LISTS IN ALPHABETICAL ORDER & ELEVATION ORDER

6.1 ALL COLORADO'S 54 OFFICIAL FOURTEENERS, ALPHABETIC.
Blanca Peak, 14,345
Capitol Peak, 14,130
Castle Peak, 14,265
Crestone Needle, 14,197

Crestone Peak, 14,294
Culebra Peak, 14,047
El Diente Peak, 14,159
Ellingwood Peak, 14,042
Grays Peak, 14,270
Handies Peak, 14,048
Humboldt Peak, 14,064
Huron Peak, 14,003
Kit Carson Mountain, 14,165
La Plata Peak, 14,336
Little Bear Peak, 14,037
Longs Peak, 14,255
Missouri Mountain, 14,067
Mount Antero, 14,269
Mount Belford, 14,197
Mount Bierstadt, 14,060
Mount Bross, 14,172
Mount Columbia, 14,073
Mount Democrat, 14,148
Mount Elbert, 14,433
Mount Evans, 14,264
Mount Harvard, 14,420
Mount Lincoln, 14,286
Mount Lindsey, 14,042
Mount Massive, 14,421
Mount Oxford, 14,153
Mount Princeton, 14,197
Mount Shavano, 14,229
Mount Sherman, 14,036
Mount Sneffels, 14,150
Mount Wilson (S.), 14,246
Mount Yale, 14,196
Mount of the Holy Cross, 14,005
North Maroon Peak, 14,014
Pikes Peak, 14,109
Pyramid Peak, 14,018
Quandary Peak, 14,265
Redcloud Peak, 14,034
San Luis Peak, 14,014,
Snowmass Mountain, 14,092
South Maroon Peak, 14,156
South Mount Eolus, 14,083
Sunlight Peak, 14,059
Sunshine Peak, 14,001
Tabeguache Peak, 14,155
Torreys Peak, 14,267
Uncompahgre Peak, 14,309
Wetterhorn Peak, 14,015
Wilson Peak (N.), 14,017
Windom Peak, 14,082

6.2. ALL COLORADO'S 54 OFFICIAL FOURTEENERS, BY ELEVATION.

Mount Elbert, 14,433
Mount Massive, 14,421
Mount Harvard, 14,420
Blanca Peak, 14,345
La Plata Peak, 14,336
Uncompahgre Peak, 14,309
Crestone Peak, 14,294
Mount Lincoln, 14,286

Grays Peak, 14,270
Mount Antero, 14,269
Torreys Peak, 14,267
Castle Peak, 14,265
Quandary Peak, 14,265
Mount Evans, 14,264
Longs Peak, 14,255
Mount Wilson (S.), 14,246
Mount Shavano, 14,229
Crestone Needle, 14,197
Mount Belford, 14,197
Mount Princeton, 14,197
Mount Yale, 14,196
Mount Bross, 14,172
Kit Carson Mountain, 14,165
El Diente Peak, 14,159
South Maroon Peak, 14,156
Tabeguache Peak, 14,155
Mount Oxford, 14,153
Mount Sneffels, 14,150
Mount Democrat, 14,148
Capitol Peak, 14,130
Pikes Peak, 14,109
Snowmass Mountain, 14,092
South Mount Eolus, 14,083
Windom Peak, 14,082
Mount Columbia, 14,073
Missouri Mountain, 14,067
Humboldt Peak, 14,064
Mount Bierstadt, 14,060
Sunlight Peak, 14,059
Handies Peak, 14,048
Culebra Peak, 14,047
Ellingwood Peak, 14,042
Mount Lindsey, 14,042
Little Bear Peak, 14,037
Mount Sherman, 14,036
Redcloud Peak, 14,034
Pyramid Peak, 14,018
Wilson Peak (N.), 14,017
Wetterhorn Peak, 14,015
North Maroon Peak, 14,014
San Luis Peak, 14,014
Mount of the Holy Cross, 14,005
Huron Peak, 14,003
Sunshine Peak, 14,001

6.3. FOURTEENERS IN THIS VOLUME, ALPHABETIC

Blanca Peak, 14,345
Challenger Peak, 14,080
Crestone Needle, 14,197
Crestone Peak, 14,294
Culebra Peak, 14,047
El Diente Peak, 14,159
Ellingwood Peak, 14,042
Handies Peak, 14,048
Humboldt Peak, 14,064
Kit Carson Mountain, 14,165

Little Bear Peak, 14,037
Mount Lindsey, 14,042
Mount Sneffels, 14,150
Mount Wilson (S.), 14,246
North Mount Eolus, 14,039
Pikes Peak, 14,109
Redcloud Peak, 14,034
San Luis Peak, 14,014
South Mount Eolus, 14,083
Sunlight Peak, 14,059
Sunshine Peak, 14,001
Uncompahgre Peak, 14,309
Wetterhorn Peak, 14,015
Wilson Peak (N.), 14,017
Windom Peak, 14,082

6.4. FOURTEENERS IN THIS VOLUME, BY ELEVATION

Blanca Peak, 14,345
Uncompahgre Peak, 14,309
Crestone Peak, 14,294
Mount Wilson (S.), 14,246
Crestone Needle, 14,197
Kit Carson Mountain, 14,165
El Diente Peak, 14,159
Mount Sneffels, 14,150
Pikes Peak, 14,109
South Mount Eolus, 14,083
Windom Peak, 14,082
Challenger Peak, 14,080
Humboldt Peak, 14,064
Sunlight Peak, 14,059
Handies Peak, 14,048
Culebra Peak, 14,047
Ellingwood Peak, 14,042
Mount Lindsey, 14,042
North Mount Eolus, 14,039
Little Bear Peak, 14,037
Redcloud Peak, 14,034
Wilson Peak (N.), 14,017
Wetterhorn Peak, 14,015
San Luis Peak, 14,014
Sunshine Peak, 14,001

Appendix 7
USGS 7.5-MINUTE MAPS COVERING ROUTES AND ROUTE ACCESS IN THIS GUIDE

including sequence number useful for ordering from the USGS (the sequence number is simply where the map is in the alphabetic sequence of all

Colorado maps, it is also called the file number).

If you'd prefer to mail order your maps, first write for a Colorado catalog of published maps from: United States Department of the Interior, Geological Survey, Reston Virginia, 22092. This catalog provides excellent order forms and lists of all the maps available for Colorado. You can also buy maps at retail dealers all over the state. The catalog has a list of these outlets. The USGS map outlet at the Denver Federal Center is a good bet if your retail outlet does not have the map you need. If you don't know Denver, the map office at the Federal Center is hard to find; consider other options.

Beck Mountain, 131
Blanca Peak, 181
Columbine Pass, 402
Creede, none
Crestone, 449
Crestone Peak, 450
Cripple Creek N., 451
Culebra Peak, 462
Dolores Peak, 533
El Valle Creek, 597
Electric Peak, 611
Elk Park, 616
Fairplay West, 634
Fort Garland, 672
Gray Head, 788
Handies Peak, 836
Horn Peak, 912
La Valley, 1074

Lake City, 1083
Lake San Cristobal, 1091
Little Cone, 1156
Manitou Springs, 1210
Mosca Pass, 1333
Mount Sneffels, 1352
Mount Wilson, 1360
Mountain View Crest, 1362
Nathrop , 2128
Pikes Peak, 1491
Redcloud Peak, 1611
San Luis Peak, 37106
Snowdon Peak, 1769
Stewart Peak, 1819
Storm King Peak, 1832
Taylor Ranch, 1871
Telluride, 1875
Twin Peaks, 1947
Uncompahgre Peak, 1960
Wetterhorn Peak, 2050
Woodland Park, 2077

Y

During snow seasons, you can enjoy Colorado's mountains with less impact on the environment.

PRESERVE OUR FOURTEENERS!

Colorado's fourteeners are priceless resources that give us immeasurable benefit. The increased popularity of climbing these peaks, however, is taking its toll: the fragile alpine environment is being damaged by erosion and crowding. As climbers, we must reduce the impact of our visits—we must climb with care and sensitivity. The following recommendations will help you reduce your impact.

1. Before your trip, learn about problems for the area you'll be in. Is there undue trail erosion? A riparian area that's being damaged? Wildlife you should avoid? Crowding? Parking problems? Private land?

2. Keep your group under 6 people.

3. If you camp, plan your itinerary to avoid over-used sites, and avoid camps during times of high use.

4. Don't use campfires in the backcountry; pack a stove.

5. Avoid traveling through undisturbed areas. Instead, use designated trails and established paths (unless you travel over snow).

6. When climbing or camping, do not build structures such as wind breaks, large cairns, rock walls, and fire rings.

7. Deposit human feces in holes 6 to 8 inches deep a minimum of 75 paces from water or camp. Burn or pack out your toilet paper.

8. Pack out what you pack in—litter and orange peels!

9. Don't feed wildlife.

10. Leave your pets at home—just the smell of a dog disturbs wildlife.

11. If possible, climb during snow seasons so that snow cover minimizes all your impacts.

12. Be courteous: wait for climbers below you to move out of rockfall areas. Don't ski above other climbers. Keep noise to a minimum (except for summit yodels). Be friendly and share information about routes that prevent erosion and rockfall. Share new routes, since they spread use. Remember—we're all in this together.

13. Support—or join—organizations that help preserve our fourteeners.

bluecloverpress.com
for:

new author guidelines

(we're looking for outdoor adventure writers)

sales information

(if you are a retailer who would like to distribute this or our other outdoor adventure guides, let us know)

other great books

(we carry a number of outdoor adventure guides. check out our growing list)

updates

(we make every effort to ensure our guides are as up-to-date as possible but routes can and do change. you can check out our site for the latest reported route information changes)

feedback

(in order to bring everyone the best and most recent route information we need to hear from you. by checking in we'll also be able to alert you to new route and guidebook information)

discounts

(if you don't mind a book with a bent corner or a wrinkled page, you can get a significant discount off the normal retail price. our supply of cosmetically-challenged books is limited so check back from time to time)